ECONOCRATS AND THE POLICY PROCESS:
The Politics and Philosophy of Cost–Benefit Analysis

D0930549

ECONOCRATS AND THE POLICY PROCESS -
The Politics and Philosophy of Cost–Benefit Analysis

PETER SELF

Professor of Public Administration
London School of Economics and Political Science

Westview Press
Boulder, Colorado

169585

309.212
S 465

Copyright © 1975 Peter Self

All rights reserved. No part of this publication
may be reproduced or transmitted, in any form or by
any means, without permission in writing from the publishers.

Published 1975 in London, England,
by The Macmillan Press Ltd.

Published 1977 in the United States of America by
  Westview Press, Inc.
  1898 Flatiron Court
  Boulder, Colorado 80301
  Frederick A. Praeger, Publisher and Editorial Director

Printed in Great Britain

Library of Congress Cataloging in Publication Data

Self, Peter.
  Econocrats and the policy process.

  Bibliography: p.
  Includes index.
    1. Welfare economics.   2.   Cost effectiveness.
I.   Title.
HB99.3.S443   1976   309.2′12   76–21651
ISBN 0–89158–636–9

To my friends and colleagues, the Econocrats

Contents

Preface

This book started out as a polemical criticism of the uses of cost–benefit analysis in public decisions, and expanded somewhat as it went along. That circumstance explains the structure of the book. Part One represents an attempt to scrutinise critically the tools and methods of cost–benefit analysis, including its wish to quantify as many factors as possible in money terms. Part Two deals with the relations between economic analysis and politics, social values, and methods of decision-making. Each Part is reasonably self-contained for any reader who wishes to be selective, although the book is intended to be read as a whole.

It may be asked why the author who is not a professional economist should venture upon such treacherous waters. After all, as one of my colleagues pointed out, there is no economic position which has not been strongly criticised by other economists. There are two explanations.

First, economic techniques such as cost–benefit analysis play an increasingly important part in the making of government decisions. Sometimes they are thought of as the best or most 'objective' way of reaching such decisions. On the other hand the uses of these techniques also cause not a little puzzlement, and often a vague scepticism, on the part of non-economists, including politicians, officials, and students of politics and society. It therefore seemed worthwhile to explore the social values and the logical assumptions which underlie these techniques from a non-economic perspective; and to consider their influence upon the process of policy-making and upon other ways of making public decisions.

The work of the Roskill Commission on the third London airport first drew my attention to this problem, and some references to this *cause célèbre* are scattered throughout this book. It struck me at the time as strange that so many intelligent people should apparently accept 'trial by quantification' as the only sensible or possible way of reaching such a difficult decision. Those who were dubious about the proceedings, including one eminent Commission member who in the end dissented from his fellows, did not know how to criticise them. There seemed to be no alternative between accepting the logic of cost–benefit or falling back upon purely emotional positions of dissent. The situation was not like that really, but it would obviously have helped if more people could have reflected upon the relation of economic techniques to social values.

A second explanation for writing this book is that there is (so far as I know) no book of its kind. The many textbooks that have appeared upon cost–benefit analysis and upon budgetary techniques such as P.P.B.S. (planning, programming, budgetary systems), are all written by economists who whatever their theoretical reservations (which are many) invariably believe – sometimes quite passionately – in the value of the techniques that they are expounding. Thus students and also officials obtain a rather one-sided view of the subject. There have been a few counterblasts from a political angle, notably from the trenchant pen of Aaron Wildavsky, but on the whole the position is as described.

Now it is quite true that some theoretical economists are deeply interested in social and political theories, and have made more original contributions to these subjects than the present book can hope to offer. Indeed the invasion of other social studies by economists may be seen as something of a disgrace to the inhabitants of these other fields. However, these contributions may not be intelligible to non-economists, and some of the interesting differences between theoretical economists themselves (as these affect social and political positions) may not be apparent to some students of economics either. Moreover, the gap between pure theory and practice is everywhere wide, and nowhere more so than between the empyrean reflections of some theoretical economists and the pragmatic and flourishing techniques that are practised under the rubric of the same discipline. The practising cost–benefit analyst in full employment is not called upon to defend his theoretical position, and few would understand supposing he tried to do so. Thus the diverse speculations of economic theories, and the very limited relationship between this theoretical discourse and the successful practice of operational techniques, both serve as barriers to a reflective but unspecialised view of these techniques. If this book makes any modest contribution towards overcoming this 'credibility gap', it will have been worthwhile even if the reader does not agree with the author's critical position. Indeed the critical position is itself partly taken up in order to persuade more people (including cost–benefit analysts themselves) to think about the social and political relevance of these techniques.

The style of the book follows from the author's intentions and capacities. It contains none of the elegant equations, graphs, and mathematical demonstrations which are the standard fare of books on economics, which at least makes it readable for the non-economist. If the economist misses his tools of the trade (which doubtless could express some of the arguments in a more precise and less prolix manner), perhaps he would concede that some economic textbooks suffer from a rather too hasty treatment of basic social issues, which get channelled quickly into the calmer waters of mathematical logic without it always being apparent in the end whether the issue has been resolved. At any rate a change in style and tempo may not be harmful to those living on a heavy diet of quantification.

I have had the advantage of comments upon parts of the book from colleagues at the London School of Economics and Political Science. In particular I would like to thank Christopher Foster whose insights into the relations between politics and economics were most helpful for Chapter 5; Amartya Sen for enlightenment and encouragement; and Tony Flowerdew for many helpful points. My debt to Ed Mishan's writings is plain from my dissents. It would be incongruous to ascribe any of my opinions and errors to these individuals; and if any of them should agree with any parts of the argument it will be (as with all good economists) for reasons of their own.

I am also grateful to John Charvet for useful comments, and offer a mixed gratitude to my friend Maurice Ash who really influenced me to take up the subject. Thanks for typing the manuscript go especially to Ann Kennedy and Sandra McCulloch.

PETER SELF

N.B. Chapter 3 might be skipped by anyone who does not share or find rewarding the author's puzzlement about 'externalities'. In Part Two, Chapters 5 and 6 deal with political and philosophical issues, while Chapters 7 and 8 revert to policy problems and could be read first.

Part One

A Critique of Cost-Benefit
Analysis

1

'Econocracy' and the Policy Process

This book is concerned with the methods of making public decisions or policies. It starts with a critique of the use and effects of certain economic techniques which are now widely recommended, and often used as aids for public decisions. It is the claim of their practitioners that, whatever their limitations, these techniques at least help to make public decisions more rational; that they are a contribution towards, or even the model for, the ideal of 'rational decision-making'. I shall consider this claim critically, and suggest that in many cases the use of these techniques is productive not of greater rationality, but of irrationality and confusion.

I have first to explain and justify my use of the harsh word 'econocracy', although the explanation can only become clear as the book proceeds. The word most certainly is not meant as an omnibus attack upon the activities of economists, either working within or outside of government. Clearly there are essential activities of modern government – the whole field of national accounting and the management of the economy, for example – which depend upon expert economic advice. Again in criticising the claims made for economic techniques, I am not meaning to say that public decisions are best made by hunch or intuition, or without the use of appropriate economic and statistical data (though there are important questions as to what data *is* appropriate or useful).

A critical view of 'econocracy' will be stated in this chapter in a bald and simple way with refinements left until later. The meaning of the word can be suggested through a comparison with *technocracy*. The latter word refers to a familiar and rightly criticised way of thinking which in its simplest form attaches exaggerated importance to one or more technical factors that are relevant (or thought to be relevant) to some decision.* A simple illustration will suffice here. A senior official in the British Department of the

* Technocracy is often supposed to be a vice of technical experts, but this is not quite fair. As any bar conversation will show, ordinary men are often liable to this excess. The point is that it is the experts who influence decisions, and particularly when grouped together into an influential technical service or *cadre* sharing the same training and outlook their influence can be considerable and sometimes pernicious. The subject cannot be pursued here but it is a pity that the best-known book on the subject, Jean Meynaud's Technocracy (New York, 1969), seems to view technocracy as equivalent to all action taken by public officials which eludes political control. This is a quite different notion.

Environment recently asserted that future development should be steered to the maximum extent possible to the North of England for two reasons; first because there was more water there and secondly because agricultural land was of poorer quality than in the South.

Both of these are valid reasons as far as they go, but clearly (one would have thought) they are not adequate reasons for the policy advocated. In economic terms they imply that if more people insist upon living in the South, they must expect higher bills for water and possibly for food as a result; but people and firms may be quite willing to pay these extra costs in return for the economic, social, climatic or other advantages of a southern location. Of course there may be long-term conservation arguments for the policy recommended, but these would need demonstration, and would be to a large extent speculative. If this particular official had been around, Los Angeles would hardly have got started at all, let alone been allowed to grow to a city of six millions with hardly any water nearby.

Economists are natural critics of technocracy. Dealing with the allocation of scarce resources among diverse ends, they are quick to appreciate that technical factors are rarely adequate to settle a decision.* Instead they will ask what are the costs and benefits of some decision, or in different language what 'opportunity costs' in terms of alternative uses of resources must be sacrificed to reap the benefits that the decision is expected to produce. In principle they employ a common measuring rod to measure these costs and benefits that is usually expressed (though it need not be) in monetary terms.

We must leave aside for the moment the many thorny questions of theory and practice that relate to the validity of economic measurement, however these are expressed. It is sufficient to note that much of the rationale of economic science is, or is supposed to be, that of bringing a diversity of factors into some common language of accounting. It is also true that ordinary opinion concedes to economics some validity for these operations, otherwise it would be impossible for example to attach any credence whatever to a cost-of-living index. Some theoretical economists do deny much or any credence to such indices, because of changes in the utility of money and other reasons, while public opinion is often rightly doubtful about the 'significance' of such figures. Without plunging into the complete scepticism which some economic theories themselves invite, it should be plain in a general way that the economist's apparent possession of a measuring-rod for the values registered in diverse situations must be paid for by critical doubts about the nature and significance of this unit of value.

One reason why economists are useful in government is because of their ability, as E. A. G. Robinson puts it, to see the 'interconnection of things'. Instead of assuming that phenomena must stay in their separate administra-

---

* Strictly of course a technical factor is never a determinant of any decision and becomes authoritative only when linked with a purpose that is not itself questioned; for example, because we accept that bridges ought not to collapse we also accept engineering opinion on this point as fully authoritative. However, technology is always a constraint upon possible decisions – if the knowledge to construct aqueducts and dams had been lacking, Los Angeles could not have grown in any case.

tive compartments, they seek relations through common tools of economic analysis.[1] Unfortunately though, an ability to ask useful questions does not imply an ability to give valid answers, and there are familiar situations where a good critic makes a very bad master. *Econocracy*, as I use the word, is the belief that there exist fundamental economic tests or yardsticks according to which policy decisions can and should be made. Thus stated, econocracy is much more ambitious, and consequently more dangerous to the public, than *any* kind of technocracy.

Econocracy does not refer to wholly *instrumental* types of economic advice. An economist is acting wholly legitimately in principle when he attempts to forecast how much inflation or how much unemployment is likely to result from some proposed measure. If a choice must be made between 'more unemployment' or 'more inflation', the economist can reasonably advise what measures seem most likely to produce the kind of 'trade-off' between these alternative evils that a Cabinet or President prefers. Of course it is hard indeed for economists to keep their advice strictly technical and objective; not only may their own values subtly influence their judgements about causes of social behaviour which are intrinsically dubious and debatable, but also the economic theories to which the economist subscribes usually have some normative content. For example a 'growth economist' tends to see unemployment as the greater of the two evils mentioned, whereas an economist who was reared upon equilibrium theories may be more worried about inflation. But whilst in such cases a mixture of allegedly technical advice with subtle personal or theoretical value judgements may carry a smack of econocracy, this may not be too serious a danger if the limitations and possible bias of the advice are sufficiently understood. The economists in question do not usually pretend that they possess final tests of the right policy, and their biases are sometimes known and admitted.

The supreme example of econocracy that I shall discuss is the art or technique known as cost–benefit analysis. The general idea of 'C.B.A.' is to express some or all of the factors that are considered relevant to some decision in terms of a common denominator of money so that their magnitudes can be directly compared, their benefits added, and their costs subtracted. In itself this procedure does not seem very impious to the extent that it is practical; but in so far as cost–benefit analysts claim (as they often do) that they possess objective techniques or yardsticks for recommending a policy decision they are in fact asserting an enormous amount. They are claiming in the first place that it is possible to quantify in monetary terms all sorts of factors that normally are not so expressed; secondly that the money terms used in the analysis really do possess the common property which they appear to have (e.g. that the £ or $ sign means the same thing in one part of the analysis as in another); and thirdly that these figures represent measurements of some concept of community welfare which can or should stand, if not as a unique criterion for decision-makers (the 'social welfare function'), then at least as one important criterion of the best policy.

Now clearly not all cost–benefit analysts make these elaborate claims for their art. On the contrary, many are pragmatic people concerned with finding techniques for measuring as many things as possible in money terms. But it still remains true that something like this list of claims is implicit in their work. Theoretically and logically the list should be expressed in reverse order; first come the theories of welfare economics, then the elaboration of a common yardstick of value, then the conversion of all sorts of factors, attributes, and experiences into this yardstick. Practically and pragmatically this logical order is reversed. Some analysts, like many practical men, think that a technique of this kind can be useful even if its theoretical basis is extremely shaky. I will deal with this viewpoint later. For the moment my concern is with the more comprehensive and explicit exponents of cost–benefit analysis who qualify as the 'econocrats' of my title.

C.B.A. is only one of several economic and budgetary techniques that have come much into vogue during the last decade, and some of the following critique would apply to these other techniques also. C.B.A., however, is much the most voracious of this wolf-pack. *Cost-effectiveness analysis*, for example, sticks in principle to the relatively modest aim of examining what use of resources will be most economical and effective for achieving some specified goal. Famous examples are the studies undertaken during the McNamara regime at the Pentagon to determine which package out of a variety of costly weapon systems would best meet the specified goal of an adequate nuclear striking force. In C.B.A., however, prior goals are not and need not be set; in principle, C.B.A. offers a device for the 'discovery' of policy goals through the process of listing benefits as well as costs, and relating them together in some supposedly coherent way.

However, cost-effectiveness analysis easily shades into C.B.A. because goals often cannot be precisely described. In the Defence example, 'an adequate nuclear capacity' cannot be made into a fixed goal since there are obviously questions that must be asked about the precise amount of destructive power that it is worth the United States buying, about the side-effects of different weapon systems, and so on. A partial kind of cost–benefit analysis might be said to result, although in this case qualitative and hypothetical 'benefits' have to be weighed against quantitative schedules of alternative costs so that the result is far removed from the C.B.A. ideal. Conversely C.B.A. is sometimes deliberately structured to show costs and benefits in relation to a series of specified goals, and may then come closer to cost-effectiveness analysis. These various types of exercise are sometimes collectively described as cost–utility analysis.

In attacking econocracy as a vice worse than technocracy, I have in mind the *apparently* much greater rationality and comprehensiveness of an economic as opposed to a technical approach. Economics, which deals with the allocation of scarce and transferable resources, is very much concerned with the logic of choice. The mathematical bias of modern economics adds to this interest, and economics is now formidably entwined with complex problems of mathematical logic. Logic of course has always been important and often a source of grave confusion in the study of economics,* but the

* This point has been amply documented in L. M. Fraser, *Economic Thought and Language* (London, 1947).

older traditions of the subject were more literary and humanist and had close affinities with philosophic and psychological speculations about the nature of human motives and behaviour. In an attempt to be more logically and mathematically rigorous and more self-contained, economists have tended to sever the links with related fields of social study. To some extent other social sciences have attempted to follow the same course, though seemingly with less success. The effect or tendency of these developments has been to fragment the study of human behaviour into unrelated compartments, and to dry up the well-springs of general social speculations from whence all of the classical and some of the modern theories of society have in fact emerged.

The paradoxical result has been to establish two completely contradictory tendencies within modern economics. One tendency is to create a completely technical, value-free science which makes no assumptions and delivers no judgements whatever about the nature of human motives, satisfactions, or welfare. These phenomena are just 'given data' which cannot be investigated by economics, and need not affect economic analysis when this is formulated with sufficient logical rigour and objectivity. The opposite tendency is to attempt to turn economics into a master science of human values, capable of disclosing and quantifying these values according to some objective criterion of value known to the economist. This latter group are the econocrats, and cost–benefit analysis represents the ideal method of realising their ambitions.

It may be asked *how* economics could polarise in this way without the emergence of a fierce internal controversy among economists themselves. This question has also puzzled the author. There are possibly two explanations. One is that the common interest of modern economists in mathematical models and techniques produces at least the appearance of a common methodology. The other, broader explanation is that the theoretical foundations of economics, as opposed to its techniques, are in a confused state. The beguiling notion that there exist theoretically 'optimum' conditions of production, distribution, and exchange still exerts its spell in modern economics, even upon those who would like to define 'optimum' somehow in a purely technical way. This conceded, and the idea of the intrinsic rationality of the market being simultaneously dismissed (as it now often is), economists are easily led on into a kind of paper-chase that seeks to track down those ideal economic conditions which (it is assumed) must somehow underlie specific pieces of economic advice or analysis. The intrinsic logic of economics appears to be such that, once it claims *any* title at all to objective normative standards, a consistent theorist is led on to construct a whole ideal world whereby his most modest assertion can be justified. Since almost every economist has some frail disposition to function as a pundit, traditional economists cannot easily repudiate the aspirations of the cost–benefit analysts, even though some can and do take a donnish delight over exposition at a theoretical level of the weirder contortions of welfare economics.*

* A cruder explanation is that dog does not eat dog. Economists have plenty of incentive to cling on to the bonanza received for advice tendered to modern governments. Possibly too, some traditional economists view paternalistically the attempts of

These speculations do not affect the main line of the argument here, which is that the apparent rationality and logic of economic thought can be harnessed very skilfully, and very delusively, to buttress the claims of cost–benefit analysis and similar techniques. So much is this so that in ordinary parlance these techniques are sometimes almost equated with the concept or ideal of 'rational decision-making'.

It is easy to see how this comes about. First of all the economist sets up a logical model of choice. In its simplest form, this amounts to tracing all those consequences of a possible decision which are judged sufficiently important and foreseeable to bother about (of course the economist may not do this task unaided – see later). Then the listed consequences are evaluated in terms of the 'costs' and 'benefits' which they will confer upon various members of the public or upon the community at large. The same procedures can then be followed in relation to the outcomes of any *alternative* decisions that are judged to be practical (once again there is an awkward problem of selection here). Finally some or all of the various costs and benefits of the various possible decisions are quantified in monetary terms and compared with each other. If only some items are treated in this way the analysis is partial, if all are covered it is comprehensive. That course of action can then be chosen which offers the greatest surplus of benefits over costs, after making some allowance for any 'qualitative' factors which have not been quantified. In an ideal cost–benefit analysis, admittedly rarely claimed to exist in practice, the selection of the best decision would end as a simple exercise of addition and subtraction.

Superficially, as has been said, this whole exercise *looks* very rational. It seems preferable in the first place to use a logical choice model rather than to rely upon a more casual survey of relevant considerations, or worse still upon intuition. In so far as factors can be reduced at all plausibly to common monetary terms, they can be brought into quantitative comparisons with each other which is otherwise impossible. The precision of quantitative over qualitative methods of analysis appears to many people as an obvious gain in rationality. Even if only a partial analysis is possible, at least (it will be said) the policy-maker's work is assisted by knowing the score on those items that *can* be quantified. (He can then attach what weight he likes to the other items – the analyst tends to wash his hands of such untidy problems.) Admittedly many awkward bridges must be crossed in the course of the analysis – which possible decisions to examine, which consequences to trace, how accurately these consequences can be foreseen and measured even in crude terms (e.g. the number of passengers flying from a future airport), how far the analysis is to be followed through in time and in space, and so on. But, it can be countered, most of these problems have to be faced, or assumptions made about them, in any type of rational analysis. They are not

younger colleagues to cut their teeth on cost–benefit analysis at what may charitably be supposed to be the 'frontiers of the subject'. But these, I would stress, are only speculations about the failure of modern economics adequately to confront its condition of schizophrenia; and the lucid criticisms which economists themselves have offered of welfare economics receive some attention in the next chapter.

problems of economic techniques, which are *additional* to the non-economic problems of rational analysis. However difficult these additional economic problems may be, at least (it will be said) an economic cost–benefit analysis offers a *more* rational approach to decision-making than any alternative method that anyone has yet produced.

Alternative methods of decision-making get some attention later in the book. Here only two points need be made about the alleged rationality of this procedure. First, the economist has not (and to be fair does not claim) any monopoly of the use of logical decision models. Other types of choice model can be employed than the one lightly sketched above, and are in fact used in other varieties of C.B.A. itself. But the question of *which* model to use is not (save within certain narrow limits) a purely logical one. As will emerge, different ways of constructing decision models reflect different kinds of policy judgement which, when traced to their ultimate source, reflect in turn different sets of political and social values.

Even as a simple logical device C.B.A. certainly seems more rational than making decisions by hunch, and economists sometimes stress this point to their advantage. But as a logical device C.B.A. need not in fact involve any economic measurements at all, merely a qualitative listing of the advantages and drawbacks of different decisions. Very probably of course parts of the analysis will be backed up with relevant statistics, including economic statistics, but this data can be presented as supplementary or illustrative material whose relevance is for the ultimate policy-maker to assess.

A seachange comes over the analysis as soon as 'advantages' and 'drawbacks' are converted into 'benefits' and 'costs' and measured on some allegedly common basis. At this point the three basic problems already mentioned at once arise and the consequent doubts can be summarised as a single question: has the economist got any genuine yardstick for measuring objectively a diversity of factors other than the very limited criterion provided by market prices or other forms of conventional financial data? If he has, then (as I hope to make clear) he has indeed at least found the philosopher's stone of wisdom. If he has not, then the result may be less, not more, rational than would a primarily qualitative form of analysis, because of the spurious appearance of reliability which a quantified set of data conveys.

In this event the accusation of 'econocracy' is justified. For the economist is borrowing the respect which ordinary opinion accords to economic calculations for strictly limited purposes, and applying this accumulated respect and credibility to what may have to be called fraudulent uses. He is, wittingly or not, playing a confidence trick with the symbols of monetary exchange. Of course the theoretical welfare economist is not a confidence trickster, in fact he is often high-minded, but he is committed to the discovery of some ideal ('optimum') set of economic conditions that transcend the ordinary market economy, with the aid of which he can measure intrinsic values.

To repeat, many economists would not recognise or accept this account of the foundations of cost–benefit and similar techniques. There is on this point a split between idealists and pragmatists. E. J. Mishan is one representative of the former school. In *Cost–Benefit Analysis*[2] he stresses several times that the economist has access to objective principles or criteria which will enable him (though many technical difficulties are conceded) directly to determine and to measure human welfare.* In his view therefore the economist ought not to be swayed by political or social expressions of opinion, since it would seem that his judgement (if properly applied of course) is separate from and superior to other sources of value judgements. Econocracy indeed! But in a sense Mishan does no more than express the intrinsic logic of welfare economics, and theoretically speaking his only problem would seem to be the obtuseness of other economists who will not interpret his tables of stone correctly.

The pragmatic school, on the other hand, accepts that C.B.A. must operate within the contours of a political process of some kind. On this view the analyst must accept that any information which he can provide may legitimately be overruled by the values of politicians or other decision-makers. He may even accept that his information should be limited to those factors or interests which the policy-maker considers to be relevant to his decision. The pragmatic school is likely to eschew grand theory, and perhaps to accept more readily than the idealists that there are many 'intangibles' which cannot be quantified.

By contrast, at least with the idealists, the pragmatists sound sensible and in many ways are so. But nagging questions persist. If the analyst accepts that public decisions *should* be made through the political process, is there any real point to his work? Will not the push–pull of rival interests or the workings of majority rule or any other political system accomplish its logical results perfectly well without the analyst's intervention? One answer often given is that a good C.B.A. can *clarify* the costs or benefits to various interests of a possible decision, thereby reducing political confusion and uncertainty. The adequacy of this defence will be considered later when it may turn out that C.B.A. more frequently obscures rather than clarifies policy issues. Such scepticism apart, it is possible to produce a sophisticated defence for the pragmatic use of cost–benefit analysis, but this defence has to be based upon a specific view of the policy process which is a subject not usually discussed in much depth by analysts (see Chapter 5).

Supposing economists do content themselves with the role of producing useful information for decision-makers, what is the status of this information? How objective can it be? Economic techniques are flexible enough for costs and benefits to be analysed and reckoned in a wide variety of ways. Some of these ways can be shown to involve logical fallacies, yet may still be used for partisan reasons.[3] The cost–benefit studies produced by Federal agencies in the United States used to inflate benefits by such simple devices as

---

* This is an exaggeration. Mishan concedes that the economist must utilise for his purposes one or two ethical principles which must be assumed to be self-evident. They are not so of course (see later). But the position is still 'econocratic' because plainly these basic ethical assumptions must also be accessible to politicians and other decision-making bodies. Yet apparently only the economist is in a position to utilise them to reach a right conclusion.

(for example) crediting to an irrigation project the increased incomes of all the manufacturers, shopkeepers, etc. who would supply the irrigated farms. This sort of reasoning, which is defensible at all only when there are extensive unused resources, may have helped to sell public projects to friendly Congressmen and gullible citizens, but the use of C.B.A. as propaganda can hardly improve the quality of public decisions.

Such cases apart, C.B.A. lends itself easily to at least moderately partisan positions. Every slight variation in the methods of analysis and calculation will affect the results of the analysis and without any intentional bias at all a great variety of outcomes are usually possible and plausible. Bring in the usual context of partisan policy debate, and it is plain that economists will find it hard to avoid some policy bias deriving from their own organisational position or the interest of their clients. An economist employed by a welfare agency is hardly likely to underestimate the indirect benefits to be had from better welfare services, and one advising an airport authority will probably not dwell upon the adverse 'externalities' caused by aviation.

However, the policy bias of an economist, like that of any other expert, is a question of degree, and sometimes may be largely or completely absent. This should be especially the case where an independent or non-partisan body is set up to investigate a problem, when a great deal may be expected of cost–benefit analysis. The Roskill Commission on the third London airport perhaps represents the classic case of an attempted impartial trial by quantification of this type, and any bias on the part of the Commission's analysts could be said to be technical or professional rather than institutional or political.* In the event the use of C.B.A. failed to satisfy these high expectations, and the idea that C.B.A. can play the role of 'impartial umpire' over such complex policy issues seems to have receded in Britain since its high watermark at the time of Roskill. This idea never gained so much credibility in the United States, where the concept of impartial reviews is more suspect and where C.B.A. has been easily assimilated as one weapon to be employed in the pluralist conflict of interests.

These comments are not meant to suggest that all C.B.A. exercises are wholly partisan in some sense or another. The 'objectivity' of the information furnished by C.B.A. is compromised in varying degrees by possible policy or organisational bias on the part of the analyst, as well as by any intellectual bias which his techniques introduce or enjoin. But this statement is true to some extent of *any* expert advice, and it qualifies but does not destroy the notion of objectivity which remains central to the value of information in rational debate. The objectivity of a C.B.A., however, is much more dependent upon the value judgements incorporated in the analysis than is true of most types of expert information.

---

* At any rate in theory. In practice both the Commission and the analysts were necessarily biased to some extent (by their terms of reference) in favour of the presumed benefits of another large airport, while their use of C.B.A. techniques developed specifically for transportation purposes produced a sectoral bias towards the interests of transport users. See Chapter 7 for a full discussion of this case.

When a scientist makes propositions about the feasibility and performance of a supersonic plane or a new explosive, there is a clear sense in which his proposition will prove true or false and it can often be tested. In a different way raw information of a descriptive or statistical type is in principle value-free, except for the (sometimes important) bias which leads people to collect one kind of data rather than another. The statement 'statistics can be made to prove anything', which is not true, refers to the ease with which statistics can be deployed selectively to support particular arguments. But there is still a sense in which they are true or false. Thus the agricultural acreage of England and Wales can be estimated with fair (but not complete) accuracy for various definitions of 'agricultural', and can then be expressed as a proportion of total land acreage, urbanised acreage, world agricultural acreage, and so on. Decreases in the agricultural acreage can now be expressed in various relationships so as to suggest that the agricultural acreage is falling either rapidly or slowly, but the facts stated may all be true and an intelligent man will know how to survey the same data from different angles.

Prices ruling in a market are also facts, and can be explained by inter-actions between consumer demands and the conditions of production, which is the realm of descriptive economics. It is true that economic theorists have always been deeply enmeshed with normative problems of value; for example, the utility theorists ascribed a special kind of social value (the maximisation of consumers' satisfactions) to the operation of fully competitive markets. But to describe market phenomena we need not introduce such theories.

Policy analysis is specifically concerned with social values, and any information which it utilises must be thought relevant to some value judgement. However, there is a sense in which the information produced by a C.B.A. might be claimed to be factual and objective. For example, the analyst might trace the consequences of a public policy for some group of beneficiaries, and test the willingness of this group to pay for the benefit in question. This figure could now be presented as having, in principle, a comparable status to market data about consumer demands. Of course 'consumer demand' may not be regarded by policy-makers as a sufficient or desirable criterion for their decision; or alternatively they may believe that consumer demands about public services or decisions are conveyed better through the *political* process than through techniques of economic calculation. Such issues can only be tackled theoretically through high-level debate about the nature of social welfare or the public good. Economists like to contribute to this debate but (it may be said) there is no necessity for the economic analyst to insist upon the superiority of his particular concept or interpretation of social welfare. It is sufficient for him to explain his starting point and assumptions, produce the results, and leave it to policy-makers to give their own rating to this particular contribution. Naturally the analyst is disposed to believe that his social perspective *is* valuable, and that his techniques are suited to his purposes, but these are the tendencies of any technical expert.

This defence of C.B.A. accepts that the economist starts from a particular normative position or assumption about social welfare, but then argues that in so far as this position is understood and shared by others and is accurately applied through the economist's techniques, the results will constitute valuable information for policy-makers which is objective within the limits stated. This is a reasonable defence for C.B.A. if the premises are true. Moreover, it seems clear that some economic concept of social welfare is, if only in a vague and uncertain way, widely accepted by other participants as a relevant or important criterion of public policy; consequently the analyst's contribution should have relevance to the decision. The problems of principle about this argument arise over the difficulties of understanding and clarifying the economic concept of welfare, and of ensuring that there is a logical relationship between the chosen concept and the applied techniques. Techniques cannot function rationally in a vacuum or if they incorporate vague and contradictory policy criteria. Actually it seems to be the case that both economists and policy-makers, though in different ways, show considerable disagreement and confusion about economic tests of welfare, and that the assumed neutrality of techniques is much compromised by this circumstance. But examination of these points comes later.

Whereas then the idealistic school of C.B.A. believes that there is some supreme criterion of social welfare to be interpreted and applied by economists, the pragmatic school gains in realism by accepting that an economic criterion of welfare may be only one of several possible tests of policy. A modest approach to C.B.A. will recognise not only the many logical pitfalls over the use of techniques but the influence of value assumptions, and will spell out the analysis carefully and cautiously; and it may also take care not to extend the process of economic quantification beyond limits imposed both by technical credibility and certain normative considerations. All this is difficult and patient work, and economists are not actually remarkable for their modesty. In any event even the most modest analyst must rest his work ultimately upon some concept of social welfare, to which subject I now turn.

2
The Dilemmas of Welfare Economics

A. Introduction

The foundations of modern economic techniques reside in theories of welfare economics, and some examination of these foundations is necessary for the rest of the book. The discussion here is in no way technical, my main purpose being to demonstrate and consider the logical and political assumptions which are implicitly, and sometimes explicitly, present in these economic theories.

Welfare economics can be viewed in two ways which arouse different reactions. On the one hand surely it is right and proper that economists should be specifically concerned with human welfare. Economics is supposed to be a 'useful science' and if the economist can suggest measures for the improvement of human welfare, his advice ought surely to be welcomed. Even if an economist's interest in welfare is grounded in humanist rather than professional reasons, and comes from the heart rather than the head, it should not be spurned on that account. We are or should all be citizens and humanists before we are technicians.

On the other hand there is the body of theoretical doctrines and arguments known as welfare economics. Here we enter territory of a different kind. If the economist is arguing that there exist objective standards of human welfare which he (and possibly he alone) is in a position to specify and interpret, then his theories are foolish and possibly dangerous. It may be, however, that he is merely working out in the language of formal economic analysis the kind of normative judgements that ordinary citizens make. In that case his work will be useful to the extent that he can increase the precision and clarity of such ordinary judgements; but it will be harmful to the extent that, through a passion for logical rigour and quantification, he denies or perverts more common-sense types of value judgement. Further, he will have to recognise that he is operating in a field of value judgements within which it is just as natural for economists to be in disagreement as for ordinary mortals; and value judgements which he translates into esoteric language are derived from his position not as an economist but as a citizen.

Turning aside from this position that an economist *could* adopt, we need to examine the larger theoretical claims that welfare economists have advanced. We then discover a body of extravagant theorising which encounters a whole series of logical difficulties and obstacles that cannot in fact be resolved; or rather that at best can only be notionally resolved through still more artificial sets of assumptions until all contact with the world of reality is lost. Despite these setbacks, which the more candid welfare economist readily admit, the idea still persists that an end to the rainbow can be found...somewhere, someday.

Does this situation matter? In a sense perhaps not. Why should not welfare economists play with their logical toys like medieval schoolmen if they wish to do so? The only snag is that in this case there exists also a thriving corpus of pragmatic techniques whose rationale can only be found ultimately in the realm of economic theories; and however much the fallacies and contradictions of welfare theories are demonstrated the practitioners still go on with their job as if nothing had happened. Perhaps a medieval comparison is after all in order. The purchase and sale of indulgences then continued irrespective of any theological difficulties about its ultimate justification.

It is not my purpose here to essay a full review of welfare economics. For one thing the more elaborate algebraic postulates and arguments exceed my capacity, but in any event the demolition job has already been done by economists themselves. Nobody, one would have thought, could read a book such as I. M. D. Little's *A Critique of Welfare Economics*[1] and still suppose that a coherent body of economic theorising about the nature of human welfare can be produced. The only limitation of this work is that in his conclusions, as perhaps in his later books, the author shies away from the destructive conclusions of his own logical analysis. Critics cannot bear finally to destroy the thing which they have spent much effort in criticising.

My purpose here is more modest than that of Little or other professional critics of welfare economics. My concern is with the relationship between economic theorising and types of political or social judgement. I shall conclude, as already indicated, that on the whole welfare economists are mirroring in their own special language policy opinions and arguments which can be expressed in simpler language. There is no objective science of welfare economics unless it can be grounded in a universalist ethic capable of winning general acceptance.

B. Utility and Welfare

The true intellectual ancestor of welfare economics was not primarily an economist but a political thinker. Jeremy Bentham's notion of a felicific calculus bears a striking resemblance to the ideals of cost–benefit analysis. Bentham's notion that all human behaviour was regulated by the two 'sovereign masters' of pleasure and pain offered a basic unit of accountancy (pleasure ranking as a + and pain as a −) in terms of which all human experience might theoretically be measured. Thus in principle qualitative differences of experience could be reduced to standard units of pleasure–pain, and Bentham gave some simple rules for their measurement. From these postulates followed the famous dictum 'quantity of pleasure being equal, pushpin is as good as poetry' which so offended the more fastidious John Stuart Mill. His basic criterion of public policy, 'the greatest happiness' (more strictly pleasure) 'of the greatest number' – although illogically defined (what is the greatest number?) suggested appropriate rules of distribution which for Bentham included the assumption that the happiness of every individual was equally relevant. The concern of modern welfare economics with standards of value, methods of measurement, and rules of distribution is all quite explicit in Bentham's thought.[2]

The classical economists who were writing around the time of Bentham shared a somewhat similar view of human motivations, but did not produce specific economic theories of welfare that would fit with the notion of a felicific calculus. Their discussions about economic values were dominated by controversies over the respective roles of labour, land and capital, although Adam Smith and others demonstrated the capacity of a competitive market system to maximise consumers' satisfactions. But the notion that the felicific calculus might achieve a precise expression though the behaviour of consumers under ideal market conditions emerged only with theories of economic utility and equilibrium that were developed in the late nineteenth and early twentieth centuries.

At first sight the economic concept of personal utility seemed to offer an excellent basis for the construction of a welfare calculus. Utility was conceived as the satisfaction or pleasure which a consumer obtained from each unit of his outlay upon goods or services. The notion was particularly fruitful when applied to the idea of *marginal utilities*; if the competitive system was working properly, every consumer would be receiving an equal utility or satisfaction from each marginal unit of his outlay. The utility received by a consumer from any particular product was supposed normally to decline as his more elemental want for it was satisfied, while the supply price of the product was supposed usually to increase as more of it was demanded. A standard graph in the economic textbooks of the 1930s showed a falling demand curve cutting a rising supply curve, which was the equilibrium point for matching the marginal utilities of consumers to the marginal costs of producers.

The above is a crude version of the economic theories about competition, equilibrium, and utility that were current thirty years ago. The crudity perhaps does not matter because my aim will be only to explain how utility theories led welfare economics into a blind alley. It is now widely accepted that a tenable welfare calculus cannot logically be constructed on the basis of utility theory, but a review of the reasons for this failure should help to illuminate the curious directions taken by modern welfare economics.

Before proceeding there is one familiar criticism of the 'marginal utility' school* which needs to be refuted. This is the comment that the exercise of

* The theory of consumers' sovereignty and marginal utilities is often wrongly ascribed to the classical school of English economists (Adam Smith, David Ricardo, James Mill *et al.*). This is a natural error for laymen because of the identification of these writers with theories of competition and *laissez-faire*, and the association of some of them with Bentham and the Philosophic Radicals. In fact, the classic writers espoused for the most part a labour theory of value, which though now discredited in

ational choice by ordinary consumers is an unrealistic assumption which vitiates the rest of the theory. While 'rational economic man' is an artificial construct, it may still be valid for certain purposes. The point to my mind is that, under the conditions postulated, the consumer has the *opportunity* to exercise his options as rationally as he pleases. To the extent that he acts capriciously, one can only conclude that he is not too concerned with the degree of satisfaction he receives from economic goods, perhaps having other sources of satisfaction (I am of course assuming conditions that permit reasonable knowledge of the market and absence of duress on the part of advertisers, etc.). Such behaviour is not necessarily irrational in a broader sense, and merely shows the limited relevance of 'utility' to his happiness and perhaps to his welfare. There is nothing wrong with the old belief that the individual is a much better judge of his economic satisfactions than anyone else, or with an ethical belief in the validity of the consumer's freedom of choice, so long as this does not prejudge questions about the desirable range of collective goods.

For the concept of personal utility to serve as a satisfactory basis for a welfare calculus four requirements must be met. First, appropriate conditions of production and exchange must be present (originally defined as perfect competition'); secondly it must be meaningful to add together the units of utility received by an individual consumer into a total sum; thirdly, it must also be possible to aggregate the utilities of different individuals; and fourthly, the notion of utility itself must serve for an adequate expression of welfare. In point of fact none of these requirements can be adequately met, so that the idea of a welfare calculus based on utility collapses and new theories become necessary. Even if utility theories are no longer taken seriously (though in fact the word itself continues to be fully employed in economic discourse), these four issues touch on matters that are still central for welfare theories.

i) The 'Optimum' Conditions of Production and Exchange

Marginal utilities of the money spent upon each good by a given person only have equal value under conditions of perfect competition which never did fully exist and are patently not present in the modern world. Realisation of this led to the formulation of new economic theories of monopoly and oligopoly during the 1920s and 1930s which are not my concern here. Faced by this situation welfare theorists, instead of modifying their claims, have increased their bids. Now it is claimed, not that welfare will be maximised under a perfect market system, but that the market system itself must be judged and if possible transformed by reference to the ideal postulates of

orthodox economics has possibly more in common with the theories of values implicit in cost–benefit analysis than does the marginal utility school. On this point see below p. 33. The utility school will perhaps in retrospect be seen, from the viewpoint of welfare theories, to have constituted a most unfortunate and unproductive diversion of effort. On the history of the schools see Eric Roll, *History of Economic Thought* (London, 1938) chapters 4, 7, 8 and 9.

welfare theory. As Mishan puts it: 'competitive markets are to be justified by reference to the propositions of welfare economics'.[3]

What do these propositions look like? They can still be based upon the notion that price should equal marginal cost, only the cost in question is no that to an individual firm but to society as a whole. Price should equal marginal *social* cost. This allows and indeed requires the injection into the price of any commodity or service of the indirect social costs or benefits of its production. It is easy enough to see that there often are such costs and benefits; many economic activities produce loud noise, noxious fumes, traffic congestion, dangers to health and safety, etc. and some (fewer) activities have indirect benefits, for example the reduction of juvenile delinquency which may follow upon the establishment of a sports centre in a new housing estate. We arrive at once in the complex world of cost–benefit analysis, and all the questions about what 'externalities' to include in any equation, and how to measure them, can be left for later consideration.

Here we are concerned with the theoretical construction of a positive welfare system which can incorporate within its pricing system appropriate allowances for externalities. Now in principle, if 'spillovers' can be defined in an economically meaningful way (see next chapter) their incorporation will raise the responsiveness of the system to individual demands (the welfare principle). But the difficulty of the task becomes plain when we recognise the absence of adequate guidelines for listing and measuring the 'spillovers' in question. It is true that we-ean appeal to the principle of an individual's 'willingness to pay' a sum of money in order to achieve or avert some desired effect. But his willingness to pay for any purpose is logically dependent upon his income and all his other expenditure decisions, which can only be guessed at in the absence of actual conditions of economic exchange.

The linked notion of 'opportunity cost' proves similarly to be purely formal. We can assert that the 'true' price of any activity consists in the sacrifice of the best alternative use (for the individual or for society as a whole) of the resources devoted to it. We can, it is true, recognise certain rare cases in which the social opportunity cost appears to be nil or small; as example would be the capital resources sunk in a railway branch line if the track and equipment cannot be transferred to other uses, if the land has little use for other purposes, and if pollution and other burdens are negligible But this is an exceptional situation* since usually the resources required for any activity could be used in very many different ways or combinations of ways, with diverse consequences for the satisfaction of individuals, and there is no positive theory to tell us which is the 'optimum' way to use these resources for the benefit of society. This is not to deny that 'opportunity cost

---

* We should note that it is also a situation where a private entrepreneur would behave very similarly because he cannot recover his sunk capital costs in the railway line. The public case differs because there may be favourable spillovers from the branch line which can be used to justify an operating subsidy as well as the capital write-off which would anyhow be rational. Opportunity costs are dependent upon the perspective of the actor, and naturally therefore they are much more easily identified by a private entrepreneur than by a government acting for society as a whole.

is a formally valid concept, only it looks as if it could make more mileage over decision-making than is actually the case.

None the less, economic theorists persist with the notion of a price system grounded in ultimate welfare values. Here is an example: 'There exists, then, some set of prices, called "shadow" or "accounting" prices, which reflect the true *social* opportunity costs of using resources in a particular project. These shadow prices are not necessarily observed in actual market behaviour. As their name implies, they exist rather like Plato's universal.'[4] The reference to Plato is well taken, for it would require a philosopher-king or rather a bureaucracy of such gentlemen to decree the appropriate set of shadow prices.

Of course, most welfare economists would be more modest than the above quotations perhaps reveal. The notion of shadow prices can be utilised, no doubt usefully, in a variety of more restricted contexts. In practice, the economist's aim is not usually to rewrite the entire set of market prices but to amend them more pragmatically so as to eliminate or reduce certain 'distortions'. The interesting question is the nature of these distortions. According to the older utility theories, consumers could collectively maximise their possible welfare only if competition were perfect (equilibrium theories), whereas modern welfare theories make maximisation depend upon the absorption of indirect welfare effects which must, at the very least, be identified and measured wherever possible (see next chapter).

It would seem that old-fashioned equilibrium analysis of perfect competition offers a more internally coherent and intelligible set of recommendations than modern welfare economics can achieve. This is because welfare economics raises (and does not seem able to answer) a whole series of theoretical problems about such matters as the treatment of time, risk, and uncertainty; external effects; compensation tests and equity; etc. which form the staple fare of cost–benefit textbooks. The explanation for this difference is that theories of perfect competition assume either explicitly or tacitly a psychological theory which suffices to maximise consumers' welfare as a result of the competitive interplay of universal motives of self-interest and self-improvement. Modern welfare economics makes no such psychological assumption and instead requires public decisions on a large number of issues for achievement of an 'optimum' state. As a consequence economists have to find prescriptions for collective decisions on subjects which cannot be clearly answered by any kind of *economic* theory.

At the same time 'perfect competition', however intellectually persuasive it once may have been, can be criticised not only for neglect of social costs but also because competition itself may be claimed not to maximise welfare (thus Galbraith argues for the superior welfare effects of certain forms of oligopoly[5]). Welfare economists then have many reasons for wanting to rewrite market prices, and since they cannot actually do so cost–benefit analysis offers the substitute course of notional calculations as a guide for public decisions. But this recourse to government intervention still remains supposedly based upon complete respect for the preferences of individual consumers which have now to be elucidated according to a formidable set of special 'welfare' assumptions. Thus very different beliefs about the functions of markets are associated with the same kind of faith in 'consumers' sovereignty' which welfare economics has inherited from the utility theorists.

(ii) *The Summation of Individual Utility*

Compared with the broad question of supersedence of competitive conditions by ideal welfare conditions, the problem of defining and adding the units of utility received by an individual is a rather technical issue. (It is also less important than the next requirement.) Consequently I will deal with it briefly.

The technical problem here is that, while it could be argued that marginal utilities could be measured by prices (under the right conditions), no such confident assertion could be made about non-marginal utilities. If a man consumed six units of some good, it could not be assumed that he gets the same utility from each unit. The general belief, as noted earlier, was that he would get greater satisfaction from consuming the first unit rather than the last, which is the basis of the theory of 'consumers' surplus'. In other words the consumer was getting a *greater* utility than he was paying for.

But how much greater? There seemed no way of knowing. This and other difficulties relating to the price system, and to the point that money itself could not be assumed to have a constant utility, led some economists to abandon utility theory altogether. They no longer inquired into the motivations or satisfactions of consumers at all, but contented themselves with plotting the behaviour of consumers as registered through price and market mechanisms. A more modest response to the same problems was to discard the notion of *cardinal* additions of utilities and substitute the idea of *ordinal* measurements. In this situation one could talk of a consumer having different preference levels which could be arranged in an ascending order and mapped (at each level) by means of an indifference curve; but one could not measure the differences between these various levels.[6]

We need not follow these theories further. They seemed useful for some of the purposes of descriptive or positive economics, but they were not satisfactory for the needs of welfare theory. Welfare theorists have tended to retain, and indeed to make a great deal out of, the notion of 'consumers' surplus'. Their difficulty is to know how this surplus, if indeed it exists, is actually to be located and measured. It is not registered through the price system. It therefore occupies a shadowy world of implicit values whose configurations, even in pure theory, are anything but clear.

(iii) *The Aggregation of Individual Utilities*

This requirement is essential for the policy-maker using utility to construct a welfare calculus. He is required in some way to add together the satisfactions received by different individuals in order to know which policy to favour; but how can he know that a unit of utility has equal value in each case?

First there is a psychological problem. The satisfactions experienced by different people from the same commodity or from a similar kind of experience appear to differ, so what right have we to add them together? This difficulty has led some economists to conclude that any interpersonal comparisons of utility are impossible. As Little points out, this is going too far. We do habitually make such comparisons in ordinary life, for example when distributing presents among friends or members of a family, and we do not think that such comparisons are pointless. Little suggests that we make *ordinal* comparisons but shrink from *cardinal* ones. Thus it seems reasonable to say that Johnny will get more satisfaction from a bicycle than Susan from a doll's-house costing the same amount, but rather silly and artificial to contend that Johnny will get ten units of utility and Susan will get nine.[7]

As welfare economists nearly always recognise, there has to be some formula for the distribution of utilities if a welfare calculus is to be used at all. The issue cannot be dodged. If by default one accepts the existing distribution as satisfactory one is simply approving or endorsing the *status quo*; and if the *status quo* works all right in this respect why tamper with it on any other point? Bentham's dictum that the happiness (utility) of every person should be treated as equally important corresponds to a widely accepted ethical rule. According to the 'law of diminishing utilities', which does no more than reflect a common-sense assumption, a rich man gets less utility from his last unit of outlay than does a poor man; consequently total welfare could be increased through a redistribution of wealth which, if we attend only to this consideration, should presumably proceed until all incomes are equal. The felicific calculus turns out to have strong, indeed revolutionary, implications of an egalitarian kind.

Bentham refused to draw this conclusion. This was because *his* theories of pleasure and pain, like those of most classical economists, strongly stressed the social necessity of what today would be called 'incentives' – the spur of hunger to make men work and the pull of Smithian self-improvement to increase their efforts. It could then be claimed, as it still is today, that *inequalities* of wealth must be accepted for the sake of *maximising* total wealth. If this line of argument has any validity at all, then at some point more utility would be lost than gained through a redistribution from rich to poor; but there is nothing in welfare theories to tell us where this point will occur. Certainly one can study the subject empirically by observing the behaviour of different social systems and trying to draw conclusions, but that is a different matter.

Some will say that, even if total wealth (or total utility) is reduced at some point by redistribution, the result would still be a more just and hence perhaps happier society; others will contend that justice is not simply a question of the incomes received by individuals but of their *right* to such incomes which should be based upon skill, effort, or some other criterion of desert. We need not enter this debate which transcends the normal criteria of welfare economics; but merely to mention it perhaps shows the aridity of formal economic thinking about the distribution of utilities. Thus economic thought derives any vitality it has from its connexion with a much broader policy debate that can be expressed only in qualitative terms (albeit with illustrative economic data), and that cannot be put through the hoop of utility theories.

Actually, whether we are talking of cardinal or ordinal comparisons, the root of the problem is the old philosophic puzzle about solipsism or subjective idealism. When Lionel Robbins contends that, because we cannot know private states of mind, we have no right to assume that a poor man gets more satisfaction than a rich man from a square meal,[8] he is treading the same path which led Bishop Berkeley to doubt the existence of an external world outside of his own mind, and caused David Hume to contend that we have no logical reason to expect the sun to rise tomorrow morning. The philosophic sceptic confines knowledge solely to introspection just as the naive empiricist or behaviouralist confines it solely to observation. Neither position is tenable because knowledge necessarily depends upon an inter-action between the two elements (introspection and observation).

If it is possible to infer that other individuals have some similar wants or needs to my own, then it is reasonable to form beliefs about their experience of pleasure and pain; and naturally acquaintance with and sensitivity to other individuals enables these beliefs to be developed and enlarged. But it still must be admitted that interpersonal comparisons are more convincing in relation to the satisfaction of elementary wants and increasingly dubious in relation to sophisticated types of experience. Moreover, in the nature of the case we are in the realm at best of very plausible beliefs and opinions not certainties. This is no doubt what explains the greater plausibility of ordinal over cardinal comparisons.

Public policies seem necessarily to involve interpersonal comparisons of pleasures and pains, but not as a rule in a very exact way. Moreover, questions of 'utility' become entwined with questions of justice. Thus it would certainly be a generally agreed opinion (whether or not it is an empirical 'fact') that poor men get greater utility out of a square meal than rich men; but how far this belief justifies a transfer of cash or kind from rich to poor would depend also upon concepts of justice dealing with the relation between needs and deserts. In the many less-certain types of interpersonal comparisons of utility, ideas of justice seem to play a still stronger role. Thus in the earlier example of deciding whether to give a present to Johnny or Susan, many parents would stick to some notion of 'fair shares' which did not seek to measure the satisfactions of the two children; or at any rate the opinions (which would certainly be present) about the children's respective capacities for pleasure could play a minor or uncertain role in the decision. Thus the apparent inability of one child to enjoy himself might actually be a reason for giving him the present or for sharing the money equally. The decision would be guided by the need to show affection to both children and to assist their individual development, and probably not primarily or certainly exclusively by opinions about the utility effects.

These common-sense examples suggest that the goal of utility maximisa-tion is not in practice the sole or dominant criterion for personal decision, but no more than one possible factor in a 'multi-valued choice'.[9] The inevitable uncertainty of beliefs about interpersonal utilities, save in obvious cases, merely reinforces this conclusion. Public policies have to proceed on the basis of suppositions about aggregate or average effects, since detailed information is lacking, but this circumstance need not affect such validity or acceptability as the utility principle possesses.

Thus one can accept that interpersonal comparisons of utility do occur and are certainly not nonsensical. What cannot be conceded is that these comparisons are capable of being at all precise, or that they provide a sufficient criterion for public policy. Economic error on this point seems to have occurred through an invalid inference from resource flows to personal satisfactions. Since resource flows can be calculated with some precision, it is tempting to argue that these are corresponding personal satisfactions of an equally precise nature. The theory gains plausibility from the assumption of a rational consumer selecting goods so as to maximise his satisfactions, but 'satisfaction' in this context properly refers to the benefits of a free choice and not to some actual level of pleasurable experience. The individual's pleasure might have been greater if he had chosen differently, and anyhow he will not and cannot measure his personal state in the precise way that he (necessarily) allocates his resources. In some modern welfare economics, the idea of utility has to accomplish a great deal more, because instead of being a possible inference from the satisfactory functioning of a self-regulating resource system, it must act as the independent basis for contriving a satisfactory flow of resources. It is as if the ghost of Banquo had to order the menu at that unfortunate repast in Macbeth's castle.

iv) *The Meaning of Utility*

Finally does the concept of utility stand in any meaningful way for welfare? If not, how *could* welfare be defined? These questions, already touched on, must be more explicitly answered.

Utility does not seem to be a satisfactory term, except perhaps in relation to certain technical debates about the functioning of prices and markets under specific conditions. If we take utility as standing in some sense for the satisfactions received by individuals, we run into all the difficulties of knowing what these satisfactions really are, of measuring them and adding them. This realisation has caused the descriptive or positive school of economists virtually to drop the term, and to withdraw from offering any propositions about the relationship between economic activity and human welfare. In doing so they may safeguard the technical purity of their subject, but they also throw out the baby with the bath-water. For most people would not be interested in economics at all if they did not think it had some relevance to human welfare.

Possibly we can attach some normative meaning to utility if we define it rather differently. Instead of standing *for* personal satisfactions, utility can be viewed as the *opportunity* to choose satisfactions. Two men who have equal spending power can be said to have an equal opportunity to choose the satisfactions they want, to the extent that these are obtainable through economic purchases exercised under appropriate market conditions. If the spending power of each man is now doubled, it is again reasonable to regard this in the same limited sense as a doubling of their opportunities. In this sense utility harks back to its historical and still valid connexions with the theory of the market as a mechanism for the correct registration of consumer's choice.

The relation of this sense (or indeed any other sense!) of utility to the concept of *welfare* is another matter. The opportunity which a man has to spend £10,000 a year does not, in ordinary parlance, guarantee his welfare; and if in fact he spends his income on drink and gambling, we would suppose him to have a low level of welfare. This is because welfare at its plainest does relate, as utility when made intelligible does not, to the consumption patterns of a society. A welfare society is one in which considerable priority over the allocation of resources is accorded to nutrition, health, housing, social security, and so on; and a welfare state is one where the government plays a dominant role in bringing these results about, particularly in relation to the maintenance of minimum standards. Thus expressed, welfare remains a vague term. If someone wishes to include cultural opportunities in the definition of welfare few would object, although we might protest if wine-tasting were included. Welfare is therefore grounded in normative and sometimes teleological views of human needs, is surrounded with a large penumbra of vagueness and controversy, but expresses a certain weight of received opinion.

Familiarly enough the value of welfare is often in conflict with the value of individual freedom of choice. This is the traditional line of conflict between welfare socialists and the defenders of the market system and consumers' choice. None the less each contender may have a valid normative case within his own territory. There is no need to deny the advantages to be attached to consumers' choice in order to assert the case for substantial expenditure upon collective goods. The controversies concern the balance to be struck between individualist and collectivist spheres of activity, the ground-rules which should apply within each sphere, and their mutual inter-action.

What have economic welfare theorists to offer to this great debate? Not much perhaps. Their historical mistake seems to have been that they took over a concept of utility, which arose as a device for explaining certain factors of market situations, and tried to apply the notion to a much broader context of human affairs. In the process they lost contact with what welfare arguments are actually about and, intent upon finding a unique welfare function they smother (in books only of course!) some unavoidable conflicts of human values, instead of playing the genuine rationalist role of clarifying issues and narrowing areas of disagreement.

If utility has not much to do with welfare, it has even less to do with happiness. Happiness almost by definition is a *summum bonum* which cannot be measured, certainly not by economics. Of course economic tests do have *some* relevance to happiness. For example, an improvement in the standard of living, as measured (however imperfectly) by economic indices, would generally though not universally be regarded as contributory to happiness; and again most would accept that the poorer the society the truer this is, and the richer the more dubious.

It is true that welfare economists do not identify utility with wealth either, and they can accept that a reduction of material wealth is consistent with increased utility if (for example) people obtain greater satisfaction from the increased leisure than from the missing goods. But this statement merely refers us back to the earlier idea of utility as being no more than a subjective reflection of actual resource decisions. We seem to occupy a circular universe in which changes in utility are the result of shifts in resource use, and yet utility is also the supposed basis of resource decisions. However this conundrum be resolved it seems clear that utility as an economic term of art is quite different from 'happiness' as ordinarily understood.

C. The Pareto Test

It might seem that I have said enough, for the purpose of this book, about the defects of theoretical welfare economics. But it is necessary to look at one more theory or proposition which is important because it seems to many cost–benefit economists to offer a kind of minimal theoretical platform for the practice of their art. This is the Pareto principle which now usually occupies a central place of honour in any discourse on welfare economics, and which (while admittedly not saying a great deal) seems to offer a neat way out from the logical dilemmas or dead-ends to which utility theories have led.

A Pareto improvement takes place 'if some economic re-arrangement makes one or more people better off without making anyone worse off'; or (in an alternative formulation which avoids the cloying word 'economic') 'if one or more individuals in society can be made "better off" (i.e. reach a more preferred state) without any other individual being made worse off'.[10] Pareto optimality' will exist if no further changes of this kind are possible, but of course both logic and common sense suggest that an optimal position is most unlikely to have arrived. Hence the Pareto principle provides a nice theoretical cover for the economist to propose desirable social changes, the more so as at first sight it seems merely churlish to question the value of making a Pareto improvement.

If we are to apply this principle we must have some means of knowing how much worse off people will be made by some proposed social change, and of verifying that their losses can be fully covered from the benefits received by another group of people. If again we are to avoid the difficulties of interpersonal comparisons, thus making the Pareto principle watertight against possible objections, we must accept that only the affected individual can say how much worse off he will become as the result of some change. This approach to compensation utilises the 'consumers' surplus' concept. Suppose, for example, property owners must be bought out to make way for a public project. In addition to the market value of their property which (we will assume) is automatically paid them, it can be claimed that they lose further 'amenities' or advantages special to themselves that are not reflected in house prices. The attempted measurement of this 'consumers' surplus' is one approach to paying compensation according to the Pareto principle. The problems of this compensation principle are considered in Chapter 4.

The Pareto principle is not nearly as unexceptionable as it sounds, for reasons relating to rules of distribution. If the existing distribution of welfare is unequal, we might judge that it is desirable for some people to be made worse off in order to improve the lot of others; such a change would not pass the Pareto test even though we might rank it as of higher priority than many changes that *would* pass this test. The more generous the compensation principle, the fewer are the cases which can pass the Pareto test. In other words, the Pareto principle is strongly biased towards the *status quo*, and to those sets of possible future developments which are consistent with the *status quo*.

So far as cost–benefit analysis is concerned there is a final objection to practitioners relying upon the Pareto principle; namely *that they are not allowed to apply it*. Since compensation on Pareto lines is not as a rule actually paid to those made worse off, the analysis cannot do more than suggest that a given change *would* accord with the Pareto condition if this were to be honoured (which it will not be). As already indicated this limitation may not always be such a bad thing, but this point will hardly help to justify the resulting analysis on its chosen basis.

D. The Logic of Preferences

To many economists the discussion to date will have an old-fashioned ring because nothing has been said about the concept of preference. Much of modern economics seeks to get away from *any* ethical or psychological assumptions and to ground itself in the logic of choice. The theory is that we do not need to say anything about an individual's wants or motives in order to establish the nature of his preference in a choice situation. Individual preference is now taken to be the best available guide to individual welfare, and social preferences to social welfare. The ultimate criterion of C.B.A. is 'what society prefers', which is usually required (in line with the basic philosophy of individualism) to be derived in some way from the total set of individual preferences, although the 'social welfare function' can of course be derived in other ways.

The considerable logical and mathematical ingenuity that has now been expended upon analysing the concept of preference may be useful for the purposes of descriptive economics, games theory, and other parts of the discipline. For welfare economics, however, there is the prior problem of explaining why and in what circumstances a declaration of preference is an adequate guide to the welfare (or happiness or goodness) of the individual making it.

The concept of preference is linked inseparably to the logical conditions of rational choice. Unless these conditions are satisfied we cannot speak the language of preferences, although we may suppose that individuals have desires or inclinations which they have not formulated coherently. The necessary logical axioms are often described as connectedness, transitivity, reflexity, and continuity.[11] The important points here are that the individual must connect the alternatives with each other, he must rank them transitively (e.g. if he prefers A to B and B to C then he prefers A to C), and he must regard any state that is close to one alternative (say A) as standing in the same relation as does A to the other alternatives. There is room for argument as to how adequate or necessary these axioms are for the existence of rational choice. For example, the axiom of transitivity is logically compulsive only if each state is viewed in an identical light under each pair of comparisons. Since often in practice this condition is relaxed, one can understand how preference orderings which do not satisfy transitivity may yet seem not altogether irrational to an individual making them. In comparing each pair of alternatives he may be mindful of somewhat different criteria, although it is true enough that for properly logical choice he must keep his criteria uniform and constant.

In a normative sense these requirements might suggest that any desires which are not logically expressed as preferences cannot be covered by a welfare calculus. Actually there are two different problems here. Some individuals may lack the intellectual skill needed for expressing wants as preferences. In that case, unless one accepts a distributional rule of intelligence, the correct course is presumably to help them (of course if one tries to stick to a purely behavioural view of preference, this strategy is impossible). A second and overlapping problem is that individuals may *choose* to behave illogically, but even so their votes or market purchases will still count towards the result. They are not disfranchised by reason of their logical incoherence, whether or not they can be said to be exercising 'preference'. Actually, as has been suggested, logic of meaningful choice can be specified only in a very formal way, so that varying degrees of rationality can be and are attributed to actual behaviour depending upon one's assumptions about an individual's motives or intentions.

Starting rather too easily from the concept of individual preference, welfare economists usually make heavy weather of the further move to social preference. This is because the lion of Arrow's so-called 'impossibility theorem' now blocks the path. Arrow started from the position that a collective choice rule is necessary for combining any set of individual orderings of alternatives (one ordering for each individual) into a composite social ordering of the same alternatives. Arrow then argues that no choice rule can be found which satisfies a reasonable minimal list of acceptable assumptions.[12]

The logic of Arrow's theorem has been extensively analysed. It has been questioned or modified on various points but not convincingly refuted. For our purposes, however, the crucial question is the nature of the 'reasonable assumptions' which Arrow introduces into the attempt to move from individual to social preference orderings. To a considerable extent these assumptions represent applications to group decisions of the logical axioms said to be intrinsic to the notion of preference as rational choice (for example the transitivity axiom). Now it is easy to show, as in Condorcet's famous paradox, that each individual may obey the rule of transitivity without there being any possibility of finding a transitive group preference through majority or plurality forms of voting. Similarly Arrow is concerned to find a rule which is consistent with any logically possible set of individual rankings, at least for a limited range of three alternatives. It emerges that this cannot be done but that one can get closer to Arrow's aim *if* the individual orderings themselves satisfy certain standards of mutual consistency. For example the 'single-peakedness' restriction upon possible individual orderings requires that all individuals agree that one of three possible alternatives is not the worst one, and this restriction can be generalised into a requirement that some alternative exists which is neither the best nor the worst nor the medium choice of any individual.[13] By means of such a restriction the possibility of a transitive social preference ordering between three alternatives is improved.

It is easy to see that logicians are wrestling here with the political problem of consensus. The degree of 'consensus' can be logically tested in various ways, but in a crude sense it seems plain that the more congruence there is among individual opinions the more meaningful will it be to talk of 'consensus'. This raises the question as to how far any consensus which can be discovered derives from shared social values and norms, and how far it is an adventitious result from points of similarity in the preference rankings articulated separately by individuals. This is a sociological not a logical inquiry, but it has some relevance to the Arrow problem because the latter starts from the assumption that 'randomness' in the distribution of individual preferences must be protected as far as possible, that is no social dependence shall be assumed. Thus the discovery that there can then be no logical method of deriving a unique social welfare function will hardly surprise most people – indeed the amazement would be due if the result were otherwise; but the demonstration comes as a disappointment to those welfare economists who hope that 'individual preference' can do the conjuring trick of offering an indubitable standard of value which 'individual utility' could not manage.

The same problem can be reached from consideration of the interdependencies of individual preference orderings. An individual's ranking of alternatives will often depend upon (*a*) his assumptions about others' preferences and (*b*) his choice of values. Thus if I accept egoistic values I might regard the question of wage increases under inflationary conditions in the following way. My first preference might be to get the largest possible wage increase for myself and as little as possible for everyone else, my second preference might be that wage restraint should be applied to everyone, and my worst alternative would be that others do better than me. But the first preference might be impracticable, and *if* I could assume that others would accept restraint it might be better for me to choose the second alternative. If my values are different and I accept the welfare of others as having relevance for my rankings. I might well start with the second alternative or even with some version of the third one. This raises the question of whether or not economists should assume egoist values (see Chapter 6). Whether they do so or not, an individual's preference orderings cannot be isolated from his assumptions about others' behaviour, and the assumptions that he makes will depend upon the institution rules and social norms of a given society. This is true even in relation to conventional market behaviour, because the individual must assume that property will be respected, contracts enforced, and so on. Of course this interdependence factor need not prevent individual orderings (however these are arrived at) being taken as the raw material for a social-welfare function. Only the process has become circular because assumptions about social welfare *must* (empirically, not logically*) be fed into the individual preference function, and further elucidation of these assumptions then becomes logically necessary to the determination of any S.W.F.

In the real world the exercise of choice is confined to a variety of specific situations offering limited (usually narrow) sets of alternatives. This does not destroy freedom of choice as one value among others, but the recognition of this value turns upon rational interpretations of motives which are not provided by behaviour itself. The theory of 'revealed preference' rests upon a mechanistic assumption that, if certain logical conditions are satisfied, it makes no difference how an individual understands or values the choice which he appears to be making; but in this event it is not clear why we should attach any value to the supposed exercise of choice, even though a purely mechanistic treatment might perhaps be sufficient for certain predictive purposes. (In fact one has doubts; as Sen points out it is hard to make much of revealed preference without the 'peep into the head' which that theory is designed to exclude.)[14] Often the meaningfulness of choice depends upon an assumed background of social values. For example if I vote for candidate A rather than B, it will usually be assumed that I prefer A (or his party or his policies) to B, and the assumption will be true *if* I am playing the 'election game' according to certain democratic values which are encapsulated in these institutional arrangements; but it might be that my preference, within the alternatives available, was for B and that I voted for A from a belief that this would hasten the collapse of A's party or of the whole political system.

The welfare theorists tend to abstract from these restrictive conditions

---

* We use 'logically' here in a purely formal sense. However, to my mind, some of the more curious diversions of welfare economics derive from the philosophic (Cartesian) belief that nothing should be believed which cannot be demonstrated by formal logical deduction. As Descartes himself understood, a starting-point for *any* conclusions at all about reality must now be provided by some self-evident axiom, which he pinned down in the doubt of his own existence. The concept of 'utility' followed by that of 'preference' play analogous roles in modern welfare economics to Descartes's intellectual self-doubt. These concepts are then developed in an incredibly thin and rarefied zone of abstract thought. A difference is that utility or preference are suggested as ultimate tests of empirical *value* whereas Descartes was interested in a test of empirical *knowledge*. But this difference is not so great because welfare economists often assume that value is a question of fact, meaning that it is there to be discovered, thus also committing what is known in philosophy as the naturalist fallacy.

and to posit an individual who can order social states in any way he chooses, subject only to the technological and resource limitations of his society. They do so for the highly abstract purpose of examining the mere *possibility* of a social-welfare function erected on this foundation. They then discover that there is no unique S.W.F. but that various versions of this concept can be erected theoretically upon the basis of different collective decision rules. It is simpler, logically speaking, to posit a S.W.F. as determined by a dictator, when the Arrow problem will not apply, although the exercise seems rather barren as a basis for social prescription. These criticisms do not of course imply that the logic of collective choice is *itself* a barren subject because it may be interesting and useful to *clarify* the implications of possible decision rules; but this relatively modest task is far removed from the ambition to use some concept of preference as a surrogate for human welfare.

This blow to welfare economics need not be fatal if a much modified and more pragmatic position is taken. It can be accepted that no collective choice rule is wholly satisfactory for the combination of individual preferences, but reasons can be given for arguing that some rules are better than others. The individual now has to get the best choice rules he can and accept the consequences for the treatment of his particular preferences; and he will be more likely to accept this situation if it is understood that his preference rankings are not independently articulated but represent at least in part his responses to choice rules which already exist. His attempts to apply his preferences and to change the rules are related elements within a single process.

However, this process is essentially a political one, and the logical tools for its analysis belong to political rather than economic science. Where does this leave the welfare economist? He can pragmatically assume such collective choice rules as happen to exist and construct his welfare calculus on this basis. That position abandons part of his claim to possessing an independent yardstick of welfare but not all of it, because he might still claim to possess superior tools for measuring individual preferences within the framework of assumed collective rules (see Chapter 5). Alternatively and additionally the economist can criticise the choice rules currently in existence and try to deduce the consequences of alternative rules. The basis of his criticism here is none too clear. Once the claim to an unambiguous welfare calculus is dropped, the criticism can only represent logical applications of possible ethical positions. This may be very useful but it is not provided *qua* economist.

This brief look at preference theories concludes with two points. First, it is obvious that the concept of preference raises similar problems to that of utility. There are the same difficulties over defining individual preference (utility) and over aggregating preferences (utilities). There is the distinction that preference rankings are ordinal, whereas utilities can be expressed cardinally. This fact gives rise to the logical criticism that *intensities* of preference cannot be conveyed by ordinal rankings. Utility can of course still be derived as a function of individual preference (thus theoretically avoiding its identification with pleasure or happiness), and represented upon either an ordinal or a cardinal scale. But the aggregation of cardinal utilities leads back to the earlier problems of interpersonal comparisons which preference theories hoped to avoid. In fact C.B.A. does normally work with cardinal rather than ordinal scales so that this particular hurdle cannot be avoided.

Secondly, preference theories tend to rush quickly into logical problems and conundrums without examining their social foundations. It is only plausible to equate *A*'s preference orderings with his welfare if the conditions of his choices can be regarded as satisfactory. These conditions, however, cannot be scrutinised by any purely logical means unless we assume a situation whereby each individual first independently orders his preferences over the full range of possible outcomes, and then somehow combines the separate rankings. This is a wholly unrealistic picture. Once we recognise the circumstantial contingency and restrictiveness of actual exercises of preference, and the interdependencies of individual and social choice, we enter a realm where other principles of welfare must be sought besides the concept of preference itself.

E. Conclusion

The theoretical portions of textbooks upon cost–benefit analysis often convey an air of unreality to the perceptive reader. The author seems to have set himself an obstacle race in which all manner of objections to the *possibility* of an objective social-welfare function must be overcome. He proceeds in short bursts of argument covering vast issues, followed by lengthy exercises in mathematical logic which, not infrequently, advance the argument by very little. Warning signs reveal rocks which have to be elaborately circumvented: the problem of interpersonal comparisons, Arrow's impossibility theorem. Other signals draw us into allegedly safe harbours: the Pareto principle and once (but no longer perhaps) the Kaldor–Hicks compensation principle. It is a curious and perilous voyage, certainly the ship will be holed several times, but the real puzzle is where it is supposed to be heading.

After all the basic criterion of welfare economics is an ethical one. Somewhere there is an entity 'welfare' to be maximised, which supposedly should provide the sole criterion for public policy decisions (or at the very least – theories diverge here – a dominant criterion for a very large class of them). But what exactly is 'welfare'? The older utility theorists saw it as the sort of satisfaction or pleasure that a consumer would get from a free selection of goods and services under favourable conditions. As was shown earlier this sense of 'welfare' by no means coincides with its more conventional meaning which refers to basic standards of material well-being. Nor has the economist's 'welfare' a great deal to do with happiness as ordinarily understood although it may be an element in happiness. Still the older idea of 'utility' as welfare was in one sense rooted in the ground, because it was based upon the sort of satisfactions which a properly functioning market system could produce for individual consumers.

The more recent theories of economic welfare tend to cut the cable connecting this concept with the market system and its conditions of economic exchange, or anyhow to modify the relationship very considerably. They also part company with the idea of welfare as a psychological fact or state of mind. Instead they concentrate upon the idea of maximising the 'preferences' of individuals, which entails as we have seen a 'social-welfare function' for combining these preferences since it is *social* or public policy which has to be determined. This removal of the argument to a formal logical plane enables economists to have a field-day with the tools or toys of mathematical logic. But as the equations unroll, one begins to wonder where the ethical principle has gone. Its logical conditions or implications apart, the concept of 'preference' seems to be completely open-ended. What kinds of preferences are to be sought or anticipated, and under what social circumstances? Why should we assume that their exercise will be conducive to welfare (as ordinarily understood), to pleasure, or to happiness?

The answer is that we cannot and should not assume this. A preference is a preference – and no more; it implies nothing about states of mind or well-being except in so far as the articulation and satisfaction of preferences may be intrinsically desirable (and of course satisfaction here depends not only upon the logical problems of combining preferences, but also upon the social possibilities of their realisation). Theoretically perhaps there ought not to be a problem of realisation, because a properly structured logic of choice should deal only with realisable alternatives. In practice, the fit can never be anything like so neat: there are too many uncertainties, too many pressures for enlarging the supposed scope of the possible.

The new meaning which 'welfare' has acquired could almost be equated with some version of 'democracy'. Many writers stress the democratic basis or implications of welfare economics and C.B.A., although others disagree (see Chapter 5). The origins of this idea go back to 'consumers' sovereignty' or market democracy which was an obvious element in the old utility theories. Now the democratic element is more generalised. It is supposed to be good and right to give individuals their preferences of any kind whatever these may be (save perhaps for legal and some ethical restrictions). The lines of demarcation are now lost or very blurred between economics and politics since it is uncertain through what channels preferences ought to be assessed and conveyed. But to avoid becoming a branch of politics, welfare economics must reaffirm its possession of an ultimate truth. This has to be found in the notion that the economist can systematically map the structure of individual preferences and convert the results into a homogenous value scale. The process amounts to a sort of democratic science – a special economic version of the old idea of *vox populi, vox Dei.*

Some of the difficulties of such a 'democratic science' have already been indicated, and two in particular receive further attention in this book. First, there is the problem of making preference rankings economically operational, since they will not themselves produce the quantified (cardinal) figures which are used in C.B.A. This task has to be attempted through one of the more awkward traverses between different slopes of the welfare mountain as pictured in a typical textbook. The missing element may be provided by some version of the Pareto principle, such as the Kaldor–Hicks compensation formula,[15] which appeals to the subjective preference curves of individuals in order to get some measurement (in monetary terms) of the 'worsement' they suffer from some projected welfare change. The artificiality and frequent absurdity of such subjective tests, as well as their latent conservatism, receives attention in the chapter on quantification. The point here is that the economist having appealed to a world of purely private values whether expressed as 'preference' or as 'utility', has no logical escape route possible to the hard-headed world of C.B.A. as this is normally understood and practised.

Secondly, there is the problem of reconciling the concept of maximising preferences (or utilities) with appropriate rules of distribution. It is possible to demonstrate logically that *every* issue of maximisation is also an issue of distribution. Thus the economist cannot prescribe on any case without considering both these matters. It is here that welfare economics gets entangled with ordinary ethical judgements in ways that will be further explored in Chapter 6.

The Physiocrats and the classical economists were deeply concerned with trying to discover the true nature and causes of economic values. The labour theory of value was the favourite answer to this conundrum – the opinion that the price of any product was or should be determined by the quantity and quality of labour invested in its production. Unfortunately for the theory the movement of prices in market economies did not accord in any meaningful way with the postulate, which led most economists to explain prices in terms of the fluctuating conditions of market supply and demand, and of the logical responses to given conditions of consumers and producers. Descriptive economists thereupon abandoned the search for intrinsic economic values, but welfare economists took over the concept of utility used for a time to help explain market phenomena and sought in it a new criterion of intrinsic values. (Their failures have already been discussed.)

Thus cost–benefit analysts and their like are building upon a powerful economic tradition which once underlay (to some extent at least) the labour theory of value. Only this tradition is now monstrously changed and enlarged. The labour theorists of value at least started from a common-sense fact – that labour in one form or another was the main if not the exclusive input of production – as well as from a simple ethical idea that somehow it must be 'the sweat of our brows' which determines true values; and they confined their analysis to what may be called normal economic phenomena. But modern welfare and cost–benefit economists aspire in principle to measure any and every facet of human experience in terms of some idea of its true or intrinsic value.

It may be said in reply that the welfare economist derives his values not from the intrinsic value of objects or experiences but from the implicit preferences of individuals, as expressed under a diverse range of hypothesised conditions and as directed towards an illimitable number of theoretically quantifiable wants. But is not this extreme form of 'methodological individualism' itself a retreat into a solipsist world of private values, whose magnitude is revealable only through introspection? One is in a deeply tenebrous world of shades into which the illumination provided by actual economic exchanges penetrates but feebly. It is a Cartesian world. Certainly the Pareto principle and much else in welfare theorising invites such speculation.

This conclusion leaves open the possibility of a more pragmatic kind of cost–benefit analysis, which would help to articulate social values without becoming fatally dependent upon grand theories. This question can be left open for the time being, since it involves subtle questions about the interplay between political values and economic diagnosis which will be treated throughout the book and answered only (and then tentatively) at its end. However, at the level of theory, we have so far found little satisfactory basis for this economic mapping of social or misnamed 'welfare' values, and some evidence to suggest that the theories of welfare economists are guided by value judgements which are chosen more for their logical convenience than for their ethical or social adequacy.

3
The Puzzles of 'Externalities'

A. Government and Externalities

Much of modern cost–benefit analysis can be seen as an attempt to deal with the problem of 'externalities'. Public decisions, it is said, have indirect social consequences which are not adequately incorporated in the decision premises or assumptions. The role of logical analysis is to expose these consequences, and that of economists is to measure them where possible.

Now there is no doubt that this concept of 'externalities' refers to basic problems of policy-making. On the other hand the economists who are so ready with their measurements do not often consider the full meaning of 'externality'. The subject can be analysed logically, and also politically or sociologically, as well as in economic terms. This chapter will first look briefly at some logical and political aspects of 'externalities' before considering economic usages. Then we will return to examples of policy problems.

Logically speaking an externality might be described as a consequence of some decision which lies outside the normal or appropriate reference framework of the decision-maker but which ought somehow to be included within this framework. This definition is necessarily a normative one. Not *all* unconsidered consequences of a decision can plausibly be regarded as externalities, since a list of this kind would be almost infinite and would include many things that would generally be regarded as trivial or unavoidable. Thus the detection of externalities requires an exercise of judgement which is necessarily controversial and cannot be settled by automatic rules.

Externalities in this sense are a commonplace of personal decision-making. There will often be consequences of an individual's decision of which he failed to take account, but which subsequently he or others consider should have been considered. The phrase 'he or others' shows clearly enough the controversial element in the identification of externalities. Still there may sometimes be a good deal of agreement as to which consequences should have been considered.

The concept of externalities applies in very different ways to circumstances of business and government. In business the appropriate criteria for decision-making are provided by market or financial tests, not simply 'profit' in the simple sense but by criteria which relate to the financial conditions and prospects of the firm. The firm must of course, particularly today and if it is a large one, attend to various indirect consequences of its decisions that are of a political or social kind. These 'externalities' can be treated as constraints upon business decisions, or in some cases viewed as subsidiary goals for which the firm has some responsibility; but in any event they can be related fairly clearly to a basic core of appropriate criteria for decision-making.

When we turn to government the vista appears as much broader, grander, and mistier. There are of course political criteria which influence the decisions of government, sometimes very specifically, but these criteria are often subtle and debatable and not easily reducible to decision rules. In any case when we inquire what *ought* to be the criteria for government decisions as a whole, we tend to be referred to very broad goals indeed such as the safety and prosperity of the whole community, the maximisation of the welfare of its individual members, justice or equity as between different groups or individuals, and so on. This is particularly so under conditions of the modern 'positive' or 'welfare' state. There are still many things which (it can be contended) governments ought not to undertake, but even conservatives concede an enormously broad range to government action.

In this situation how are we to define 'externalities' in terms (initially) of a plausible political analysis? The task is not quite so formidable as it sounds because the work of government is factorised into a great number of programmes, performed by a variety of agencies, and the reference points for these agencies are at least clearer than for government as a whole. Thus we can build up a view of 'externalities' based upon three viewpoints: inter-agency relations, inadequate government powers, and comprehensive decision criteria.

(i) *Interagency Relations*

Frequently the activities of one government agency create burdens or benefits for another agency. These effects may not be considered adequately or at all in the decisions taken by Agency A, and looking at the work as a whole this seems a clear case of 'externalities' that have been overlooked. These externalities are easiest to locate when they arise in the form of transferred financial costs and benefits.

For example, a programme to relieve unemployment will (to the extent that it succeeds) reduce the unemployment benefits payable by a social security agency; therefore, it may be said, these savings should be deducted from the cost of the first programme in order to arrive at its true cost. Or, to give another example, the dispossession of a family from public housing for non-payment of rent may give rise to very much larger expenditure (than the lost rent) by public welfare agencies. In this case we are to infer that the dispossession had better not take place or at any rate only be decided upon in the light of a full public accounting.

Both these examples are quite valid, so far as they go. But even in these cases, the transferred benefits or costs are not certain or straightforward. How in the first instance are we to decide the volume of employment which an agency *has* created? If it has offered incentives to firms to employ more men, we cannot know closely (though we must try to judge) how much difference these incentives made to the firms' decisions; if the agency has effectively stimulated work in one part of the country, we cannot be certain how much potential work has been lost in other areas; if the effect of employment subsidies is to reduce the productivity of capital or labour through shifts of location, unsuspected long-run losses of employment may again occur. Equally of course the activities of the agency will have all sorts of beneficial indirect effects upon the creation of employment. In the second example, it is quite uncertain what costs have actually been saved – some or all of the costs to the welfare agency might have arisen in any event.

There is no need to be plunged into a complete sea of scepticism. Intelligent judgements can be made on many of these matters, with the aid of relevant evidence, but they are only judgements and sometimes necessarily close to guesses. There is a further, rather obvious point to add. Even if it seems clear that, when 'externalities' are allowed for, a different decision would be right in resource terms, this argument is not conclusive. In the housing case, for example, it might be thought a poor example to let a man get away with non-payment of rent (assuming he could pay) even at extra cost to public funds. If this viewpoint be too antique for consideration, many other cases can be envisaged where 'principles' might be judged more important than 'costs'.

Very often interagency 'externalities' will be still vaguer, in terms of resource costs, than in the example given; but they may be equally relevant for public policy. For example, as has happened in Britain, the development of a new town may be thwarted because the department responsible for industrial location refuses to allow firms to move into the new town, arguing that they should go to depressed areas. There is no interagency book-keeping to consult in this kind of case, and to look at the resource implications we must rely largely upon subtle judgements or guesses. Thus a C.B.A. on this subject would have to consider effects upon productivity, exports, and employment resulting from the choice of industrial location; effects upon the costs of associated infrastructure and public services; effects upon the satisfactions of workers and managers as measured (theoretically) by their willingness to pay for different 'packages' of facilities, opportunities, and environmental conditions; effects upon agriculture, the national transportation network, recreational facilities, and so on. Some of these matters are more capable of economic analysis and calculation than others, but in most cases economic estimates (if obtainable at all) will be speculative and arguable, and will depend upon a large number of often tacit assumptions about social causation and individual values.

The location of interagency externalities is *relatively* simple in so far as these can arise only from the interaction of the agencies themselves (we have not here inquired into the worth of their programmes). Even so, the question of which externalities are worth considering is still a matter of judgement. The interagency book-keeping approach helps to locate obvious cases for consideration, and provides a starting point for resource analysis but gives only uncertain answers to the questions raised. In a sense this conclusion accords with the viewpoint of cost–benefit analysis, which (like all idealistic economics) is biased towards progressive enlargement of the framework of analysis; but I have already suggested how elusive and elaborate the train of resource implications becomes, even in relation to interagency accounting.

(ii) *Inadequate Government Powers*

This gives us a different perspective upon 'externalities'. These are cases where some consequences of a government decision are clearly harmful to some section of the public, but lie outside the direct responsibilities and often the legal competence of the agencies concerned. The trouble may now be diagnosed as due to the absence of adequate public powers or methods.

A topical example is the nuisance of excessive noise created by public works such as motorways or airports. There are two different ways of tackling this problem. One way is to create a new public programme concerned specifically with the control of noise, perhaps combined with the control of other, comparable environmental hazards. This new agency would then specify permitted noise levels, regulate the lay-out of new developments so as to reduce noise, pay compensation where necessary, and so on. Its rules should of course be binding upon private as well as public developers.

Alternatively the noise nuisance can somehow be internalised as a factor in the decisions of government agencies. This might be done simply by persuasion and by increasing their legal ability to incur necessary expenditure, but it might require specific directions or decisions made by a higher authority, for example over the location of a proposed airport.

But before any of these decisions are made there will be a natural tendency for politicians and officials to inquire just how significant and deleterious is the noise nuisance. Various ways exist of answering this question; politicians can consult their mail or commission social surveys, doctors or scientists can advise about the effects of noise on health, sleep, and productivity. One further method is to commission an economic study which will express the noise nuisance as a hypothesised monetary cost. Whether or not the resulting figure is at all objective or plausible, this sort of economic measurement of an 'externality' fits nearly enough into the framework of policy argument. Its results may influence government policy either in general or over a particular decision, but they are unlikely themselves to form sufficient grounds for action.

(iii) *Comprehensive Decision Criteria*

So far we have taken a limited view of the existence of 'externalities'. From a broader perspective however, the world of government is crawling with these creatures. Part of the trouble is that much of the work of government is accomplished in indirect ways, such as the use of subsidies and regulations, not to mention advice and exhortation, which in various ways influence or constrain the acts of citizens and of private firms or organisations. These influences are not themselves 'externalities' because they are intended; but many of the *further* consequences which occur under the influence of government inducements and controls can be viewed in principle as 'externalities';

either because of their feedback upon public programmes or because of their significance for general welfare. Unfortunately such causal chains are enormously difficult to trace, and become matter for hazardous guess-work.

It may be objected that we are tracing purely logical relations which have little significance for economic analysis. But this is not so because comprehensive cost–benefit analysis is concerned in principle with *all* costs and benefits that can be discovered (at any rate all 'significant' ones – again a question of judgement), hence with the interrelations I have described. Moreover welfare economics is dedicated to the notion of a basic welfare calculus and criterion, so is led naturally to question the 'value' of particular programmes. Finally it should be noted that *all* the relationships I have mentioned do have resource implications, even though these cannot usually be known. It thus comes about that, as Aaron Wildavsky once remarked, for some economists the whole world is 'externalities'.

Of course, in practice, the utopian vision of tracing and measuring all these externalities is quickly discarded, even by cost–benefit economists. Still the influence of this comprehensive approach to resource analysis reveals itself in two ways. One is the continued temptation, already noted, to widen the analysis. The end of the rainbow is always just over the hill, but never is it actually found.

The other way is the fascination exerted by the idea of a *comprehensive* cost–benefit analysis for settling a particular issue. Instead of being bound by established programmes, policies, and precedents, why not (it is asked) take a look at *all* the costs and benefits that will result from a particular decision or policy, in so far as these can be ascertained? The same approach will mop up 'externalities' that have not yet been adequately considered, since these factors can now be brought into the grand equation.

In point of fact a *tabula rasa* of this kind is impossible, alike in political and logical terms. The problem has to be structured, decisions made as to which factors to include and whose interests to consider, and so on. In the end it may be claimed that political constraints are usually so considerable that much is to be gained and little lost by *attempting* a comprehensive approach, whatever its logical or analytical difficulties. In other words the dangers of utopianism may be less than those of sheer inertia.

I shall return to this argument, which certainly has plausibility, at a later stage when it will also be necessary to say more about different models of government decision-making. Here it is sufficient to note that the demonstration of 'externalities' reaches its logical climax in the case for comprehensive forms of analysis, but that this approach (whatever its therapeutic or shock value to the political system) opens up a vista of endlessly receding consequences and connexions.

B. Economics and Externalities

The forms of policy analysis which I have just sketched seem a soggy tool for coping with issues of 'externalities'. In contrast welfare economics appears to offer a much more precise instrument for the definition, detection, and measurement of some at least of these phenomena. Hence the frequent impatience of economists with political or administrative forms of analysis which rest upon no clear or explicit definition of 'welfare', and which can produce no precise calculations. Actually this contrast is very misleading. Welfare economics does indeed offer a set of theories for structuring the problem, but 'externalities' still prove to be very difficult to define and to locate, let alone to measure.

The earlier policy view of an externality as some indirect effect of a decision which ought to be considered clearly will not do for economics. Economics needs to state first what an externality is, then consider what should be done about it. An economic externality might be defined as an indirect relationship between two parties which affects the welfare of one or both without being priced or economically compensated. But 'relationship' here seems so general that it ought to be qualified. One way of doing so is to stick to the unpriced effects of economic production or consumption upon the utility of other producers or consumers. This enables us to locate externalities as being, so to speak, deviations from an otherwise price-controlled market system. For example, a factory owner must pay for his labour and materials but not for any soot which he may happen to deposit upon the persons or property of his neighbours; the latter can be viewed as a case of market failure. The same approach enables one to say that an externality only exists if in principle somebody is prepared to pay something to prevent or to produce the effect in question. A gain in trade must be theoretically possible between the two parties, even although institutional or bargaining conditions may preclude its occurrence.

However, this market-based concept of externalities will not apply easily to the effects of public policies since most of these are unpriced. Hence the wish of some welfare economists to define 'externality' more broadly than as a type of market failure or imperfection. The problem is compounded by the 'indirect' and 'unintended' character of externalities as these are usually understood. The usual notion of an externality is that an individual in legal pursuit of his own gain unintentionally confers some injury or benefit upon an unrelated party; if he intends the injury – if for example the factory owner *means* to pollute the neighbourhood in order to drive away political opponents – the description of the result as an externality seems perverse, and certainly the word itself is a misnomer. Admittedly some economists deny this restriction and want to use the word to refer to *any* impact by *B* upon the welfare of *A* that is sufficient to generate in *A* a wish for adjustive action through trade, persuasion, compromise, agreement, convention, collective action, etc.[1] Thus defined, externalities comprise the entire class of significant interpersonal acts, and market exchanges are simply one way of dealing with certain situations of this type. So large a concept is not very useful.

The idea of an economic externality as an uncompensated side-effect runs parallel to the earlier general discussion of 'externalities' in public policy-making. Just as the pursuit of economic gain in the market may result in unwanted and uncompensated side-effects upon third parties, so may the implementation by a public agency of its official duties or of its prescribed or presumed policy goal result in unwanted effects upon other agencies or upon members of the public. However, as already suggested, the concept of 'unwanted' in the second case is extraordinarily hard to test against any type of economic criterion, the only usual test being political reactions or responses. Economic analysis must therefore work within some political definition of relevant externalities, or at the most provide some information to assist this process of political recognition. Moreover, since psychological assumptions about the 'intentions' of actors (whether economic or political) are very hard to apply and have very limited relevance for judging the desirability of side-effects, ethical judgements about these effects have to be made and fed back where this is appropriate into redefinitions of the legal responsibilities of both economic and government actors.

Alfred Marshall's *Principles* first considered the significance of external economies or diseconomies for rules of pricing by discussing the case of industries where the arrival of an additional firm reduces certain costs for existing firms. These gains to other firms do not reduce the costs of the incoming firm, hence are not reflected in the price of the product which (if the industry is competitive) equals the cost of production to the marginal firm. In other words, the external economies of production created by the growth of the industry are reflected in a larger 'producers' surplus' (of profit or rent), and if the aim should be to maximise 'consumers' surplus' (as some welfare economists aver) then a lower product price and higher output seem to be indicated. Logically, according to this theory, the firm which makes the external economies possible ought to be compensated by the other firms who get the benefits. If we accept the theory it is hard to apply; the relevant savings are difficult to isolate and to calculate, and the transaction would be commercially unacceptable.

However, Marshall opened a Pandora's box. One way of classifying economic externalities (i.e. external economies and diseconomies) is in terms of the parties involved. This approach gives us a list of producer-to-producer externalities (e.g. Marshall's case), producer-to-consumer ones (e.g. the pollution case), consumer-to-consumer ones, and consumer-to-producer ones, although this last type of externality rarely seems to occur. Government agencies can be fitted into this classification. Interagency externalities are a special example of the first type, and might be compared in principle (although they are far more massive and significant in practice) with the externalities which one branch of a large firm inflicts or confers, often unwittingly, upon other branches. Public agencies as already noticed are responsible for numerous, indeed innumerable, producer-to-consumer externalities which can be unfavourable (as when public agencies themselves cause pollution) as well as favourable.

Economists usually also distinguish between 'technological' and 'pecuniary' externalities.[2] The former derive from the unpriced effects of technological change, as in the pollution example or when someone with a loud transistor radio annoys other individuals in his vicinity (an example of a consumer-to-consumer externality). The free benefits or uncompensated losses which producers derive from technological changes introduced by other firms or by government intervention and assistance belong in this category. Pecuniary externalities relate to changes in output or incomes that are due indirectly to changes in the level of demand, as when increased demand for agricultural products also increases the output and profits of manufacturers of agricultural machinery. Since these pecuniary effects are *not* unpriced and are absorbed by the economic system, it is usual to exclude them from cost–benefit analysis so as to avoid double-counting. More precisely, pecuniary effects are excluded if they represent only transfers of wealth between different sections of the community. Of course the distributional effects *are* relevant for welfare economics (see Chapter 6), but they pose different problems from technological externalities and cannot be treated in the same way.

However, pecuniary externalities are definitely relevant to the present discussion if they represent a use of resources that would otherwise lie idle. The most obvious example is the 'multiplier' effect of public projects over creating employment in depressed areas. If the workers thereby indirectly employed in service and other industries would otherwise have been idle, this welfare gain ought to be added to the direct benefits of the public project. The difficulties about this particular argument are (*a*) the practical ones of knowing how much of this labour would have remained unemployed and for how long (for example, some workers would move to jobs in others areas if the public project did not exist) and (*b*) the theoretical argument that increased employment could be brought about by selective measures of demand management, and therefore ought not to be credited as an indirect effect of a particular project. The first objection refers to the familiar problem of actually isolating and calculating an economic externality, the second one to the equally familiar problem of knowing precisely which public measure (or combination of measures) has brought it about. But neither objection removes the point that *if* men who would otherwise be idle can find work as an indirect consequence of public policies, this is a favourable externality of a non-technological kind.

The attention which some economists bestow now upon 'technological' externalities is a reflection of urgent social problems and stresses. Because of the mostly harmful effects which the uses of modern technology have upon 'free goods' such as water and air, and upon social properties such as the quality of the environment and the safety of the streets, some economists have naturally and very rightly concerned themselves with the social costs of these processes. But this concentration of effort does not alter the fact that, in principle, the economic notion of externality covers *all* indirect effects upon welfare which could be but are not priced or priced effectively in the realm of market transactions. Economists have a practical problem over where they should place the limits of their investigations.

The naivety of too comprehensive an economic definition of externalities can be seen from the frequent textbook example of the 'problem of envy'.[3] The writer will point out, for example, that a jealous woman might be willing to pay some sum in order to see a rival less well-dressed, or to remove her from the vicinity. The analyst will then wonder whether this is a legitimate theoretical use of the willingness-to-pay principle, and will ponder that society might not approve of this sort of application. Not only would society not approve, but no one is likely to find the formulation meaningful unless perhaps he is thinking of bribery or gangsterism. It is similar thinking which causes some economists to argue that the only and sufficient test of a welfare gain is whether the gainers can fully compensate the losers in money terms. However valid the proposition may be in relation to some definition of commercial transactions, it becomes obtuse when applied to the whole possible world of 'externalities'. For in many circumstances money is simply not commensurable with a loss of personal welfare, not for the reason that no price can be found (anything *can* be priced under certain assumptions), but because the two kinds of assets – money and the lost personal satisfaction – are simply not interchangeable. In some circumstances the paradox can exist that a higher money payment will *reduce* subjective welfare or happiness (see p. 84).

Of course many, and probably most, welfare economists, would not take up such an extreme position. They would concede that there are cases of welfare loss or gain which simply cannot be expressed in monetary terms. Such cases fail the test of quantification in a C.B.A. But how many such cases are there and where should the line be drawn? By *ad hoc* judgements or by some set of ethical or social principles? An economist might answer that the only limitation can be the professional one of his own capacity to measure externalities, and of the willingness of others (political leaders perhaps) to accept these measurements for certain purposes. But because of the ubiquitous relationship between welfare effects and the use of resources, economists are often asked or allowed to measure almost everything and can invariably find *some* technique for doing so. The true situation is not that these are exceptional cases which fail the test of quantification on social grounds, but that monetary quantification usually provides only a specialised and partial test of welfare whose usage has to be judged upon non-economic grounds (see Chapters 4 and 6).

To consider the economic problems of defining and measuring externalities let us return to the familiar example of the smoking factory chimney. Suppose that the citizens who suffer thereby are prepared to pay total sums of between A for partial and B for complete abatement of the nuisance, and that the factory owner will accept between X and Y for complying with their requests. So long as the line AB lies above the line XY or intersects it at some point, an optimum change for increasing total welfare can be discovered by economic analysis.

In more complex cases the welfare equation becomes harder to set out. Suppose that several private firms and public agencies are polluting a river or lake, as often in fact happens, and that the victims of the pollution include some determinate individuals (e.g. fishermen) and also a large number of indeterminate individuals whose welfare will be lowered, perhaps only in the long run, as a consequence of the pollution. There can now be no proper information at all about the sums which affected individuals would be willing to pay to be free of pollution, except perhaps for the fishermen. If the consumers' willingness to pay to abate the nuisance is in some way guessed at, then the consequent 'demand curve' might be related to a 'supply curve' derived from the cost to each producer of abating or removing his contribution to pollution. This requirement would introduce a bargaining situation among the producers, with each seeking to maximise his compensation or minimise his contribution. An alternative approach would be to determine the obligations of producers according to technical measurements of their contribution to river pollution. However, this arrangement would not be economically 'optimum', inasmuch as it would take no account of the cost and demand curves of the various producers, for example of the varying value of their outputs in relation to the social costs of pollution.

In such complex cases, which frequently arise in relation to technological 'spillovers', the derivation of an economic-welfare equation becomes highly indeterminate because the relevant data is just not obtainable. None the less, the theory of welfare economics still stands in these cases for an intelligible and defensible point of view – namely that the correct solution is the one which most accurately balances the costs of various forms of pollution against the benefits of various forms of production. Welfare economics is not committed to the social or 'civic' viewpoint that pollution is an evil which ought simply to be abolished, because some pollution at least will be worth incurring wherever its nuisance costs are outweighed by its productive benefits. The problem is that both costs and benefits accrue in complex and often indeterminate ways to large number of individuals, who are often the same people (citizens who suffer from pollution also benefit from cheap production).

Accepting this general theory of welfare economics for the time being, one runs up against not merely the practical problems of analysis and measurement which have been illustrated, but also the dependence of economic measurement upon institutional and sociological assumptions which arises even in the simplest cases such as the factory chimney. This requires the economist to utilise simplifying assumptions which require consideration.

(a) *The influence of law.* So far we have tended to assume that the victims have to compensate the producers of pollution if they want to abate the nuisance. We might just as well, and much more reasonably, have made the opposite assumption. Which assumption is the more *realistic* will depend upon the provisions of law, and actual laws have diverse requirements. Sometimes producers are allowed to treat natural resources as a common property which they can use or foul at will, sometimes they are constrained by regulations, sometimes (but in rather special cases) they have to pay compensation to injured parties. Our concern here is not to review these legal possibilities, but to consider what difference they make to the theories and solutions of welfare economics.

Whether 'consumers' of pollution have to compensate producers or vice versa, there should in theory be a welfare gain from any bargain struck between the two groups. However, the welfare effects will be different. In the former case the consumers will obtain only as much improvement as they are prepared to pay for, but if there is competition the output and prices of producers should not be much affected. If the compensation they receive can be used to pay for cleaner but more expensive methods of production, there will be no effects on price or output; if, however, output must be curtailed the final effects will depend upon the capacity of new firms to enter the industry under the postulated conditions. In the latter case 'consumers" welfare will be increased to a greater extent, but the industry's output will fall and its prices will rise to cover the compensation that must be paid or the pollution controls that must be installed. In this case prices and output will move towards or perhaps beyond the welfare 'optimum', if this is defined to include the indirect social costs of technological methods of production. This legal situation appears therefore to be preferable in welfare terms. Finally many intermediate stages can be envisaged under which the law places obligations upon both groups.

Even ignoring bargaining costs the amounts to be paid in compensation will also vary with the different legal situations. An individual will expect a different sum for tolerating a nuisance that can be inflicted upon him only with his permission, from the sum which he will be prepared to pay to prevent or remove a legal nuisance. The former sum will normally be higher (this of course is a deduction from psychology rather than economics). The reverse situation will apply to producers. It follows that the 'social cost' of pollution varies with the state of the law and also with the initial situation. Since the Pareto principle to which welfare economists frequently appeal is concerned only with changes from a given situation, it will follow (as Mishan points out) that the *continuation* of pollution may be Pareto-optimal even where the *creation* of the same situation would not be Pareto-optimal. In other words the measurement of welfare changes (and hence their desirability) is dependent upon the initial situation and the state of the law.

(b) *Bargaining costs.* In practice, it is quite unrealistic to ignore bargaining costs although these do not usually figure in the theories of welfare economics. A numerous and quite possibly indeterminate group of 'consumers' cannot organise themselves effectively to bargain with producers. For one thing the 'free rider' problem is insoluble, for example the inclination of most individuals to spare themselves the trouble and the cost of a contribution which in any one case will make a negligible difference to the result. A bargain can usually be reached at all only if a few individuals are strongly affected or are prepared for philanthropic or political reasons to take the lead (and in the latter case they will probably try to get the nuisance banned or controlled, not compensated). Buchanan and Tullock see the rationale for government intervention as deriving exclusively from the existence of bargaining costs; if these costs did not exist freely negotiated agreements would be the right way of treating externalities. The same authors argue that the price to the individual of government intervention can be viewed as another type of adverse externality, namely his consequent liability to taxation and coercion. The optimum position for any individual will depend upon the relationship between bargaining costs and the possible adverse effects upon him of government intervention.*

It would seem much more legally effective and reasonable to require producers to bargain with consumers, instead of the other way round, because there are relatively few producers, they have access to relevant legal and economic expertise, and they have a stronger and clearer incentive to reach agreement. However, there are obvious problems over deciding *which* consumers precisely have a right to compensation, and over dealing with the obverse of the 'free rider' problem, namely the ability of strategically placed consumers to hold out for very high compensation if their consent is legally required. Therefore under this legal situation the price of the product in question can be pictured as likely to rise *above* a welfare optimum. It is of course this situation which has caused all governments to fix and standardise the compensation payable for 'injurious affection' arising from railroads, highways, gas mains, and so on. It is hardly to be expected that most pollution problems or other technological spillovers can be treated more exactly. This implies substituting more rough-and-ready rules of compensation for the concept of an optimum welfare price.

(c) Social norms. When technological progress was widely admired and approved, and when its adverse spillovers were less widespread, there was not a great demand for compensation or public control. In the 1970s the climate of social opinion is rapidly changing. Indeed many people hold that sources of pollution ought to be banned or tightly controlled, whether or not this accords (as it usually will not) with an optimum position as defined by welfare economics.

In considering whether the onus for pollution control and compensation should be placed upon producers or consumers, welfare economics might seem logically disposed towards the former position. In this way producers would be made to absorb their indirect social costs, and prices and output would move towards the welfare optimum (an 'externality' would then be effectively 'internalised'). In practice, as was suggested above, to place the legal onus upon producers could be argued to increase the price of their products unduly because of bargaining problems, so that only a rough-and-ready adjustment could be effected. However, modern welfare economics is often guided by the Pareto principle which appears to require that producers who now benefit from their right to cause pollution must be compensated if this right is removed or modified.

Mishan reasonably criticises the *ethics* of this sense of the Pareto principle.

---

* This calculation is obviously impractical for any individual – there are far too many uncertainties – and the purpose of the authors is to establish appropriate constitutional or social decision rules on these matters which will command the widest possible (preferably unanimous) consent. The argument is interesting here as using the size of bargaining costs as an index to the practicality of a market solution, and also as introducing a still more stretched usage of the word 'externality'. See J. M. Buchanan and G. Tullock, *The Calculus of Consent* (Ann Arbor, Michigan, 1962) chapters 5–8.

He argues that whether or not such compensation payments are actually made, the costs of adverse technological spillovers in a C.B.A. ought to be calculated by reference to individuals' estimates of the loss of welfare which they have suffered in comparison with their previous state. (This as he shows seems likely to be different from the sums which they would pay to 'buy back' that state of affairs.) The general implication of this position seems to be that laws should be assumed to be prohibitive of technological developments which impinge involuntarily and harmfully upon the welfare of individuals.[4] Of course, welfare economists cannot themselves change the state of the law but they can (indeed as we have seen must) make some assumptions about legal conditions for the purpose of their calculations. These assumptions can either be no more than the *status quo* which seems to be the Pareto position, or a more ideal set of legal assumptions which appears to be the standpoint of Mishan. These different treatments of 'welfare loss' will in turn affect the desirability (in welfare terms) of public projects or policies.

The question of whether welfare economists should *notionally* rewrite the law when making their calculations raises the basic conflict between idealist and pragmatic applications of welfare theories. In the present context the question is how adequate Mishan's (or anybody else's) reformulation of legal principles would be for the purpose of welfare calculations. One problem is to judge whether some loss of welfare is sufficiently substantial and recent to warrant inclusion, because many fairly trivial or remote losses would not (to ordinary opinion) seem worth bothering about. Even if more ideal legal conditions are assumed they only become relevant if a sufficient welfare loss or gain can be deemed to have occurred. It seems impossible for economists to answer this question without the guidance of social norms and public opinion, because the individual's own *awareness* of his loss or gain depends upon these circumstances to a considerable extent.

Moreover, A's loss of welfare is generally a result of B's exercise of freedom. This is true at the individual level when B's acts of smoking or giving a party inflict a nuisance upon A, and true at a global level when the wish of many Bs to fly cause nuisances to many As. This is not simply a conflict between freedom and welfare because B's exercise of freedom can also be said to impose a certain loss of freedom upon A; he is constrained by A's acts. Welfare economists attempt to reduce these issues of freedom to units of welfare. In so doing they are following the tradition of economic thought which assumes or postulates the 'freedom of the consumer' subject to certain ethical and social restraints that are imposed by law. Economics has not normally bothered itself about the nature of these constraints, except for a tendency to favour keeping them to a minimum where market transactions are concerned. But this traditional treatment will not suffice when economics concerns itself with the measurement of a myriad of 'externalities' which lie outside the market system and which are normally judged according to social norms or principles. Economic measurement can only plausibly be extended to externalities at all in cases where the existence of a market can be predicated as possible and desirable in principle, and where its conditions can be specified.

The first of these conditions eliminates many cases which are primarily the province of social norms or ethics (such as the 'problem of envy') and puts a question mark after all those cases which public opinion and most individuals do not normally judge in economic welfare terms. The vagueness of this criterion seems to be unavoidable because, unless there is a perceived loss of welfare which can be traced to some determinate source, there is no empirical basis for its measurement. The second requirement (the need to specify appropriate institutional conditions) seems to be incapable of solution by welfare economics, because different assumptions yield different measurements. Though welfare theories may *point towards* optimum positions, they cannot specify which institutional arrangements would produce the optimum.

Mishan's notional rewriting of the law of nuisance according to what he terms the 'law of exact compensation' illustrates a basic quandary of welfare economics. His 'law' is actually an ethical position which requires that any involuntary loss of individual welfare should be fully compensated. The practical problems of applying such a principle are formidable and as already indicated would have to be worked out through legal and judicial interpretations guided by public opinion. At the theoretical level this 'law' is similar to the Pareto principle over requiring full compensation for losers, but much more drastic over setting aside the network of established rights which the Pareto principle is usually presumed to honour. As applied to the law of externalities the Pareto principle may appear as much too restrictive, and the Mishan principle as far too utopian. Ultimately all such principles have to be judged by non-economic criteria (see Chapter 6). The only way out seems to be to recognise that economic measurement must be dependent upon assumptions which cannot themselves be decided on economic grounds, but that it may still be a useful act to plot the economic consequences that are linked with alternative assumptions. At a pragmatic level it is obviously unwise for economics to get too far away from the existing state of social norms and public opinion. These social factors have to be consulted in order to determine what externalities it is reasonable to try to express in economic terms. But it does not follow that economists must simply be bound in their calculations by the existing state of the law; they can at the least often suggest reasons of economic welfare for changing the law and show some of the consequences of doing so.

Moreover, the existence of 'cultural lag' in the state of public opinion and particularly in the state of the law gives a fruitful leverage to reformers of all kinds, including economists acting in a reformist capacity. 'Cultural lag' is indeed very obvious in relation to some technological spillovers, which are still treated according to legal and market assumptions that can no longer be regarded as socially acceptable. On such issues economists are favourably placed to act as social reformers because they are assumed to be speaking 'scientifically'. The onslaughts upon the evils of environmental degradation made by such writers as Mishan in Britain and J. K. Galbraith in the United States command respect for this reason among laymen (economists themselves are usually more sceptical). Many of the essential elements in these critiques could just as well, and often more logically, be expressed in non-economic language, but this would sound less impressive. The economic analysis is convincing enough when it is directed towards the deficiencies of *laissez-faire* and market doctrines, but becomes less adequate when it purports to substitute a rival body of welfare theories.

This section can now be summarised. An economic treatment of externalities* can follow one of two routes. It can seek to internalise some of these factors through amended rules of market pricing, but the difficulties of organising appropriate markets generally defeat this course of action. Sometimes pricing of externalities cannot be introduced because of the widespread and somewhat indeterminate nature of welfare effects. Where these effects are assignable, there remain the problems of dealing with legal conditions and bargaining costs. The legal framework may be changed, and it is a reasonable task for economists (in conjunction with sociologists, lawyers, and political scientists) to assist with reform proposals. But while legal reforms might make some headway over 'internalising' the social costs of adverse spillovers, they could hardly overcome all the difficulties which preclude the absorption of externalities into a coherent system of market pricing. Corrective action therefore primarily turns upon the use of public regulation and of fiscal incentives or taxes, which can only make use of economic welfare theories in a very rough-and-ready manner.

The alternative economic route is to reveal the social costs and benefits of 'externalities' through cost–benefit analysis, so that public policies can be guided accordingly. The first problem here is that of collecting relevant data, which runs into difficulties both of assigning welfare effects and of disentangling valuations from normative beliefs (or alternatively of incorporating these beliefs in a systematic manner – see Chapter 6). Additionally the economist must make assumptions about legal and institutional conditions, and it is hard to know what he should assume since it is the unsatisfactory state of these conditions which partly accounts for his services being enlisted. Economic measurements are therefore bound to be conditional and arguable even if the underlying approach of the welfare economist to these questions be accepted. But some figures may still be better than no figures, and economic measurement may still be serviceable where it can be related consistently to a policy context.

---

* The discussion here of economic theories of 'externalities' is necessarily limited and condensed. In particular a distinction ought to be drawn between problems of finding prices which would correspond to those of a market if such existed (which it does not), and problems of rewriting all and any prices to allow for theories of consumers' surplus. The two issues become entangled because of the tendency of welfare economics towards trying to measure externalities according to concepts of consumers' surplus which do not enter into actual market prices. This is *one* reason for the high rates of return upon investments which C.B.A.s often show in comparison with orthodox financial types of appraisal.

C. Transportation and C.B.A.

We will now consider applications of the economic concept of 'externalities' to public policy analysis, and we will use the burgeoning field of transportation studies for this purpose. The discussion will be concerned less with the details of techniques than with the logic and policy assumptions of types of cost–benefit analysis. It will emerge that the validity of any measurements in a C.B.A. is closely dependent upon how the issue is 'structured', and that far too little attention is usually given to this subject by economists themselves.

Before proceeding it will be as well to expose an ambiguity about the idea of a 'technological' externality. Unless our perspective is completely deterministic, the effects of any technological change will depend upon human reactions to its availability and upon institutional arrangements for coping with change. In point of fact there does seem to be a sufficiently constant element in human behaviour for some technological developments to have similar behavioural effects in a wide range of social contexts. This result looks like technological determinism and perhaps can be explained by some general human tendency to exploit the immediate opportunities of technological development and to discount longer-term effects which conflict with short-run advantage. The ripple effects of technological change, however, depend upon complex social and institutional reactions, and become more variable and less predictable as one widens the analysis.

Consider the familiar example of the technological externalities of the internal combustion engine. We can analyse the ripple effects of the growth of motor traffic as these impinge upon progressively broader realms of social behaviour and adaptation.

Stage 1. The makers and buyers of motor cars interact to cause increasing production of a personal convenience good which is profitable to sell and useful to own.

Stage 2. Roads are publicly provided in response to demand. Traffic congestion and accidents create a need for extensive public regulation which interacts with the habits and norms of road users.

Stage 3. Motorisation reduces the usage of public transport and impedes its operations, which then deteriorate. (Demands for public subsidies.)

Stage 4. Motorisation influences the location of homes and workplaces, encourages urban spread and dispersal, and changes the shape and structure of cities. It also has certain blighting effects upon zones closely affected by road traffic. (Demands for comprehensive planning.)

Stage 5. Motorisation combines with other factors to influence sex mores, crime, and other aspects of social behaviour. (Possible effects upon climate of policy-making.)

Now all of these developments (except the first stage) could be loosely described as 'technological externalities' of the automobile, but obviously they vary enormously in the directness and certainty of the postulated effects which are related to complex factors of social behaviour and institutional response. Thus stage 2 occurs directly and universally because of inescapable processes of social interaction, although the scale and effectiveness of public regulation varies. Stages 3 and 4 are effects of a more indirect nature. Although broadly present everywhere, and obviously related to levels of income and economic development (which influence both the scale and the uses of motorisation), the effects also depend upon the responses to motorisation of a given social and political culture. Moreover, other *technological* factors are also influencing both the size and structure of cities and methods of public transport. On the other hand the blighting effects of motor traffic listed under stage 4 represent a more direct type of relationship. Finally stage 5 is the least determinate of all because so many other factors are influencing behaviour, and because the relationship postulated may be fairly direct (e.g. the assertion that crime has increased because fewer people walk or use public facilities) or extremely oblique (e.g. the assertion that a motorised society stimulates private greed and reduces civic spirit, hence leading to more crime).

Thus a 'technological externality' represents a behavioural response or reaction to a technological change. Responses vary from the relatively direct and determinate where only minimal behavioural assumptions are needed, to increasingly complex and arguable types of relationships. Economic analysis tends naturally to concentrate upon the more simple cases and is bound to flounder with increasing complexity. Thus it may seem sensible to say that motorists impose costs upon pedestrians by knocking them down or impeding their movement, but dubious to suggest that motorists impose costs upon householders and the police through creating an atmosphere favourable to burglary. In principle, of course, welfare economics recognises no social rule* which can restrict its analysis in this kind of way; *all* welfare effects for which people would pay ought ideally to be measured, and theoretically speaking the analysis only runs out of steam for lack of data. In practice C.B.A. is much more restricted, and this circumstance should require analysts to explain why they are measuring some externalities rather than others. This justification calls for a kind of policy analysis which economics does not itself supply.

Public policy analysis deals with the complexity of externalities in a

---

* One way to find such a rule would be legal and ethical definitions of responsibility. Thus for Meade an externality arises where an individual suffers loss of welfare from a decision to which he would not willingly consent. This approach like Mishan's (pp. 143–4) bases economic calculation upon a presumed ethical principle. In practice many welfare effects seem definite enough but have multiple causes so that responsibilities cannot be clearly assigned, while the idea of responsibility is itself complex. Thus Meade contends that employees have agreed to any adverse welfare effects that result from the terms of their contract, but that citizens have not agreed to the adverse effects of government intervention. This doctrine would completely undermine the concepts of political and legal legitimacy as normally understood. These attempts to modify the otherwise completely comprehensive definition of an economic externality do not seem very successful.

rather different way. There is the same natural tendency (as in economic analysis) to concentrate upon the more direct and determinate effects, but a greater willingness to attend to more speculative relationships. It matters less than to the economist that these relationships cannot be properly isolated and measured. But policy analysis even when systematically carried out by public authorities (as we are here assuming) is necessarily pragmatic and selective. Thus 'externalities' will be assigned to different policy areas, depending upon institutional perspectives and responsibilities as well as upon prevailing beliefs about relevant relationships. To return to the ripple effects of the automobile, stage 2 is the province of agencies concerned exclusively or primarily with such effects (road-building and traffic management). Stage 3 effects will first be tackled through changed public transport policies but eventually may form a major argument for comprehensive transportation planning and co-ordination. Stage 4 effects will be tackled as one factor in urban and regional planning policies, possibly with increasing 'feedback' to transport and traffic policies. Stage 5 effects will be tackled (if at all) through quite different realms of public policy, but are unlikely to affect policies for motor traffic except perhaps through a subtle influence upon public opinion.

It is time to leave these generalities for more specific analysis. Transportation planning provides an obvious arena for the application of C.B.A. for a variety of reasons. First, roads are usually publicly financed and provided, and there is only a tenuous and arguable relationship between the taxation of vehicles and petrol and the costs of road provision.* In the absence of direct road charges there is no easy way of discovering how much consumers are willing to pay for road improvements, what kinds of facilities and routes they prefer, and so on; and linked with this problem is the issue of congestion costs. Since engineers who design roads are hardly qualified to solve these problems, there is an obvious case for utilising some sort of indirect economic analysis.

Secondly the agencies responsible for various kinds of transportation (such as highways, railways, and air services) impose significant costs and benefits upon each other, in other words present notable examples of interagency 'externalities'. These interconnexions are harder to trace, and hence call for more subtle analysis, because of the different financial frameworks of the agencies concerned; public transport and air services are usually paid for directly by their users (although they may be subsidised) whereas roads usually are not.

Thirdly, transport developments as we have noted give rise to various externalities which affect people other than the transport users themselves (but which affect them too in other capacities). Some of these effects are fairly

---

* Figures of relevant taxation and expenditure can only be compared as total aggregations, and this comparison still cannot justify even a notional assignment of specific taxes to specific services since the former may also be regarded as general-purpose taxation. A possible exception is where vehicle or gasoline taxation is assigned to a road fund, as sometimes happens in the United States. This device, although financially precarious, brings highways closer to the concept of a user-supported service at the aggregate (but not specific) level of provision.

obvious, such as noise and fumes, others are much subtler, such as effects upon the structure and functioning of cities, access to social and work facilities, and so on.

These three types of problem require successive enlargements of the framework of analysis. In the first case attention is focused upon demand and supply for road facilities and upon transactions between and amongst road users. In the second case the same questions are considered in relation to all transportation facilities and users. In the third case the analysis comprehends the relationship between transportation and (necessarily) selective aspects of environmental planning, together with transactions between users and non-users.

This statement of the relationships to be analysed poses some awkward problems. In the first place one must be careful to specify the meaning and the incidence of costs or benefits in each type of analysis, since otherwise the scope of the analysis may shift without the logical implications being admitted or perhaps even realised. Secondly, however, these distinctions do not offer any clear guide for comparing externalities of a different logical status; for example, the congestion costs which motorists impose upon each other are different in principle from the environmental costs which motorists impose upon others, yet public policy options must consider both types of cost. Finally a restricted framework of analysis is more manageable but (because of what is left out) will be logically relevant only within narrowly defined policy contexts; but the more comprehensive analysis encounters difficulties which cannot be resolved by economic tools of analysis.

C.B.A. studies have tended to start with the narrower issues (as defined above) and to move cautiously and uncertainly towards the broader ones. This is understandable; tools of measurement are best applied to problems that can be appropriately, which usually implies narrowly, defined. But behind this issue of the scope of such studies, there lies some uncertainty as to how transportation itself should be viewed. If it is viewed as a complex but ordinary consumer service which could be provided by the market but happens often to be publicly provided for technical reasons, then one seems to have a good specification for the use of C.B.A. within a limited context. There is then no need to struggle with the sort of 'intangible' values which arise in the case of such public services as education or health. But if one attends to interactions between transportation and environment then a 'commercial' treatment of the former subject becomes inappropriate, and many intangibles* enter the picture. We will now consider the logic of different treatments of 'externalities' within successively wider policy contexts.

---

* I am using intangible here to refer not to the difficulty of making an *accurate* economic calculation but to the difficulty of finding any appropriate or plausible *method* for calculating some economic value. However, a value which can be calculated may sometimes seem to an observer to have more doubtful significance for policy-making than an intangible factor which *cannot* be calculated.

(i) *Road Investment and Pricing*

While there is no direct market evidence (unless toll roads exist) about the sums which road users would be prepared to pay for improved facilities, a surrogate for such evidence can be sought through estimating the costs which would be saved by new or improved roads. Reductions in congestion costs can be calculated on the basis of predicted savings in vehicle operation and in the time spent on travel for which a money value can be calculated in various ways. The costs of accident reduction can also be calculated.[5] These figures can then be combined and weighted to produce the return in cost savings to road users which a given road investment is expected to produce. This in outline has become the standard method used by government departments in Britain and elsewhere for evaluating and comparing possible road projects.

Central to this analysis is the notion of congestion costs. These rise with the number and pressure of road users upon a given quantity of road space. An extra motorist on a congested road inflicts externalities upon all the other road users in the form of time delays and higher running costs. If one accepts this logic there seems to be an obvious case for applying the rule of marginal-cost pricing. The marginal *social* cost, which is the relevant consideration for welfare economics, can now be defined as the extra cost imposed by the last (marginal) motorist upon all other motorists. This analysis not only provides data for estimating returns on road improvements, but also suggests the desirability of introducing some form of differential charging for the use of congested roads (or, more realistically, for roads within some area defined as congested). Expert proposals for overcoming the technical problems of road pricing have been made in Britain and elsewhere and are receiving political consideration.[6]

Although this general analysis and presumption appears at first sight to be persuasive, its logic requires close investigation. The same sort of marginal social costs occur whenever a crowd assembles, for example at a football match or a bathing beach. In these cases the result is assumed not to matter, presumably either because the mutual inconvenience is less significant than on the roads or because crowding together can be an actual pleasure for some people on some occasions. This leads one to wonder whether road users actually mind the inconvenience quite as much as economists assume. (No doubt many will say it is a nuisance but that is hardly conclusive.) If they do mind, why do so many motorists sit patiently on the most crowded roads on a Sunday when there are so many alternatives open to them? Why do so many people make crowded journeys to work on the roads when they could exercise some influence for employment to be located in less-crowded centres?

These psychological reflections at least cast some doubt upon the validity of using estimates of possible cost savings as a surrogate for the economic preferences of road users themselves. Ingenious ways can be found of deriving a market price for time savings in particular circumstances, but the doubtful propriety of generalising time values from special cases is obvious (see also Chapter 4). There may be many cases where individuals would put almost a zero or even a negative value upon time savings. There is also an awkward problem as to how far economic costs of congestion are inseparably linked with economic benefits; for example, whether burdensome delays to travel in cities such as London, Paris or Tokyo are not an inevitable concomitant (at least to a considerable degree) of the locational advantages of these places. This is not to deny that traffic improvements are possible in large cities, but only to ask *how far* congestion costs are removable in such cases. To the extent that they are not, it might be said that individuals are prepared to pay for them for the sake of locational advantages.

Two general justifications can be offered for special road charges. One is that they will have a favourable effect upon total consumers' surplus – in other words, the gain to the remaining motorists from reduced congestion will outweigh losses to those squeezed off the roads. Even if measurements of congestion savings exaggerate potential benefits to road users, they are so considerable as to suggest substantial beneficial effects for the remaining users; but the loss to those squeezed out cannot be guessed at without knowing their alternative options (see pp. 57–62). Secondly, it may be said that the congestion savings represent an obvious gain in economic efficiency and productivity. Once again the size of this gain would depend upon the adverse locational effects (if any) of preventing some traffic from using the roads.

Whatever the justification for road charges in congested areas (in principle the case is a strong one), the use of congestion savings for calculating highway benefits in cost–benefit analysis warrants careful scrutiny. The possibility that benefits to road users are thereby exaggerated may be thought not to matter greatly so long as the intention is only to compare one road project with another. Any comparison of road benefits with the returns from other investments is very misleading because of the specialised conventions employed in road economics (the very high rates of return which these calculations usually produce does at least suggest an exaggeration of benefits). But even within a comparison of road projects, an exaggeration of congestion savings will confer a differential advantage upon road projects in congested areas because the savings appear to be so high in these cases.

There is also the important question as to how fully and quickly congestion savings will be cancelled out through the attraction of additional traffic on to the improved roads. Better road conditions have the effects of encouraging more car ownership, more or longer journeys, and shifts of homes and workplaces to take advantage of easier travel. It seems extremely difficult to separate out this 'generated traffic' effect from the growth of traffic that would occur from other causes, but particularly in populous urban areas there is a large potential demand for more car trips if it is possible to make them. In these areas, however, rising congestion costs stand in the way of indefinite growth and produce some sort of 'congestion ceiling'. For these reasons it would seem that congestion gains are usually short-lived in urban areas, and that the real benefits of road investments lie in the extra journeys that are thereby made possible.

C.B.A. usually deals with this 'generated traffic' by assuming that it will share in the benefits of road projects but not to the same extent as existing traffic (because the values of the new journeys must be less than existing journeys or they would already be being made). Some arbitrary proportion (often 50 per cent) of the benefits assigned to existing traffic is then credited to this generated traffic. Perhaps the benefit is kept relatively low out of appreciation of the ambivalent role of such traffic in relation to time-savings and vehicle operation. A method whereby 'benefits' quickly dissolve into 'costs' as traffic grows is something of a quicksand for logical analysis. Whatever benefits the new roads yield, they cannot very plausibly be represented in terms of time savings. Since road projects in urbanised areas are also very expensive, this apparent overloading of benefits will still as a rule leave them with lower returns than much lower-cost projects such as intercity highways. Still the methodology has probably given some succour to a number of urban road projects which would not have ranked so highly on a more logical appraisal of the effects upon road conditions.[7]

If road charges are introduced the situation changes. The charges can be fixed so as to keep congestion costs below some prescribed level, and if congestion increases they can be raised. Some market information now becomes available to indicate whether further road investments are economically worthwhile; for example they will be worthwhile (in terms simply of the preferences of road users) if they could be paid for out of higher charges. In this situation then there is less need to use indirect measurements of benefit for the purposes of investment appraisal. But the logic of C.B.A. calculations, as they are now typically made, will fare no better in this situation than in the previous one. Logically, as before, the benefits of a new road investment will usually lie somewhere between (a) enabling an existing volume of traffic to operate at a reduced level of congestion and (b) enabling more traffic to operate at the same level of congestion. If there are road charges these can be manipulated so as to try and bring about the preferred mixture of results, but except in a full case of (a), the benefits consist only partially (if at all) of congestion savings.

The costs of accidents can be reckoned in many ways but the hardest problem is to assess the economic worth of human suffering and loss of life (see Chapter 4). Whether this factor is treated as an 'intangible' or given some notional figure, it must still be combined somehow with the congestion savings to produce the estimated benefits of a road investment. The problem is the harder because the two tests of benefit are sometimes contrary. A speed-up of traffic flows will not necessarily reduce accidents, indeed in itself it will tend to increase them, whereas road congestion reduces the lethal power of the automobile. A cost–benefit analyst naturally cannot resolve such problems, he can only show the assumptions of his calculations and leave politicians to change the weightings of different factors if they wish. But politicians and other outsiders rarely if ever look closely enough at the logic of a C.B.A. to exercise this oversight, so that the conventions of the analyst in fact settle the treatment of accidents and their weighting in the equation.

This exploration of a standard but narrow issue of road economics illustrates some of the difficulties of treating 'externalities' in a C.B.A. even where there appear to be good grounds, and some suitable evidence, for making the attempt. The measurement of congestion costs and accident savings to compare the benefits of different road projects can be claimed to be at least a useful *aid* to decision-making so long as the underlying conventions are understood and treated comparably in each case. But closer inspection reveals the slipperiness of congestion savings as a guide to realisable benefits, and suggests that the benefits of some kind of projects get exaggerated in terms of the supposed criteria. In practice, the reconciliation of road-safety and traffic-flow criteria cannot easily be tackled through the general formulations of a C.B.A., but depend upon a mixture of traffic measures and design criteria which have to be worked out on the ground. The general or implicit social valuations on such matters (which is what C.B.A. seeks) are intrinsically too vague and ambivalent to be expressed other than within wide margins, which explains the amount of controversy (*and* the scope for imaginative integration of conflicting considerations) which arises in individual cases. C.B.A. itself cannot settle the controversies or provide the practical and professional imagination needed to resolve them.

(ii) *Transportation Planning*

We will now widen the analysis to cover interactions between private road users and users of public transport. This is an arena of obvious and substantial mutual 'externalities'. Increased road traffic impedes bus operations and frequently worsens the load factor for public transport, causing higher costs and poorer services. Conversely, investments in public transport remove some traffic from the roads and reduce congestion costs, unless and until equivalent new traffic is 'generated'.

C.B.A. studies can be said to have done a useful job in exposing the importance of 'externalities' of this type; but at the same time both their conventions of measurement and their policy assumptions seem easily to lead them into exaggerating the favourable effects of public transport improvements. This is certainly the case with British studies. In the well-known Victoria Line Study by Foster and Beesley,[8] well over half of the total benefits that were assigned to construction of this proposed new underground railway in London were credited to travellers not using the Victoria Line itself. Part of these gains went to other parts of the London transport system (e.g. buses and other sections of the underground), but far the largest element referred to the gains in speed and operating costs of private road traffic. This element equalled 35 per cent of expected total benefits from the line. (Benefits to those motorists expected to switch to the new Line came to another 13 per cent.)

This measurement of so large a favourable 'externality' is obviously most dubious for reasons raised in the last section. Supposing the posited time and vehicle operating savings *were* realised, we cannot know how much motorists would actually pay for them if a market existed; and the doubt is increased in this particular case by the high valuations put upon time costs.* Moreover, the argument that congestion savings will probably only be temporary is met by the authors with the assertion that, as traffic grows in London, the value of the Victoria Line will tend to *increase*. In other words its value over preventing road congestion from getting still worse will at least equal or outweigh its tendency to generate more traffic. Consequently the authors assume that savings to existing road traffic will last for the 50-year period used.

Not untypically the Victoria Line Study combined elaborate conventions of quantification with a cavalier treatment of the vital question of policy perspective. Unfortunately there is no empirical way of distinguishing between journeys which a project such as the Victoria Line 'generates' (e.g. those which would not have occurred in its absence) from new journeys which it merely 'absorbs' (e.g. those which would have occurred anyhow). There is empirical evidence to suggest that the 'generational' effect is likely to be considerable in the circumstances of London,† and to the extent that, for this reason, new traffic pours on to the emptier roads the congestion savings listed in the analysis will be cancelled and replaced by the benefits of the extra journeys themselves. On the other hand, the capacity of the Line to 'absorb' further road congestion costs will depend upon the degree of congestion which motorists will tolerate and how far this exceeds the level existing when the Line is built. A crude assumption that the factors will 'cancel out' simply will not do, because the benefits of having more journeys under equally congested conditions are *not* the same as the benefits of making the same journeys under considerably less-congested conditions. While the ripple effects of the Line could only be guessed at, an elaborate calculation of time savings which could not in practice be realised seems an inadequate basis for evaluation.

The Victoria Line could not be a commercial proposition, partly because London Transport was not prepared to charge a differential fare upon part of its system but mainly because the benefits to road users could not be recouped. Consequently it had to be publicly subsidised. This arrangement

---

* Leisure time was valued at 75 per cent of working time which would now be regarded as excessive and, altogether, time savings of one sort or another accounted for nearly 50 per cent of total benefits which shows the reliance upon this method of measurement.

† London is a large circular area with a fairly even spread of development declining in density from the centre. Car ownership has been rising rapidly. The latent demand for more car travel is considerable, but is constrained by the generally congested road conditions varying of course with proximity to the centre and major sub-centres. Thus any sudden relief to roads in one sector of the conurbation is likely to be exploited fairly quickly as a result of (1) the attractions of extra journeys, (2) the incentive to buy a car, (3) the incentive to change house or workplace. Empirical observations support these deductions.

meant that all affected travellers using both public and private transport would be gainers, but the question for the government ought to have been whether greater gains would flow from a comparable investment within London or elsewhere. From this standpoint one C.B.A. was of little use; even if one accepted its conclusion of a positive balance of social benefit, the project was only worthwhile if it rated well with other projects calculated on similar conventions and assumptions, and in fact no comparable studies were commissioned. If they had been it would have been logically essential to clarify the policy treatment of 'generated traffic' whose impact would certainly vary between urban areas. The Victoria Line ought to have been assessed not only in terms of the balance between public and private transport, but in terms of the balance of advantage between increasing the mobility of travel in London and in other urban areas. It would not be fair to criticise the authors of the study for not asking questions which were outside their remit; still their somewhat unrealistic definition of the project's benefits did rather obscure this wider issue.

British C.B.A. studies conclude that the role of public transport should be substantially increased because of the high congestion costs attributable to private road users. For smaller cities at any rate a programme of road construction usually shows up as worthwhile because the costs to the public authorities are less than the apparent congestion savings to road users or to their employers. However, an alternative policy of relying primarily upon an extensive changeover to public transport (usually buses) tends to emerge as the better course because it would also produce substantial savings in travel costs without requiring as much or perhaps any expenditure upon road construction.

This preferred policy would clearly improve the welfare of existing public transport users but its effects upon that of existing motorists are more arguable. Thus measurements of time and other savings cannot allow for the comfort and convenience of making a complete journey by car where such is possible. This consideration is sometimes met by a separate ordinal ranking for 'comfort and convenience', while another ordinal ranking may also be added for environmental considerations (see next section). While these ordinal additions represent gains in the adequacy and coverage of the analysis, they make it harder still to assess the significance (in policy terms) of the fully quantified part of the analysis. Congestion savings become a sort of Trojan horse for introducing a powerful dose of precise quantification into an increasingly complex issue, without their adequacy for stating consumers' preferences being sufficiently stressed. It is usually accepted that motorists would have to be lured on to public transport by substantial subsidies, but this is treated as only a corollary of the failure to price congested roads.[9]

To understand these transportation problems it is natural to utilise general behavioural models. Mishan offers an explanation of this sort which he dresses up in rather superfluous language about 'consumers' surplus'. He suggests that, when few people have cars, journeys will be easy and quick, and public transport in cities will also generally be good. An individual buying a car might now calculate that he will receive a 'consumers' surplus' of £x from his purchase after averaging benefits and costs of his anticipated journeys under existing road conditions for the car's life. As others follow suit and roads become congested his expectations will be cruelly disappointed. However, in the next phase of the cycle the purchase of a car may still appear to yield as good or better a consumers' surplus as in the earlier phase. This is because, although motorists' costs have soared in relation to the benefits, the alternative option of public transport may have deteriorated still more in terms of the frequency, speed, and reliability of travel. In the final situation public transport may have disappeared almost completely, and the only choices are to buy a car, use taxis, or walk.[10]

The use of consumers' surplus here seems mainly relevant to understanding the paradoxical implications of this concept. Otherwise it seems to have been brought in to give an economic veneer to what is essentially a brief essay in social psychology. Thus the developments posited by Mishan depend primarily upon two non-economic assumptions: (*a*) that car purchasers, at any rate initially, are extremely short-sighted and (*b*) that when they regret their bargains, they lack the energy or initiative to change course and re-establish the demand for public transport. Both postulates are plausible up to a point but are probably exaggerated in Mishan's illustrations.* We cannot know how great the exaggerations may be without some clearer guide to motorists' actual preferences than the use of congestion costs offers. By treating all motorists as spineless jellyfish Mishan makes his economic analysis of road costs more plausible; or in other words crude psychology is brought in to aid the incomplete economics, the whole operation being camouflaged by talk of consumers' surplus!

These strictures are not intended to suggest that the case for more use of public transport in cities is wrong. On the contrary (in the author's view) it is very much the right policy. But it is so for reasons which, in terms of their social relevance and cogency, come close to reversing the order (though not all the contents) of the analysis offered by some economists. Thus economists usually start with the congestion costs inflicted by road users upon each other, move on (carrying the luggage of congestion costs with them) to the interactions between road traffic and public transport, and finally may add some points about the more 'intangible' environmental costs of traffic. But if we look to the social effects we may perhaps be less concerned about the mutual frustrations of motorists or at any rate less disposed to accept hypothesised time-savings to them as a suitable yardstick for 'community benefit'. But the impact of motor traffic upon public transport, and equally or more so upon environmental conditions, has patently substantial and deleterious social effects, whether or not these effects can be plausibly measured by economists.

An economic structuring of issues in line with the technical scope for quantification may be thought not to matter if its practical implications coincide with those that are suggested by general social arguments. For example, supposing road pricing were to be introduced on the argument that

---

* It is surely grotesque that Mishan should assume a car purchaser who can make elaborate forecasts of his consumers' surplus but is apparently unable to foresee that they will be wrong!

it would maximise the consumers' surplus of road users, its introduction would still have beneficial effects for public transport and the physical environment; or again, supposing economists do exaggerate the favourable congestion savings of public transport facilities, this could be considered as a desirable policy compensation for other (environmental) advantages of public transport that cannot so easily be quantified. If cost–benefit economists offer subtle scholastic arguments for sensible policies why not welcome their assistance? Where a coalition of interests want something like the same result for different reasons, it is politically expedient to use a variety of arguments to suit all tastes. Politically speaking, economists have served to make road pricing respectable to business- and efficiency-minded people who would be little swayed by assertions about the environment.

Nevertheless intellectual rigour must also be treasured and will certainly be needed in other contexts. Since plausible economic measurement is possible only for some factors, and proves upon inspection to be somewhat 'soft', the main value of an economic approach is to point *towards* a welfare optimum rather than to specify the optimum itself. But the pointers can be ambiguous. Thus the existence of very high congestion costs can be used to produce evidence of very large gains from road investments, but an alternative interpretation (Mishan's) reaches a precisely opposite conclusion – namely that the benefits of such investments are largely illusory and only seem to exist because roads have not been properly priced in the first place. Mishan's logic is here much more sound. But, following Mishan's logic, it now becomes quite wrong to credit *public transport* projects like the Victoria Line with substantial favourable externalities to road users (this is true whether the benefits are defined as less congestion or as more road journeys). Instead the 'externalities' of such a project will consist of the compensation thereby offered to public transport users who have been disadvantaged by the absence of road pricing, and of favourable environmental 'spillovers'. The practical conclusions of the two viewpoints may be rather similar but they would hinge upon quite different interpretations of the significance of congestion costs!

On the whole economic welfare theories can provide only vague guidance for transportation policies. This is because relevant data does not exist, and in some respects *could not* exist to specify anything like an optimum position. This is not only a problem of, for example, the difficulty of costing environmental externalities. It arises more fundamentally when, as Mishan's analysis suggests, psychological, sociological, and political considerations have to be introduced into the search for an optimum. Our opinion as to *how myopic* are car owners must influence our opinion as to whether the preferences which they apparently demonstrate should be corrected for costs which they may not have foreseen.

A simple formula, such as the idea that all relevant externalities should be priced and charged for, might if it could be applied achieve something like the optimum welfare position. On this basis a road user would be charged *both* the congestion costs inflicted upon other users (including users of public transport) *and* his share of environmental costs as well. The relevant charges as we have seen could only be very artificially determined, and would vary widely with the conventions adopted, but they would certainly tend to rise steeply with the growth of road traffic. At least there is a respectable economic argument here, when properly understood, for redressing a state of affairs which ought never to have been allowed (in welfare terms). To the extent that such corrective action is now possible, the functioning of transportation markets could be improved. But strong action along these lines is politically difficult, and C.B.A. cannot provide a very adequate or reliable guidance about alternative remedies. Essentially and in the end these remedies are the product of broad social valuations applied to a complex mass of phenomena, with economic techniques playing less the role of midwife than of gadfly. We are in the realm of social engineering wherein no single intellectual discipline can give very much guidance but logical clarity of analysis remains of supreme importance.

(iii) *Transportation and Environmental Planning*

A still broader framework of analysis is provided by the interactions between a total transportation system and its physical environment. We cannot delve far into the vast topic here, especially as it recurs in Chapter 7. However, a few points will serve to round off the present analysis.

The elusiveness but importance of the environmental externalities of road traffic have already been noticed. Some of these effects are certain, observable, and sometimes physically measurable (for example noise and fumes), but difficult to measure economically. One should therefore not confuse the economic problem of measuring an 'intangible' value with uncertainties about the nature of causation or impact which actually may be harder to analyse for factors which *are* measured by economists.

But in addition to these more obvious effects, methods of transportation have considerable but subtle and somewhat speculative influences upon environmental conditions generally, including the size, structure and functioning of urban areas, access to social and work facilities, and so on. Important social effects include the tendencies of public and private transport facilities to favour different activity patterns: in the former case concentrated residential areas and centralised facilities, and in the latter case low-density housing and dispersed facilities. The 'modal split' thus becomes critical for urban planning. Conversely, other factors influencing the physical pattern of development, particularly over the location of homes and workplaces, greatly influence the demand for various transportation facilities.*

Of course these tendencies reflect the varying opportunities to satisfy

* Colin Clark analyses the tendency towards lower housing densities which has occurred in almost all urban areas under the influence both of mass transportation and of rising car ownership. However, public transport problems put a limit upon this movement for some social groups, and road congestion in the larger cities (but not smaller ones) has some similar effects. These problems encourage the removal of workplaces as well as residences to suburban and 'exurban' zones where a more mobile life can only conveniently be enjoyed by car owners. See Colin Clark, *Population Growth and Land Use* (London, 1967).

individual tastes which are presented by different transportation facilities, so that the actual patterns will reflect variations in these tastes due to cultural or income factors. But it does so happen that technological and economic conditions create a significant split in the opportunities available to users of public and private transport.

Faced with these complex patterns of interaction, it is possible to take up one of three policy positions with different implications for the use of C.B.A.

(a) Environmental costs and benefits may be incorporated as far as possible within a transportation analysis. The actual results tend to be disappointing, because so many environmental effects elude measurement and the result of costing only a few items (and these very speculatively) may be to reduce or confuse the importance of environmental considerations. Also economic techniques such as the use of time costs which may be defensible up to a point within limited policy contexts (such as road priorities) change their meaning and lose validity when transferred to a supposedly comprehensive framework of analysis (see Chapter 7).

(b) It may be decided that an integration of transportation and environmental planning is actually too difficult, and that it is better to tackle their interface by means of appropriate shock-absorbers. For example, standards and other measures may be promulgated for warding off excessive or inequitable traffic intrusions; such as stringent compensation requirements for properties affected by motorways, designation of pedestrian routes or precincts, conservation areas, noise regulations, land-use controls over main transportation routes, and so on. In this event transportation planning might reasonably treat environmental constraints as given factors, and not need to add them into cost–benefit equations. But the policy problem is to decide whether reasonable constraints of this kind are actually in operation. Usually one would judge that they are not.

(c) Comprehensive guidelines for both transportation and environmental planning may be laid down on the basis of broad social judgements. For example, attempts can be made to plan cities so that social facilities are equally available to users of private and public transport. This can be done either by planning for two different movement patterns which do not conflict with each other (to some extent anyhow) and which are related to different sets of facilities that are hopefully of comparable quality; or through restraining and controlling private road users so as to facilitate access to facilities located at nodal points upon a public transport network; or through investing sufficient money in both roads and public transport to keep pace with the consequences of private locational decisions and travel preferences. The first policy runs the danger of actually creating a two-class city with public transport users allocated inferior facilities, the third policy is enormously expensive, the second policy runs into political conflicts with car owners although seemingly the most promising as well as according with the conclusions of cost–benefit analysts. Actual plans for cities represent interesting examples of and variants upon these three solutions.*

* Thus in Britain the *South Hampshire Study* (1966) favoured the first solution as did the first tentative plan for the large new town of Milton Keynes; but the final

C.B.A. finds it difficult to get adequate leverage for the analysis and evaluation of these broad-based urban plans because many of their consequences are hazardous to forecast and difficult to measure at all plausibly; while in addition much will depend upon interpretations of the significance of different types of cost or benefit. In practice, therefore, the plans tend to be based upon simplified assumptions about desirable goals and the means to their realisation. This approach need not be dubbed as 'irrational' if it is related to empirical evidence and to logical analysis of the general effects of possible policies, because a more fine-grained evaluation may be impossible. Certainly the results are to be preferred to the unwarranted conclusions that are often drawn by analysts from carefully quantified data. The use of C.B.A. can only be helpful in this context if it is linked with careful exploration of the policy significance of different treatments of 'cost'. One can illustrate this point by considering briefly the *distributional* aspects of C.B.A. figures.

When the analysis is concerned solely with interactions among private road users, the only distributional problem is the familiar one of income inequalities, and this problem can reasonably be treated in precisely the same way as it would be in relation to ordinary market demands; that is corrections have to be sought through general measures of income redistribution. When public transport users are introduced the same principle will still apply for income inequalities, but two further problems of distribution arise: (*a*) many individuals (the elderly, the handicapped, for example) cannot *physically* utilise the alternative of car ownership, and (*b*) there is a discontinuity or 'jump' between the two transportation markets stemming from the fact that sufficient capital is necessary to join the group of car owners (this jump is comparable on a smaller scale to that between rented and owner-occupied housing).

In principle this second consideration may be viewed as simply another aspect of general income distribution. However, if one accepts that public transport deteriorates because of the indirect (technological) impact of car ownership, and does so at a faster rate than the opportunities open to car owners, the gap between the services available through the two types of transportation will widen; and this is undesirable for the satisfaction of consumer preferences. This is the essence of Mishan's argument about the rising consumers' surplus from car ownership. Whether or not one accepts this argument (which would require difficult empirical analysis) its plausibility at least reinforces the other special disabilities of public transport users. It so happens also that these users as a group are relatively poor in relation to car owners, so that poverty and physical disabilities run together.

When environmental externalities are introduced distributional issues become more complex. The nuisances and hazards of motor traffic are inflicted in varying degrees upon almost everyone and thus widely affect motorists also in their capacities as pedestrians, pedal cyclists or residents. But there are also more specific geographic effects. An uncompensated effect

plan for this new town leaned strongly towards the third solution because of its assumption of and belief in a very high level of car ownership, while the official county plan for South Hampshire used a mixture of the first and second approaches.

occurs where the residents of one area are subject to especially heavy traffic intrusion and blight. This occurs with many villages and small towns located on main arteries, and more extensively in relation to the inner areas of large cities.

Whether or not these people own a car, and many of the poorer ones do not, they lie athwart the radial lines of communication into the centre of the city. The suburban car owners drive through these areas, utilising their own particular 'trade-off' between the nuisance of a journey to work and the desirability of a relatively spacious home. The blighting effect upon the inner areas is seen in the invasion of residential areas by commuters' cars and in the congestion, fumes and hazards of high-roads which must serve both as through routes and as local shopping centres. If funds and politics should permit major new highways to be driven through these densely occupied areas, nuisance effects can be reduced only at very high expenditure (which will not be to the liking of suburban motorists), and much land will be taken that is also wanted for local purposes. The Americans have a name for this situation: 'corridor communities'.

How does or could C.B.A. deal with these distributional issues? Certainly it is concerned, whether or not effectively, with income effects (see Chapter 6). But relative poverty is only a reinforcement, although admittedly sometimes an important one, of functional disadvantages which accrue to some groups through the growth of motor traffic. Can these disadvantages be labelled as 'costs' having the same logical status as, for example, the congestion costs which one motorist imposes upon another? It seems doubtful whether they can be because the burdens under discussion are of a different type. Ultimately they can be traced to differences in the structure of opportunities open to individuals. Thus a motorist living in a suburban area might be able to trade off the benefits (to him) of more motorisation against the costs (to him) of worse public transport and/or more environmental disruption. But such equations have much less or little meaning to individuals who have no alternative to public transport or no ability to move from a blighted inner area. The costs and benefits no longer appear as commensurate.

Admittedly welfare economics can deal in theory with this as with any problem. The plight of the public transport user can be viewed as a case of 'market failure', for which the cure should be the creation of a substitute market price so as to allow for the uncompensated effects of motor traffic upon his welfare. A compensation formula could also be worked out for the inhabitant of a 'corridor community' which would suffice to restore his welfare level to a pre-traffic-blight position. In practice, it is extremely difficult to suggest or arrive at any figure for this purpose, but that is not the only difficulty. We seem to be dealing here with 'costs' of different types, measured or estimated in different ways, which cannot plausibly be aggregated or combined in a general equation. Some analysts certainly recognise this fact and suggest that the aim of a C.B.A. should be to show the *incidence* of costs among different groups, not to add them up. It will then be for the policy-makers to do their own evaluation (see Chapter 6).

However, this gain in realism does not get C.B.A. out of the wood. It still looks as if the different estimates of costs represent attempted economic answers to different policy problems, not usually considered conjointly. One test of the relationship of costs can be found by looking at political responses. Vehicle owners are a high proportion of the population and have the inbuilt tendency of any group to oppose new taxes or controls which did not exist when they bought their vehicles; and many also hold the traditional and legally sanctioned viewpoint that the 'King's highway' should be free to all (although parking charges have now eroded this principle). On the other hand, a lot of road users increasingly see the need to tackle congestion costs and can find common ground with public transport users over the case for a more 'balanced' transportation strategy. These issues are not deeply divisive, but remedial action is slow-moving because of the reluctance of politicians and officials to offend entrenched interests. By contrast, the environmental effects of road traffic can be deeply divisive, because those adversely affected may share no sufficient degree of common interest with the road users. Inhabitants of inner cities may see traffic blight as an uncompensated loss to themselves, and also (as has happened in London) they may perceive an intensive conflict between the claims of highways and housing for available money and land.

Analysing the policy process one would describe 'traffic congestion' and 'public transportation' as two issues that were initially quite separate but which are increasingly, though very partially, becoming merged into a 'transportation issue'. Environmental reactions to traffic problems take the varying forms of compensation issues, local protest issues, and budgetary issues. Traffic blight in the inner cities usually gets allocated to the broader realm of poverty problems and loses contact with the transportation policy realm. Clearly this analysis is a very crude presentation of the handling of policy issues.* But if C.B.A. is to tackle transportation issues comprehensively, its techniques need to bridge the 'policy gulfs' which derive partly from the sequential treatment of issues in different policy arenas and partly from the existence not only of disparate but of disparately felt and understood interests.

The first of these problems belongs to the exploration of political–economic relationships in the second half of this book. The second, as we have seen, involves for C.B.A. complex questions about the 'weighting' of the analysis to allow for distributional values. Such considerations can easily be presented schematically and quantitatively, the difficulty being to define the relevant factors and give them appropriate weights. This subject is treated in Chapter 6. Here we will merely note that a comprehensive approach to C.B.A. has the intrinsically laudable aim of integrating issues that are politically compartmentalised, although the difficulties of doing so successfully appear formidable indeed.

* No mention has been made of the structure of political behaviour, or institutional effects, or of the varying perception of issues by different participants – for example 'expert opinion' (or some of it) can see connexions between issues which are quite obscure to the general public. My aim was no more than to suggest the kind of political differentiation of these issues which has probably occurred in most Western countries.

4
The Quest for Quantification

A. Introduction

Numeracy is increasingly esteemed in modern societies, and (some cynics might add) literacy is increasingly devalued. The first of these developments can, in principle, only be welcomed. Social, economic and scientific statistics play a vital part in the processes of decision-making, and the work of modern government would be impossible without the collection and use of vast amounts of quantitative data. Problems about the use and misuse of statistics need to be widely studied and understood.

The subject of this chapter is not the general uses of quantification, but attempts, mainly by economists, to express the widest possible range of preferences or values in terms of some common scale of quantification. The usual scale to be adopted is hypothesised money values, which will receive most of our attention, but the quest can also be pursued in simpler ways. At the end of this chapter we will consider the idea that a numerical rating or weighting of preferences somehow adds to the rationality of decision-making.

When people buy and sell in a market, their diverse preferences are converted into a monetary scale. The preferences of individual consumers are not revealed clearly or unambiguously by market transactions,* but the prices ruling in the market offer a meaningful interpretation of the relative worth of different goods and services as settled by a complex interplay between the preferences of consumers and the costs of production.

But if it is meaningful to assign prices to pears and peaches, as a means of choosing between them, why should it not be valid to assign prices to the various outcomes of a public policy or decision? (The policy can of course only be priced by reference to its results.) No doubt the task is enormously more complex, but in principle are we not still dealing fundamentally with the prefences of individuals who stand to gain or lose from the policy in diverse ways? Why not plot these gains and losses as precisely as possible, and convert them into the only suitable or tenable common denominator, one that has already shown its great merits for comparable purposes?

---

* If a housewife must pay 4p for a peach or 4p for a pear and buys only the peach, she unambiguously prefers the one to the other in an ordinal sense. But if she buys one peach at 4p and one pear at 5p we cannot say that she has a 5:4 preference for the pear over the peach. The peach might be the preferred fruit, but she could still logically buy a more expensive pear as well rather than add a second peach or some other item. To know all this we would have to know her subjective preference curves, but she never formulates these explicitly but only as a sort of fluctuating response to market opportunities.

Moreover, if we do not attempt some conversion of diverse effects into common units of accountancy, how can we logically relate the evaluation of one factor to another? Are we not left to flounder in a sea of hunches, intuitions, and other subjective judgements? Shall we not be left with an extreme precision over the analysis of means and a sorry vagueness over that of ends? Conceding the many snags of monetary evaluation, as most economists will do, is this device not still a potential source of increased rationality in policy analysis? Can we afford to neglect it? What alternative have we?

These are some of the broad arguments which economists and others advance for the extended application of monetary evaluation to policy choices. We are here in a very intricate field of discussion in which it is easy to get into false positions. For example, it is an obvious fact that policymakers and citizens have continually to decide whether some unquantified benefits (x) is worth some quantified resource (y). Often the choice is not explicit, and it seems useful to clarify the implicit prices being placed upon benefits in all such cases. It may be helpful also to compile different indices of effectiveness of a public policy (not necessarily in monetary terms) and to compare these with the different resource costs, which may themselves be reckoned in different ways. In other words, a considerable variety of what may be loosely termed cost–benefit studies have a useful place in government decision-making, and deserve more attention than they will get here. How are we to distinguish then between valid and invalid uses of monetary quantification? It is this question that the chapter explores.

B. Values and Costs

Has everything its price? To many people it seems wrong or even impious to set a monetary value upon all sorts of phenomena that are not normally so valued, ranging from the enjoyment of a view to human life itself. To the cost–benefit analyst, this question is misconceived. Wherever the logic of choice prevails, A has somehow to be balanced against B and if the choice is helped by using a common medium of accounting what crime is being committed? The analyst would repudiate the charge that he is decreeing the value to be placed upon some result; he is only helping to elucidate the preferences of others. Even so, economists differ as to how far quantification can reasonably be pushed. Some draw the line fairly narrowly not necessarily for ethical reasons but from opinions about the intrinsic limitations of economic or mathematical forms of analysis.

Consider a solitary monk who devotes all his time to either prayer and contemplation or growing his own food. The economist would say that the opportunity cost to the monk of an extra hour spent in prayer is the food thereby forgone, and vice versa. There is nothing wrong with this formulation as an exercise in logic, but the monk is unlikely to see the issue in this light. Assuming that his eyes are fixed upon a higher reality, and that he views prayer and contemplation as the purpose of his life, he will see the necessity to grow food as only a constraint upon his chosen goal. Food then becomes an input into the monk's only valued output which is prayer and contemplation. The monk still has the problem of managing his resources so as to maximise his output over time, but the output cannot itself be valued because there is nothing to compare it with.

An individual will say that something is invaluable or priceless if no circumstances would persuade him to part with it for the sake of some other consideration. The monk might reduce the time spent on prayer if, because of a bad season for example, he could not achieve a bare subsistence in any other way; but, unless of course his value system changed, he would never give up prayer altogether or (possibly) reduce it below a certain amount. A man may consign himself and his family to hunger and even starvation rather than give up some cherished purpose, principle, or object. True, if circumstances are exceptionally bad, he may instead conclude that another 'absolute' consideration such as feeding his family should take priority over the original consideration. This is another way of saying that, save for the exceptionally single-minded man, almost all personal values are relative.

What has all this to do with C.B.A.? Not much except to help clear the ground. The expression 'everything has its price' is sometimes understood in the cynical sense that a sufficient sum of money will persuade a man to part with anything – his home, his principles, or his wife; the evidence is against the view and it needs no more attention. The truer statement is that almost all individuals have multiple goals or values which often conflict. This conflict itself is more a subject for philosophy or psychology than economics. Economic analysis enters in from the further fact that most goals at any rate require the use of scarce resources. My use of scarce resources to pursue a goal can be described as its cost; and if some of these resources could be switched to one or more other goals that I also value an opportunity cost is involved – namely the various degrees of goal achievement or satisfaction that these resources used in a different way could produce.

Because of the intrinsic scarcity and flexibility of resources, almost all choices can be treated from one standpoint, as economic equations relating goals to resources. Unfortunately for economics the value which I place upon my goals cannot be inferred from the resources which I devote to them, save in a very specialised or tautological sense. Take a simple example where I have two goals (playing golf and playing music) which compete for my scarce resources of time, energy and money. Suppose I devote ten times the resources to golf as to music, can we infer that I value golf ten times higher? Clearly we cannot because I might (for example) like both of them equally and devote all that effort to golf simply because that is necessary to bring me up to a minimum standard of proficiency. A further switch of resources to golf may signify that I have come to prefer it to music or merely that my golf has become relatively worse. We could not say anything about my personal valuations without knowing my motives, purposes, and standards. We could, of course, say that in terms of a cost–benefit yardstick my willingness to pay for golf is $10x$ and for music x, which is informative about my demand for scarce resources. But except in this restricted sense it is uninformative about how I value the results.

The classic problem of C.B.A. is that it seems much easier to measure costs than benefits. This does not imply that it is actually easy to measure costs. In our simplified examples we have been treating costs as means and benefits as ends. But the world is not so simple and in terms of values we can make no such assumption. In ordinary reasoning what we treat as 'means' and what as 'ends' derives from a mixture of analytical convenience and the *relative* importance attached to various activities and experiences. The simplifications of logic become misleading if they are assumed to give an accurate picture of motivations and values.

Sir Geoffrey Vickers has criticised the 'goal-orientated' school of psychologists for this false simplification. For example, if I go fishing it is artificial to regard all the acts which lead up to the actual catching of a fish as *means* towards this eventual goal; all the more artificial perhaps as I may then throw the fish back into the water! Sir Geoffrey prefers to say that I enjoy using my capacities in certain relationships with my environment; and on this view I may value the process of driving or cycling to get to the fishing-place in the same way (if to a lesser degree) that I value fishing itself. My goals themselves might be described as driving, cycling, and fishing *not* catching a fish.[1]

This correction of the crudities of means–ends analysis creates fundamental, as opposed to simply technical, problems about the 'costs' side of a C.B.A. as well as the benefits side. We can see this from an actual example. Some cost–benefit studies of public recreational facilities, faced with the difficulty of discovering what their users would be willing to pay for what is in fact provided free, argue that the benefits to a user must be at least equal to the costs he must pay to get to the facility. But this overlooks the fact that a user may not view the journey simply as a means for the recreational benefit, but may (and sometimes certainly does) enjoy the journey also as one element perhaps in a family 'outing'. The case is on all fours with Sir Geoffrey Vickers's example.

This point leads into a fundamental criticism of economic analysis, namely that it is prone to divide the world into two halves labelled respectively 'costs' and 'benefits'. For example, work in economic analysis is often treated simply as the necessary means (cost) towards the end of consumption (benefit). But some people at least still value the act of working more than the act of consuming, which led Bernard Shaw to the conclusion that those who enjoy their work should pay for the privilege of doing it! A cost would then logically be changed into a benefit.

This situation is fully recognised by the more sophisticated cost–benefit analysts. They would agree that the allocation of items as costs and benefits is to some extent artificial depending upon the framework of valuation employed. For example, the Roskill Commission listed all the items in its analysis as costs on the argument that the benefit of having an airport *somewhere* must be taken as proved (for which it was much criticised – see Chapter 7), and the cost attributable to any of the possible sites was related to a figure of 0 for the site which showed up best on each count.

Moving beyond technical issues of valuation procedure one plunges into deep water. The basic issue seems to be whether it is the aim of C.B.A. to plot the whole skein of human values in economic terms, or as much of this map as possible, or whether the aim is to assess costs in fairly conventional terms and compare them with benefits many of which at least are accepted as being 'intangible', that is to say incapable of economic measurement. This presentation is admittedly a great simplification since there are many possible intermediate positions. The ambitious approach can be qualified in a variety of ways. The more modest approach can be augmented by arguments that some or all of the 'intangibles' on the benefit side of the equation can be subjected to economic measurements which provide meaningful information to policy-makers even though final judgements exceed the economist's capacity to make recommendations.

The modest approach assumes that we can at least measure costs in a meaningful way even though we often cannot do the same with benefits. This compels us to take a fairly conventional view of costs that excludes for example the 'psychic' satisfactions which some workers get from work that they enjoy. But it does not follow that this factor need be dropped altogether from the analysis since it can be transformed into benefits and grouped there with other items which are difficult or impossible to quantify. For example, if two possible methods of production cost the same amount in terms of labour, materials and other inputs but one method is expected to provide greater work satisfaction, this factor can be listed as an unquantified benefit of one method. But costs could remain the same.

It will be seen that we are seeking a 'hard-headed' definition of resource cost, but even this is difficult to find. The imperfections of conventional market and financial data usually lead economists to urge that costs should be measured in 'real resource' terms. However, the concept of real resources is basically a physical one, for example a project will require so many man-hours of work, tons of material, and so on. Paradoxically the appeal of 'real resource' arguments lies in their reference to *non-economic* data. The rationality of the analysis is increased, not by converting new factors into money, but through qualifying the significance of money figures by reference to 'real' phenomena.

The concept of real resources therefore provides not so much an alternative framework of accounting to conventional forms of economic measurement, as a necessary *corrective* for some of the limitations of those measurements, for example transfer costs (e.g. when money is simply redistributed) do not entail any direct burden upon real resources. The cost of land is only a transfer cost inasmuch as total supply is fixed and a given site is merely shifted from private to public use (however, a full analysis would be more sophisticated, and ask which 'opportunity costs' are being sacrificed by using land in one way rather than another – a question incidentally that can never be very adequately answered). Another important distinction is that finance can normally be shifted from one purpose to another without friction or cost (other than administrative), whereas real resources are much less elastic, particularly in the short run.

Subject to these and other qualifications, economic measurements can provide some kind of indication of the 'real resource' cost of a project. Of course, we are again simplifying considerably in our effort to present one side of the cost–benefit equation in common-sense terms. For many welfare economists, for example, *all* costs ought to be recalculated according to the very exigent (and disputed) requirement of an 'optimum' pricing system; for example, the prices of input factors should be made equal to their marginal social costs. Even if we were to accept the relevant theory it would be very difficult to make the necessary computations consistently and, in practice, such ideas are introduced only as partial variants of a more conventional analysis (in which capacity they puzzle the layman not a little). All of this suggests that the calculations of costs must be done on some second-best (or third-best or n-best) basis, a line of analysis which could lead us back to our earlier position of equal scepticism about both costs and benefits.

All that rescues us from this conclusion is the common-sense position that economics is able to say something about something, not nothing (or everything) about everything. A common-sense position might be that resources (meaning by this usually labour, capital and land) are ubiquitously and perennially scarce in relation to the purposes both of individuals and of society (individuals acting collectively). Economics can tell us something about the cost of using these resources in various ways, which is helpful as a way of analysing a set of constraints upon the exercise of choice. But can economics tell us anything much about the process of valuation (individual or collective) which guide these processes of choice? After these preliminary reflections it is to this question that we now turn.

C. Implicit Prices

The last section did not distinguish between circumstances of individual and collective choice. This subject belongs primarily to Chapters 5 and 6. Here we shall assume that it is meaningful to treat decisions made by governments or their agents as being in some sense reflections of social values or preferences, without committing ourselves to any particular theory of collective will.

There are some reasons for suggesting that economic quantification has a broader application to problems of collective than of individual choice. The individual enjoys or suffers a great variety of experiences which he would not normally think of expressing in money or in any common unit of account. There is no reason for him to do so. He may regard many features of his way of life and even some of his physical possessions as priceless in the sense that no monetary inducement (or none that he can reasonably hope to receive) would normally persuade him to part with them. In a crisis situation these assumptions do not apply. In some societies a man may choose to sell his liberty or even his life in order to procure food for his family, or to sell their liberty for his benefit. But we cannot generalise from such circumstances.

Collective choices, as exercised through or by a government, follow a different kind of logic. They operate in a sense at the margin or have marginal applications. For example, if there is unemployment a public project may provide work for x men. For slightly more outlay it could put $x+1$ men to work, and for the marginal individual this might make a vital difference in terms not just of his standard of living but of his well-being and dignity. For him the condition of working may in a sense be priceless. But the public policy-maker usually does not or cannot see the problem in these terms. His eyes are not fixed upon the condition of one individual unemployed man, but upon the conflict between competing social goals. His reasoning may be that more relief expenditure will reduce health expenditure or harm the balance of payments so as eventually (perhaps) to threaten the success of unemployment relief; or he may believe that a certain amount of unemployment is necessary for a sound economy, or to the maintenance of profits in which he also believes. But in any event the line must be drawn somewhere, and at this point an implicit price is being placed upon the resources which society can spare in order to create one more job.

In a sense the individual also makes his decisions at the margin – he can increase the effort and resources he devotes to one purpose rather than another and (just like society) he strikes a changing balance between 'pain-avoidance' and 'pleasure-promotion'. But his decisions are integrated by his own consciousness and experience – every move he makes directly affects himself – whereas collective decisions are distributive – the pains or pleasures they confer on some individuals are not experienced by others unless they happen to be mutually related.

As already stated it often seems more meaningful to quantify the costs than the benefits of some public decision, especially if we define costs conventionally. We can state the costs of building a battleship, but how are we to estimate the benefits from having it? We can state the costs of building schools and hiring teachers, but how are we to value the output of the schools? We can ascertain the extra cost of putting electricity pylons under instead of above ground in the Lake District, but how can we measure the presumed benefits of doing so? And so on through an endless list of possible examples.

Theories of valuing benefits in such contexts get further attention in the next section. Here we are concerned with a more modest attempt to get some answer to these conundrums which uses the concept of 'implicit prices'. This concept is derived wholly from the cost side of the equation, but the evidence about costs is presented in a slightly different way. The argument runs as follows: if society is prepared to spend £x millions in order to obtain a certain result, surely we can say that it is implicitly valuing the result at a figure of at least the same amount.

It is easy to see that one version of this argument is a conjuring trick which has already been exposed. We cannot say that because a government spends twice as much on health as on education, it values the former more than the latter. The differences will result from an evaluation of demands or needs, standards and costs in the two fields (the case is equivalent to our earlier example about golf and music). In other words, social values determine choice, and hence, indirectly, implicit prices, not the other way round.

But implicit prices still have their interest if too much is not made of them. It is interesting to enquire *why* a government should spend £x for one purpose, £y on another, and nothing upon a third. Expressed differently it is always worth knowing the costs as far as possible, because even if benefits cannot be measured in money terms other relationships between costs and benefits can be investigated. The analysis of differential costs is useful, however, only to the extent that the resulting benefits can be meaningfully compared. The benefits of defence can be compared with those of education only through broad value judgements; but the benefits of one kind of school can be compared with those of another (not necessarily of course in money terms) and both sets of benefits related to the respective costs.

A problem that bothers economists a great deal about these implicit prices is their apparent gross inconsistencies. A man's freedom from injury, it may be said, is just as important to him whether he is at work, on the roads, on the railway, or walking in the mountains; why then should the sums spent upon avoiding accidents in these various circumstances vary so widely? Again why should there be such large differences over the money spent per patient for the treatment of various complaints and diseases, when a switch of resources could enable more lives to be saved or more suffering avoided? Is not ill-health equally unpalatable whatever its causes?

Closer inspection shows that public (and private) expenditure in these and similar cases cannot be separated from a variable and admittedly often vague context of social values. For example a distinction can be drawn between risks that are voluntarily and involuntarily incurred, and it is reasonable for society to provide or require a greater degree of protection against involuntary risks. This distinction would help to explain the relatively large sums that must statutorily be spent upon protecting workers from injury and compensating them if it does occur, or upon retaining railways in a safe condition, as compared with the sums spent to protect motorists from their own follies. Unfortunately the argument breaks down in relation to the innocent victims of road accidents.

Mountaineering provides an interesting example. As it is a wholly voluntary risk the prevention of accidents in the hills would seem to have a low priority on public funds. But mountaineering is also widely regarded as a desirable risk – good for the character, pleasurable, inspiring, and so on. This means that its risks are socially acceptable and even esteemed within certain limits, and when a mishap does occur large public resources are devoted to rescue attempts. If the costs to the armed forces per mountaineer rescued or per dinghy-sailor saved were accurately estimated, they would be found to be extremely high. But these costs are cheerfully accepted, not only on humanitarian grounds, but because they require qualities of courage and endurance, on the part of both rescuers and rescued, that are also esteemed and necessary in a military context. The sportsmen and the armed services provide mutually beneficial 'externalities' for each other! And certainly without such tasks the Services would sometimes have little to do.

Health expenditure provides serious examples of apparent inconsistencies. all the more so as they occur in Britain within what is supposed to be a uniform and integrated service. Some of these inconsistencies can be attributed to the influence of scientific goals. For example, the distribution of medical expenditure on research and development shows the influence of the search for new knowledge and the utilisation of specialised skills, without close attention to the number of lives or amount of suffering that will thereby be saved. Of course, it can be said that *any* enlargement of medical knowledge may have favourable spillover effects in the long run, but this broad argument will hardly suffice where possible uses are so numerous and resources so scarce.[2]

To some extent medical policy (like any other professional policy) has to be guided by the interests of the practitioners themselves, and the full logic of consumers' needs (supposing this could be independently defined) would be difficult to get accepted: but one can still question the large differences which exist between the prices implicitly placed upon the relief of suffering in different contexts. A case in point is the large sums spent on experiments with heart transplants. Is such expenditure justified when we know that relatively modest expenditure on more kidney machines would certainly save more lives and alleviate more suffering? The argument can of course be widened beyond the medical field to enquire whether any collective expenditures upon luxuries or frills can be justified when there is so much suffering waiting and able to be alleviated. Here we have an acute version of the pain-avoiding versus pleasure-promoting issue.

Collective decisions are guided in most modern societies by an ethical principal which holds that any human life in danger must be saved if it is possible to do so regardless of cost. The rule is applied in crisis situations and emergencies, but it is not applied when the danger is not immediate even though it is plain that the failure to provide certain facilities or treatment will in all probability cost lives. It thus follows that very large and variable sums are often spent upon saving lives in emergencies, although more lives could be saved for equivalent outlays at a somewhat earlier stage. This discriminating social behaviour appears to reflect an ethical belief that it is obligatory to save a specific life that is known to be in danger (which also explains the large sums spent upon rescuing individuals from the tops of mountains or the bottoms of oceans), but that it is less-obligatory to save through advance precautions an indeterminate number of individuals whose identities are unknown, or whose fate is not immediate or absolutely certain.

Without going into further examples it is easy to see that the alleged inconsistencies of implicit prices can often be traced to the influence of various social norms which guide actual decisions in complex and subtle ways. For example, the use of resources in order to prevent or avert personal hazards to life and limb can be seen to be influenced in subtle ways by the answers to such questions as: Is the risk voluntary or involuntary? Is it socially approved or disapproved? Is it immediate and determinate or less immediate and indeterminate? It will often be difficult to explain some decision in terms of a single social rule or norm, since a variety of such norms can be relevant and may conflict.

But, in addition, the analysis to date has been much too high-minded.

Governments do not just earnestly apply social principles to particular cases; they are also influenced by political groups seeking favours or urging policies. In some contexts resource allocations may not be much influenced by political pressures (the British Health Service for example), while in others this influence is considerable. For example, the amount of resources that is devoted to saving woodland glades and pastoral scenes from unwanted development seems to depend rather more upon the influence of their protectors than upon some pure canon of aesthetic judgement.

It would be wrong, however, to put social norms and political pressures into separate boxes save for analytic purposes. Political argument is *about* principles as well as interests.

What does all this show about the alleged inconsistency of implicit prices? When the complex processes of social and political evaluation are looked at, even superficially, we can see that there are many possible explanations as to why a different resource price is attached to one decision than to another which looks rather similar; and the same analysis suggests that the alleged similarity of circumstances may prove more apparent than real on closer investigation. This need not, of course, mean that the economist must accept the explanations offered as reasonable or desirable. But basically he can only question them by changing his role from an economist to a citizen, since there is no base for such criticism except an ethical or political position. The economist can, however, function most usefully as a technical auxiliary in the process of scrutinising the social evaluations which underlie the relationships between particular configurations of resource costs and non-monetarised benefits. Meanwhile, is there any point in using these 'implicit' prices as a proxy for the valuation of intangible benefits in a C.B.A.? It would seem not. In the first place we have already amply illustrated the circular process of valuation that this course involves. Even if this were not so there seems not much reason for the economist to play the conservative and circular role of writing the implicit prices suggested by past social decisions into an analysis intended to be the basis of a fresh decision.

D. Principles of Valuation

Having examined arguments about implicit valuations in public decisions, we can turn to the economist's own methods for valuing phenomena which do not have a market price. We will examine three possible approaches to this subject which will be shown to be related, at least loosely, to different social or political ideologies. We will also consider briefly the objections to each approach and the relationships between them.

(i) *The Market Approach*

This is the conventional and most obvious approach to valuations for C.B.A. It builds on the assumption that the best (if not the only) meaning of *value* in an economic sense is provided by evidence about actual or possible transactions between willing sellers and buyers. In this way the consumer's willingness and ability to pay for something is tested against the market costs of providing him with that thing. Of course, there are all the problems about the imperfections of markets and the corrections to prices that may or may not be justified on that account. We will not go into these questions which were briefly discussed in Chapter 2 and are familiar territory for economists. The chief practical limitation upon a market approach is the paucity of data for evaluating many items which cost–benefit analysts would like to include in their balance sheets. The only way round this problem is to seek out indirect evidence about market values, but the analysis ought not to include items for which no proper evidence can be produced. The analysis can do no more than use evidence about economic behaviour as this is normally understood. What can be tried out is various techniques for inferring the prices which consumers would be willing to pay for various benefits under appropriate conditions. Some of these techniques are:

(1) *The use of analogous market prices.* Sometimes there exist reasonably analogous market prices which offer a basis for the calculation of the costs or benefits of a public decision. For example, the value of the water provided for farmers by a public irrigation scheme can sometimes be estimated in this way. The scheme itself is probably subsidised, but as Schultze says it is useful to know the implicit size of the subsidy, so that government can consider more rationally whether aid to agriculture (if such is desired) would be better given in some other way.[3] This kind of quantification raises no serious problems of principle.

(2) *Intermediate goods method.* Here some 'intermediate' measurement of benefit which can be measured does proxy for a final benefit which cannot be. For example, we cannot measure directly the benefit of some form of education to an individual but we can try to estimate the extra income which this particular education enabled him to receive. There are obvious difficulties: for example, how far is his job performance and extra income actually due to the education he received? On the other side of the account, are there not benefits from his education which are additional to income? There are cases where an 'intermediate goods' treatment has more plausibility than in this example.

(3) *Cost-savings method.* Here the size of a benefit is inferred from cost-savings; for example, the benefit of a new road is valued at the reduction of costs of those using it. There are various snags about this method, such as the treatment of traffic generated by the new road and the validity of time savings, which have already been discussed.

(4) *A partial or implicit market* may exist which suggests the sort of sums that individuals might be willing to pay for the facility in question. For example, attempts to value time-savings can be based upon the extra money travellers will pay to go by a fast rather than a slow train. The evidence in

this example is extremely dubious: it is likely to be based upon only a small number of cases, it applies only to the circumstances of rail travel and it is dealing with one element of a 'joint product' since the fast train traveller normally enjoys extra comfort as well as speed (especially if there is an extra charge). Admittedly there is a considerable variety of other indirect information about the valuation of time by travellers. The basic difficulty always is the search for a market which does not genuinely exist, and the plausibility of the method depends upon a judgement as to whether the phenomenon in question really could be bought and sold in a systematic way.

What political position or ideology is represented by this 'market approach'? Some critics will simply view it as a reflection of traditional economic theories of perfect equilibrium, *laissez-faire*, and the invisible hand of Adam Smith. However, this inference is excessive. The market approach as used here is not intended to pre-judge the question of how far goods should be supplied through market competition or collective action, or even definitively to prefer capitalism to socialism, although there is an apparent bias against the latter. The primary principle under consideration is that all benefits should be measured (if they can be) by reference to concrete evidence about the willingness and ability of individuals to pay for them. It no doubt is the case that a 'free market economy' provides the usually favoured forum for this purpose, but if there are other reasons for regulating the market or for preferring collective to market provision the same approach can still be utilised up to a point.

Indeed, it is due to the extensive substitution of public for private services and to government efforts to cope with 'externalities' that cost–benefit analysis has arisen. This circumstance is the cause of a certain dualism over the aims of C.B.A. Some economists are busy trying to apply what they think of as normal and proper methods of market calculation to the different circumstances of government decisions. Others, and these include many 'welfare economists', have in fact no fondness for the market at all. They generally wish to rewrite all the prices registered in markets according to their own ideal assumptions. Even so some of them at least will still be prepared to exalt the principle of individuals' willingness to pay as expressed under ideal exchange conditions, all the more so and on a much wider front if they have themselves rewritten (in theory only) these ideal conditions. But we need not again follow through this strand of utopianism whose ambitions are admittedly ill-expressed by any concept which refers to existing markets.

Clearly a discussion of the 'market approach' can immerse us into deep ideological water. A traditional belief in the value of perfect competition permeates this approach despite the extricatory devices of welfare-economists. But one strength of the general position being discussed is that it usually at least starts from an intelligible view of the meaning and limitations of economic measurement. Measurement has to be grounded in such evidence as exists or which can be inferred from actual exchange relationships, and the limitations of such evidence as a guide to public policy are vaguely appreciated by most people. It is true that as techniques of measurement are stretched and bent in the effort to comprehend a widening range of phenomena, these limitations are easily forgotten and the results may be interpreted as a much more adequate guide to decision-making than can possibly be the case. In principle then the position being considered occupies the same ideology as does any belief in the virtues of free markets working under appropriate conditions. Even 'mature' socialist economics accords some validity to this belief. Dogmatism comes in when it is supposed that collective decisions should be determined wholly or primarily by evidence about market behaviour. Suppose, for example, that it *is* possible to obtain some meaningful evidence about the market benefits of education, it would not follow that public policy should be based primarily upon this evidence even though *some* relevance be conceded to it. Ideology apart, limits to these techniques lies in the paucity of relevant market data, and in problems as to whether and when a market does or could exist.

(ii) *Social Efficiency*

The essence of the 'market approach' is that the valuation of costs and benefits should be traced ultimately to individual wants or preferences. If a social calculus can be established on this foundation it will consist wholly in some formula for the aggregation of individual wants. However, various other ideas about social welfare or social efficiency do sometimes figure in C.B.A. For example, the analyst (or his political master) might assume that the aim should be to maximise national wealth as represented, for example, by G.N.P. (gross national product), or to achieve a given distribution of income within the society, or to bring about some mix of the two aims. This would be equivalent to imposing a view of social welfare different from that obtainable through the market approach. Even where the two approaches appeared to coincide there might be considerable differences. For example, the market approach in principle uses the 'efficiency' criterion and thereby *should* lead to a maximisation of wealth, but wealth here may be given a much broader meaning than statistics of G.N.P. – for example if people are willing to pay money to preserve views which they find beautiful this would count on the market approach but not on the G.N.P. one.*

The approach to the valuation of costs and benefits under consideration here may loosely be termed the social-efficiency test. It is plain that the costs and benefits which accrue to society collectively frequently diverge from the resultant of market preferences exercised by individuals. For example, the introduction of collectively financed health and social security measures removes much of the supply and demand for medical treatment from the sphere of market choice. Possibly this result is fully consistent with the criterion of the aggregation of individual wants *if* we assume that some kinds

---

* This is not perhaps strictly true. If a group of people persuade the government to preserve their views through extra expenditure, this expenditure will show up in the national accounts as a service provided by the government for the community.

of wants can only be realised by political means. But in any event we have an apparent need to introduce social criteria of costs and benefits.

Suppose, for example, we want to evaluate the benefits of more effective accident prevention on the roads. Ultimately the benefits will accrue to various individuals – there is no disputing that; but not only is there no easy way of discovering their willingness to pay for this increased protection (other than through waiting for political action, which would be a circular test), the proposed action will also have complex effects upon collective social accounting. If x accidents are thereby averted, the government will save y in hospital bills and z in social security payments. The limited financial accounting has usefulness since, if the expectation is that the public financial gains will outweigh the financial costs of the prevention programme, it seemingly must be worth doing – all the 'real' benefits (as most people would regard them), for example the avoidance of suffering and deaths, are achieved at no financial cost!

The framework of social accounting could be broadened to include tangible costs and benefits which accrue to society generally whoever pays or receives them. On this approach the costs of road deaths and injuries can be estimated in terms of lost production, hospital bills, and other forms of 'real resource' costs. Of course, much of the evidence is very speculative, because side-effects and assumptions are so complex, but this is not the point here. The point is that, in principle, this approach to the valuation of social costs and benefits seems reasonable, so long as its considerable limitations are remembered.

In particular it must be remembered that we are not using any ultimate or comprehensive yardstick of measurement, but only one to be employed within rather restrictive policy assumptions. It is clear that neither financial nor 'real resource' measurements of the costs of accidents can cover in any way the personal sufferings of individuals. The answer that it is helpful to know x (tangible costs) even if we cannot know y (intangibles) is only partly helpful. For example, the deaths of old people usually represent net gains not losses in real resource terms to society as a whole. If we accept a Christian or humanitarian ethic about the equal value of all lives, we are now in the paradoxical position that the smaller is any individual's x the larger must be his y, and vice versa.

This paradox partly disappears if we read this ethical rule into the C.B.A. by averaging all interpersonal costs and benefits. Still we are not out of the wood since some cost savings are still ethically illegitimate. Suppose that the composition of accident victims was such that there was a net gain to national production from their demise, we ought not presumably to treat this as a benefit in the equation – it would simply be irrelevant. But if this is so then doubt must also be cast on the significance of any figures of production losses which relate to different cases. For the tangible costs to be averaged, intangibles must be treated consistently between every type of case.

Reliance upon C.B.A. is a two-edged sword where, as is very often the case, 'intangible' benefits are important. This circumstance produces a familiar dilemma of educationalists in the modern world. If they seek to justify investment in education on economic grounds (as some do) they may be faced with evidence that its economic return is fairly small and dubious when compared with other investment opportunities.* If now they fall back upon their traditional staple of cultural or civic arguments to make up for this deficiency, they will be accused of trying to have it both ways. After failing the economic tests which they have adduced, they will seem to be treating the cultural and other reasons as second-best or subsidiary, or at any rate as deserving less credence on their own than they might otherwise receive.

At the same time it would seem excessive (although some people do take this position) to argue that resource implications are *irrelevant* for the assessment of projects which confer intangible benefits. In a few cases the evidence does support this interpretation; for example, as was pointed out earlier, no resource cost is usually regarded as excessive (assuming the resources are available) for saving the lives of specific individuals known to be in immediate danger. But even here this position can be questioned ethically. The problem then is to know *how far* and *in what ways* resource analysis should be applied to policies whose aims are (in ordinary parlance) partly 'non-economic'? How do we weight the (economically) tangible against the (economically) intangible considerations, or is this a loaded way of expressing the issue? More will be said on this subject, but the economist's itch to 'quantify the unquantifiable', however falteringly, is one possible reaction to the frustrations of this situation.

The 'social-efficiency approach' to valuation uses many of the same techniques as the 'market approach' already discussed. For instance, the benefits of accident prevention were measured through the cost-saving method listed earlier. Many welfare economists indeed would deny the validity of my distinction between these two approaches, claiming that an ideal pricing system would reconcile both criteria. In the real world, however, there does seem to be a valid distinction to be drawn over the uses of C.B.A., even though it is somewhat blurred and techniques of calculation overlap.

Consider the earlier example of the benefits of education. On the market approach these might be tested by the willingness of parents (or scholars themselves when old enough) to pay for the education; but for a variety of reasons this criterion of benefit is not acceptable to policy-makers. Alternatively, as already noted, we might take the extra income which some form of education would yield as an 'intermediate' index of benefits received. This approach is sometimes found in U.S. cost–benefit studies but less so in Europe. It provides some guide to the tangible benefits received by the

* Of course this is not the usual finding of cost–benefit analysts working in this field who are disposed to argue that education *is* economically worthwhile in addition to its other (intangible) benefits. But I do not find their arguments convincing; they seem to be biased (like other specialised analysts) towards justifying economically the service they are studying or the organisation they serve. The reader can judge for himself from a book such as Marc Blaug (ed.), *Economics of Education*, I (Harmondsworth: Penguin, 1968).

individuals concerned, although not to their 'intangible' benefits – which incidentally might sometimes be negative if a narrow technical education restricts or perverts their mental and cultural capacities. Few people would regard these extra incomes as a sound guide to social benefit if only because of the strong influence of oligopoly or imperfect competition. Many professions keep up their incomes through imposing stringent (and possibly unnecessary) educational qualifications, and in many other cases – the French bureaucracy for example – incomes are closely based upon educational attainment as being supposedly the fairest way of allocating jobs and promotions. Because the increases simply reflect educational attainments, they cannot be much guide to the *social* benefits of these attainments; the test is circular.[4]

Thus a market treatment of educational benefits produces rather different results from a social welfare or efficiency treatment, and neither approach can suggest any adequate general yardstick. *Any* measurement of educational benefits has meaning only in a specific and restricted context which ought to be stated; and the political nature of the inferences which tend to be drawn from particular measurements should also be clarified. If, for example, an economist suggests that the higher incomes which some forms of education produce are a justification of the education in question, he is blessing a set of social arrangements which in fact may be rather pernicious for the public at large.

The ideology behind the 'social efficiency' approach is intrinsically somewhat vague. Primarily this is a tool for measuring collectively incurred resource costs and benefits of a tangible kind, and such exercises may be useful so long as their considerable limitations are understood. In particular the identification and measurement of community costs cannot be detached from their selective use within policy analysis and set up as the basis for an independent equation.

However, the approach does become ideological if some idea of collective efficiency is put above the satisfaction of individual wants. We have already noted examples of such thinking. Time spent upon travelling is no more and no less a 'cost' to individuals than is the loss of some amenity such as a cherished view from the backdoor; but the former 'cost' appears to be more significant for economic productivity which to some people may make its existence more plausible. Social-efficiency arguments, like those concerning real resources, also gain much of their plausibility from a latent appeal to non-economic criteria. Thus the inefficiency of 'congestion costs', as analysed in Chapter 3, derives not from an economic model of supply and demand so much as from a technological view of the relationship between effort expended and work accomplished. Or at any rate some kind of mechanistic notion seems often in such cases to lie subtly behind the economic analysis.

(iii) *Subjective Valuations*

This approach moves right away from observed or inferred market behaviour, and relies upon the individual to disclose his own subjective preference curve. The results, to put it mildly, are likely to be somewhat artificial. When somebody states a price he normally does so in the context of an exchange relationship which gives point and precision to his calculation; he has to estimate how much something is worth in terms of other claims upon his income. Abstract from these conditions and there is a likelihood that the replies will either be somewhat casual (the exercise is academic and there is nothing at stake) or else will be latently influenced by the possibility of a subsequent bargain (if I am later going to be paid or compensated for something, then it is sensible to value it as highly as I dare). The exercise is more defensible if the aim is no more than to test how the respondent thinks a given sum of money could best be used (for example by a public authority) where there is a choice. If one can abstract from personal interest and be given a realistic and intelligible choice over the use of scarce resources, hypothetical monetary valuations may help to clarify individual preferences in specific situations. Otherwise, subjective valuations are likely to bear little relation to the same valuations made under conditions of market exchange if such were possible (which frequently is not the case).

But of course the cost–benefit analyst may deliberately reject market behaviour as inappropriate and consider subjective valuations to be the only appropriate guide. 'Consumers' surplus' – if it exists – can only be known through subjective preference curves. But can these curves be known even by their owner (assuming he tries to be honest)? Probably not, it would seem, because their shape only materialises under the pressure of actual marginal choices, and certainly only an exceptionally intellectual individual could attempt a systematic answer according to the theoretical rules of the game.

This approach does introduce a definite political bias or ideology of a conservative kind. It is usually linked with the Pareto principle which as we have seen argues that the only policy changes which are certainly worth making are those which leave no individual worse off than he was before. If 'worse off' is taken not in a conventional economic sense but in relation to a general state of well-being then only the individual himself can judge the extent of his deprivation. An individual may get all sorts of satisfactions out of living in a particular house that are not expressed in the market price. If house-owners are asked, as they were in the Roskill enquiry, to put a figure on this prospective loss and some answer 'infinity', as some did, then logically that is an end of the matter. No development can occur. Of course the Roskill research team could not accept this answer and laid down an arbitrary maximum of 200 per cent 'consumer's surplus', which meant the house-owner's loss was valued at three times the market price of his house. This happened to be the maximum surplus that anyone *did* claim, but the figure seems simply a crude correction to a theory that cannot be applied.[5]

This treatment of losses does not follow from any genuinely 'economic' principle of welfare, but from an old-fashioned assertion of individual rights. It may be done in a good cause, such as that of defending the individual's enjoyment of environmental 'goods' such as pure air and absence of excessive noise against those who would trespass upon these particular amenities.

But the fact remains that it is basically a policy opinion expressed (like many other opinions) in economic language only because it has become fashionable to do so. Moreover, the persuasiveness of the principle seems to depend very heavily upon the circumstances in which it is adduced. To appeal to Pareto in order to protect householders against the environmental disruption of a proposed airport these days seems a useful, even praiseworthy type of argument; to do so in order to protect a group of rich suburbanites against the development in their proximity of a low-income housing estate is rather less convincing. But while political argument can quite reasonably make much of such distinctions, this theory of valuation is blind to them.

This technique also leads to confusion about the basis for public compensation, which must in fact rest not upon any economic principle but upon broad criteria of social justice. Thus when people are dispossessed from their homes it may be socially reasonable and fair to pay them rather more than the market price of their property on the grounds that many of them are not willing sellers (this assumes that the law will not allow any of them to exact the full scarcity premium which naturally occurs in these circumstances). The premium to be paid can now be tested by asking the householders what special value they attach to their present location and amenities, and the answers they return may not be wholly unreasonable in terms of this particular context of public action. But what exactly is being measured? The economist may claim that he is working with the notion of 'consumers' surplus', but this concept, supposing it is meaningful, could not be estimated with any accuracy through the chosen techniques. What is actually being done is to try to estimate, in some rough-and-ready way, the extra compensation that should be fairly awarded for a forced sale.

But the gravest criticism of this approach is that it is essentially wrong-headed in trying to assign monetary figures to deprivations which not only cannot but should not be treated in this way. Consider a village which is flooded, and its community life destroyed, in order to make way for a reservoir and dam. Some people would assert that an act of this nature should not be done at all and others that considerable extra expenditure would be justified to avoid it (but how much?). But if the village is flooded, few would suppose that *any* money payment could redress the position of the villagers. In point of fact some of the villagers may in the long run *welcome* a change to some new environment while others will probably be inconsolable. Either way, beyond some basic yardstick of financial compensation, money would simply be irrelevant. Indeed, it would widely be thought immoral as well as inappropriate to offer a very large compensation in respect of matters that money cannot compensate. Both ethically and politically the question of what resource expenditure is worth incurring to save the village has to be answered on largely different grounds from the question of what compensation should be paid the villagers if it is flooded. The only connexion is a reasonable argument that the first figure should not be smaller than the second.

Mishan is an economist of this school, and the slight absurdity of subjective valuations can be seen from his own chosen example of the true value of the loss of life and limb.[6] He rejects the idea that the value to be attached to human life or freedom from injury could be inferred from the implicit prices placed upon such factors by public decisions, because of the gross inconsistencies of these figures (as we have seen there are reasons for these inconsistencies, but it can be accepted that such implicit prices cannot properly be transferred from their specific contexts). He rejects equally the idea that the value of life can be based upon any estimates of economic loss to society (we have already accepted the considerable limits upon the relevance of such evidence). He rightly rejects also the adequacy of insurance benefits as a guide to the value of life, since these benefits can logically only be related to the supposed financial needs of dependents.

But Mishan still claims that there is one correct and indubitable method for the valuation of life in pecuniary terms. It turns out to be a complex one. First, we are to ignore the value to the individual himself of a life which he has voluntarily risked (say through mountaineering) on the grounds that he had decided that the benefit was worth the risk. On the other hand, lives that are involuntarily lost have to be valued upon a self-assessed basis divided by the extent of the relevant risk. Additionally in all cases one should include the financial loss incurred by dependents, and the monetary value of the emotional deprivation (or possibly gain?) which dependents and others will suffer. Mishan opines that the self-assessed value of life will increase in the future, but that the financial and emotional losses of dependents will decline, presumably because emotional attachments will contribute less to happiness. One has only to state this argument baldly, stripped of its complex algebraic formulae, to see that it is, at the best, a scholastic dissection of some of the elements that enter into judgements about the value of human life, devoted to an unreal enterprise. The concepts could never be turned into meaningful or acceptable economic calculations, which is the very basis for asserting that some values lie beyond the realm of economics.

We have now reviewed three possible approaches to the evaluation of costs and benefits. It would be misleading to suggest that economists themselves fall into three distinctive schools or that they would accept the analysis I have offered. Welfare economics is too convoluted a subject to yield easily to this sort of treatment. I would not wish either to be dogmatic about the utility of this particular analysis. It is no more than an attempt to translate into ordinary language some of the social or political meanings that seem to be inherent in these economic theories.

However we do the analysis we seem to return to the same riddles. These may be summarised as follows:

(i) If we look for a market basis for valuations we have the advantage of treading a well-worn road which implicitly accepts the relativity of all economic measurements (money which is the normal yardstick of measurement has itself a constantly shifting value). But we have perennial problems of coping with market imperfections and failures, including the lack of market evidence about many of the factors which it is desired to quantify.

(ii) If we try to correct our data to allow for differences between private and social costs, we are up against the elusive problems about externalities discussed in the last chapter. The willingness of individuals to pay in order to prevent some collective injury or achieve some collective benefit is closely dependent upon legal and institutional rules and the conditions of collective bargaining. Economic theorising can support the case for some political action, but it cannot go far towards the construction of meaningful measurements.

(iii) If we fall back on subjective valuations we get into different trouble. This route may take us to the conservative stance associated with the Pareto principle which is defensible only given a special political ideology, or else lead us into a maze of impossible calculations. But a reaction to this situation which eschews intangibles and concentrates upon resource costs easily (though not necessarily) becomes too concerned with limited tests of economic efficiency.

These three approaches may also be regarded as attempts to deal with successively harder problems of measurement. Once we move into the realm of phenomena which are not in the normal sense economic (that is to say the subject of regular exchange transactions), we enter a shadowy type of economic world in which it is hard to know what is or is not in principle measurable. The principle of willingness to pay is not very helpful, because by definition, W.T.P. is not being revealed in a market sense so that we have to test its existence in other ways. And even if some economic techniques can provide tests of this kind, the economist cannot bring his apparatus to bear upon all possible cases. It is necessary to concentrate upon those phenomena which arouse social concern, as well as possessing some capacity for being submitted to economic measurement.

It is often claimed that some externalities are more capable of measurement than others, and that as the economist's techniques improve more of these creatures will be successfully caught in the quantifier's net. But is this a true statement of the situation? May it not be the case that *all* externalities are equally incapable of being measured with much objectivity, but that in some cases a partial measurement for a particular purpose has a utility and plausibility which is absent in other cases?

Compare the measurement of time-savings (often regarded as relatively 'hard' figures) with that of the enjoyment of country views (usually treated as an 'intangible'). In both cases there is little or only spotty market evidence, more so in the case of time perhaps, although estate agents could provide some evidence about the sums which people will pay to enjoy a desirable view. In both cases subjective valuation is equally hard in principle and raises the same basic scepticism and doubt. The chief difference perhaps is that lost time is a cause of economic inefficiency (as conventionally conceived) in a way that does not apply to lost views – hence attracting the attention of those interested in measuring efficiency; but welfare theorists will be quick to point out that by *their* test of individual satisfactions the protection of views is equally relevant whether or not it is so important. Possibly the circumstances that time like money itself is homogeneous and measurable leads analysts into a sort of intellectual exaggeration about its economic significance.

E. Measuring the Rabbit

When analysts say that they will eventually devise new techniques of measurement they are certainly right. The problem does not lie in any intrinsic limits upon the techniques of quantification – *anything* can be reduced to a monetary figure by some device or another – but in the logic and coherence of the processes being used. And here we run into the problems of mixed techniques of measurement, which are additional to the more basic problems of logical analysis – of how an issue should be structured – which were considered in the last chapter.

Thus if I add an item measured in one way to another one measured in a different way the values I am presenting do not have the same significance. Both results may be presented in £s or $s, but the £ or $ ceases to have the degree of consistency which the use of these symbols suggests. There will as already suggested be political or social biases imputed into the answers if the techniques used rest upon particular value premises or assumptions. This need not matter so much if the techniques themselves are consistent and if their biases and limitations are apparent, for example if we are clear what question precisely is being answered and from what perspective or standpoint. But if the techniques are not themselves consistent or coherent, if they comprise an ingenious mixture whose only rationale is the urge to quantify somehow or other, then the aggregation of the results will produce all sorts of curious distortions and uncertainties that are additional to the inadequacies of the individual techniques.

Often in practice these problems are ducked by a failure to describe the techniques used in any systematic way. Discussion of methodology appears as a tiresome constraint upon the urge to produce figures. But even if (partly for this reason) the techniques used cannot be positively asserted to be mutually incompatible, it is often apparent that they are being applied in inconsistent ways. The Roskill Commission's research, for all its size and thoroughness, fell into such errors. For example, the effect of noises upon those already living near an airport site was treated as a cost, but was not extended to those who would subsequently move into the area on the grounds that they would do so voluntarily with knowledge of the consequences; but their loss would be just as 'tangible' in terms of personal experience (unless they did not mind at all about noise) as that of the equally voluntary future air passengers whose time-costs *were* reckoned. Or again the research team, after giving credit to 'consumers' surplus' in its analysis of the costs of displaced householders, forgot the concept when it came to loss of amenity; otherwise it could hardly have accepted the idea (though this suggestion was later withdrawn) that the loss of a Norman church might be based upon fire insurance, which is no measure at all of the subjective losses of those who could no longer use or visit the church. Curiously this particular idea emanated from the Church of England, which is interesting evidence about the inability of such a group to see any relation (presumably) between economic price and social value

The problem of cost–benefit analysis is often viewed as that of the relation between the quantified and the unquantified items: the former are known, the latter are not. But this is a gross mis-statement. There are all sorts of often subtle gradations within the category of quantified items. If the analyst is modest – if for example he attempts to measure no more than one or two fairly obvious 'externalities' – he increases the credibility of the quantified element. His figures still pose serious problems, not only about his techniques but as to *why* he should single out certain items for measurement when (it may be asserted) others are equally relevant; but at least he retains a grounding in conventional forms of economic debate with the result of course that the unquantified element is correspondingly larger.

If instead the analysis is extended to include valuations placed upon a wide variety of items, the reliability of the results cumulatively declines – partly because of the inadequacies and inconsistencies of the techniques being used, and partly for reasons which are not (or need not be) the analyst's fault. Thus monetary figures often have to be applied to predicted outcomes which have wide or very wide margins of error; while additionally, the uncertainties of evaluation techniques mean that a wide range of money values can be plausibly assigned to the same phenomenon. The more honestly and carefully the analyst plots these speculative uncertainties, the more indeterminate and inconclusive will be his results; but the more dogmatic he is, the more unreliable.

Thus a cost–benefit analysis ends up not with a division between known and unknown factors, but with quantified items of very varying degrees of 'hardness' or 'softness' plus the unquantified items. An item is hard when its occurrence can be reliably predicted, it can be assigned to a determinate source, and it can be measured in ways that are conventionally meaningful (for example the costs to a public authority of constructing an airport); an item is soft when converse conditions prevail (for example the time-costs of future air travellers). Of course it does not follow that the item itself should necessarily be regarded as a less-important decision factor *because* its measurement is soft; the softness refers only to the meaningfulness of a monetary calculation.

Even so there still remains the problem of comparing the quantified items (however far these are stretched) against the unquantified ones. This is the problem of 'horse and rabbit stew'; what is the use of meticulously evaluating the rabbit if the horse is bound to give its flavour to the whole stew?[7] In pure logic, even if we have quantified 99 per cent of the relevant factors in the equation, the indeterminancy of the remainder means that no inference can be drawn about a correct solution. But decision-making cannot be a question of pure logic since it involves probabilities and guesses. In principle quantification reduces the number of mental operations which must be performed to produce some answer; instead of a long series of successive comparisons, we can now regard a single figure (x) as standing for the net product of all the quantifiable considerations and consider how to trade off x against the unquantified items $(Y_1, Y_2, \ldots, Y_n)$. However we do these 'trading-off' operations (and there are many possible ways) the process is simplified when compared with the much larger number of mental operations that would be necessary if x were split into its original components.

But this simplification is acceptable only if we really do accept that *all* the considerations relevant to *all* the items contained within x can be expressed by a notional global money sum. And it is most unlikely that one could reasonably or in practice make such an assumption. In practice it is very probable that the policy-maker will feel inclined or obliged to disentangle for certain purposes the elements contained within x, and to extend 'trading-off' operations to these items. It would then seem an open question whether the analyst has done more to simplify or to confuse the process of decision-making.

To return to the mixed stew, it is of course just as possible (logically rather than gastronomically) for the rabbit to dominate the flavour as the horse. This will occur if the decision-makers are biased towards the idea that quantified items deserve more respect as grounds for a decision than unquantified ones. Admittedly they may have the converse bias, however.

The economist who seeks for an independent or objective basis with which to plot the whole world of social values in economic terms is doomed to be disappointed. He will end up with a farrago of pretentious theorising. If, however, he tries to push out the frontiers of economic analysis pragmatically and cautiously, he has more hope of success in two respects. First, he may be able to adduce some evidence (speculative rather than conclusive) about the willingness of individuals to pay for certain phenomena that are not normally or regularly expressed in market terms. Secondly, he may be able to offer measurements about the effects of public decisions upon the collective use of resources which have some relevance for policy-making although they can never logically determine it.

These roles require the economist to stick to his trade and to accept a basic distinction between economic and non-economic forms of analysis. The former covers resource factors that are measurable in various ways in monetary terms, the latter comprises social values that are themselves untranslatable into such terms, even though it is true that the realisation of such values usually involves demands upon resources that can be measured.

In a comprehensive cost–benefit analysis too many factors cannot be valued in monetary terms at all, or only very speculatively, for the results to provide much reliable evidence for a decision. On the other hand, specific economic measurements that are designed to help the application of a public policy, or to improve the policy itself, can be helpful so long as their intrinsic limitations are understood. If such an exercise be described as a sort of partial cost–benefit analysis, there seems no reason to object. To conclude this section an illustration will be helpful.

Consider a public enquiry into the location of a new town or housing development that will use up agricultural land. Since the Second World War it has been public policy in Britain to conserve agricultural land, on grounds of its possible future scarcity in relation to food requirements. Conservation policy affects the costs of development adversely, through requiring shifts of sites or increases of density, and these changes also reduce the welfare of those living in the new development areas. Thus a 'trade-off' of conflicting policy considerations is necessary according to criteria that have been only loosely prescribed and seem to vary with shifts of public policy, local pressures, and so on.

How can the economist help to make such a decision more rational? Not, it may be suggested, by a comprehensive cost–benefit analysis of a particular decision, which would flounder amidst a great variety of costs and benefits accruing to all those concerned (farmers, householders, industrialists, et al.), the treatment of 'intangibles' (community values, individual rights), differences between public and private interests and between short and long run (e.g. over conservation policy), and so on. If the analysis was objectively and carefully attempted, the results would certainly be inconclusive – unless indeed the balance of gain in terms of a common-sense social judgement was so obvious that little analysis was needed!

On the other hand, economic analysis can help to clarify some particular policies. How should the loss of agricultural land be expressed? From a public policy viewpoint what counts here may be the loss of future production, and one measure of this is the volume of resources that would have to be put into agriculture in the future to make good the loss ('food replacement yardstick'). These required resources can be calculated in various ways according to how far farmers are expected to replace the lost resources spontaneously through an intensification of their production, or how far the government would need itself to stimulate production artificially, for example through subsidies for the improvement of marginal land. The latter figure would be higher in terms not only of public finance but of real resources and there is no one 'right' or 'certain' figure to adduce as the cost of food replacement. But at least this approach provides some meaningful figures within a policy context to compare with the estimated costs of development which a conservation policy will entail.[8]

We should note the questions that this economic analysis does *not* attempt to answer. It does not deal, for example, with farmers' losses. These losses are partly economic (which must be dealt with by compensation rules) and partly personal, for example the loss of roots, local connexions, and traditional ways of life. Similarly, there are gains or losses affecting the inhabitants of the new development areas which are not subsumed in developers' costs, such as the intensity or desperation with which they need a home, their liking for a garden (which would use more land), and so on.*

* This is a considerable simplification. Distinctions must be drawn between conservation decisions which (a) reduce absolutely the number of dwellings that can be built or (b) put up the average costs of construction or (c) reduce the attractiveness of the dwellings or their surroundings. In practice all effects may be present to some extent. The general effect, however, will be to increase housing costs in terms of housing quality. Economically this can be expressed as an increase in the cost per unit of housing of average quality although the calculation is difficult. Socially speaking just as with the displaced farmers there will be frustrations imposed upon individuals who cannot get the sort of home they want (or a home at all) which elude quantification, except through the circular process of 'implicit prices'.

These social values are, as we have seen, highly resistant to any economic calculation save on a most artificial and dubious basis; but they are factors which figure naturally in political debate, and which can to some extent be independently assessed by an impartial adjudicator through the medium of the public enquiry. The economic analysis must then to some extent be kept separate from the broader social analysis of which it forms part, and this will introduce all the familiar problems of their combination within a final decision. But this problem is at any rate more manageable than an attempt to stew rabbit with horse in the same (economic) turreen. For as the example has illustrated the economists have problems enough over producing partial measurements for specific purposes.

F. The Myths of Numerology

Any discussion of the quest for quantification has to come to grips at some point with the myths of numerology. Thus to some people the essence of rationality is that all relevant factors or values should be expressed in some common unit of account so that like is compared with like. The most convenient accounting system of this kind appears to be monetary symbols, because of the substantial place already occupied by such symbols in the process of decision-making and because of the existence of a sophisticated body of economic theories which use these symbols. But this interpretation is not inevitable. If notional monetary values are too hard to estimate, or their use falls foul of other objections, it can be claimed that the unit of account can be an ordinary numerical scale of preferences, conceived cardinally and/or ordinally. In other words, for some would-be rationalists, the vital need is to express qualitative differences of judgements in some kind of quantitative scale, however crude. Rationality equals counting and measuring.

To explore the full peculiarities of this belief one would have to write a treatise on mathematical logic – a task beyond the capacity of this writer and (one suspects) beyond that of most advocates of numerology. But for the purposes of this book it is necessary to look at some of the simpler social and logical assumptions which underlie such beliefs and consider their validity.

Now it is perfectly true that, in choosing between alternatives, I can if I wish convert all the factors I judge to be relevant into a notional numerical scale. I can then end up with the finding that alternative A gets 16 points, B 14 points, and C 12 points, so I should choose A. But the weights I assign merely reflect the qualitative judgements I have already made. The evidence for this is that if I do not like the result which my numerical weights produce, I will change them. There is no independent basis for assigning the numbers that is separate from my own value judgements, so that the use of numerology cannot contribute anything new to the analysis.

It is often claimed that the use of numbers will cause me to think more carefully about the importance of the various factors, and to introduce new factors which I would otherwise overlook. But this result is not the logical consequence of using numbers – it could be done without them – and it is very dubious whether it is even a psychological consequence. The critical question here is how carefully and how widely an individual is prepared to think about his decision premises. If he thinks in a narrow way numerology will not make him reflective, and if he is reflective there is no need for numerology.

This argument has a close analogy with the claim often made for the therapeutic value of cost–benefit analysis in persuading decision-makers to think more carefully and systematically about relevant factors. But if there is such a therapeutic effect (as there well may be) it derives from the systematic listing of relevant factors and the attachment to them of useful supporting data. For this purpose there is no requirement that the factors themselves (or any of them) should be weighted numerically or in money terms. On the contrary such numerical conversions may distract attention from the *harder* tasks of examining the relationships between value judgements and relevant information, and between the value judgements themselves. The numerical weighting of the values themselves, however circular it may transpire to be, offers an apparent short cut to decision-making which has a beguiling appearance (and nothing more) of scientific rationality. Thus, while the logical analysis of relevant factors should aid rationality, their quantification can easily be a spurious and slipshod way of dodging the issues. At the best it is harmless, at the worst it distracts attention from more necessary tasks.

Our examples have so far been drawn from *individual* decisions. Collective decisions introduce some psychological or sociological differences of importance. The individual has a ready-made corrective for any errors into which a use of numerology might lead him, namely that he must live with the consequences. Thus if the results of a notional point-count on some prospective personal choice, such as which house to buy, which holiday to take, or which girl to marry, does not please him, he can correct his reckoning without difficulty. Indeed the fact that such point-counts are rarely made in relation to personal decisions, save as a parlour game, shows their essential irrelevance to the decision.

However, a collective decision-maker such as a politician or an official, whether operating singly or in a team, does not himself bear the consequences of a decision made on behalf of society. He bears only a tiny fraction of the consequences as one citizen among millions, while his personal reputation is affected in ways which may not bear much or any direct relationship to the social effects of the decision. In this situation numerology takes on a certain appeal as a recipe for protecting society from the subjective preferences of the official or politician. For the same reasons, however, the use or misuse of numerology is not subject to the corrective check of an interested personal judgement. It is true that political judgements may play something of the same role by ruling out decisions which, whatever their grounding in quantitative assessments, appear as politically unacceptable. But these political checks are not automatic, they do not operate in matters left to bureaucratic discretion, and in doubtful cases at any rate the politician may himself be over-impressed by an exercise in numerology.

However real or fancied these dangers may be it is the case that much energy is being diverted from more useful work into essentially futile exercises in numerical evaluations. Such evaluations have become a frequent feature of the reports of consultants or officials who are concerned with alternative policy options. Qualitative evaluations of such options, based upon declared or hypothesised public policies, have always been a feature of such reports, although usually approached with caution and discretion. But numerical evaluations logically require considerable precision over the structuring and weighting of the goals and values that are to be regarded as relevant to the decision. This logical structure of values is rarely if ever supplied by politicians or governments themselves. Accordingly the consultants or officials preparing the report are largely in the position of supplying their own scale of values and preferences, and then reading these off in the form of an apparently objective numerical scale.

As already suggested the worst effect is not that people are fooled but that the analysis becomes more slipshod and spurious. A typical exercise is to reel off a fairly large number of alternative courses of action (for it is also supposed, following Herbert Simon, that to multiply alternatives is intrinsically more rational) and then to evaluate them accordingly to some numerical scale or system of ordinal preferences. In consequence too much space is devoted to the mechanics of evaluation, too little to the much tougher tasks of policy analysis. As in some cost–benefit studies, the fixing of eyes upon the techniques of final evaluation shifts attention from the intervening processes and the reasoning behind them. The conclusions then become numerate but shallow.

A typical British example – many could be given – is the Docklands Study prepared by consultants for the Department of the Environment and the Greater London Council. The analysis moves swiftly to the presentation of five alternative plans which are sketchily set out and then tentatively evaluated according to a system of points awarded for the capacity of each plan to achieve certain specified goals. Both goals and points are largely supplied by the consultants, but this fact might matter less if their reasoning were clear and specific enough for the rationale of their rankings to be followed. The report had in fact rather little influence, but the use of fashionable techniques provided a window-dressing which helped to disguise the essential shallowness of the policy analysis.[9]

Of course it should be conceded that there is no *necessary* connexion whatever between slipshod policy analysis and numerical techniques of evaluation. So long as the artificiality of the numerical rankings is understood they may persuade decision-makers to consider factors which they otherwise have little incentive to think about because of the nature of collective decisions. But while this beneficial therapeutic effect *may* occur, so also is there a risk of 'displaced rationality' whereby the apparent precision of the final rankings serves to shift effort and attention from the substantive part of the analysis. It becomes an open question, appropriate to psychological inquiry, as to whether possible benefit is worth the risk.

Part Two

Political and Economic Choice

5
Economics and Democracy

A. Economic and Political Choice

This chapter switches attention to political factors which are relevant to the use of economic techniques, while the next one examines the social philosophy behind these techniques. Suppose that politics is viewed as a kind of market in which the voter as a consumer of public policy outputs is trying to express his preferences between them. On this basis the inferiority of political to economic markets needs little demonstration.

Thus the economic consumer can spend 10p on bacon, 20p on eggs, 25p on chocolate and so on, showing the exact distribution of his preferences between these commodities at the prices currently ruling. The political consumer at a national or local election by contrast must, however rational he is, pack an enormous number of separate policy preferences into a single vote. He has no way even of indicating which issues seem to him most important, or of making his position clear on any one issue. Thus he may prefer Party A on Issues 1, 2, 3 and Party B on Issues 4, 5, 6 and his analysis of the relative importance of these issues and the party differences over them may lead him to a careful selection of Party A, but none of this reasoning is apparent from his vote. Even if he concentrates upon voting on a single issue, no one (save perhaps his friends) can know what that issue is.

Explanations of voting behaviour in modern democracies are various and complex.[1] It seems to be agreed that very little voting behaviour is based upon the sort of careful review of specific issues posited above, and that the great bulk of voting follows party lines. Many studies have shown the importance of group loyalties and alignments in determining party allegiance. The most frequent identifications are with socio-economic classes, although these can take a subjective form as with the 'deferential' identification of some working-class voters with the Conservative Party in Britain. Religious and ethnic identifications can also be important, as can the voter's identification with the nation as a whole (nationalism or patriotism), and trade-offs between conflicting group loyalties have often to be made.

Voters no doubt assume that support for a party will also work to their own advantage, but when voting loyalties are traditional and cemented by family and social structure there is probably little disposition to think about this relationship. Separate individual calculations of advantage may simply not be made, and a dominant group or even national loyalty suffices. However, in Western democracies a good deal of voting was always more explicitly reasoned than this, and the weakening of traditional social structures plus the increase of social mobility has certainly increased the amount of open-ended voting (that is voting not settled by some strong or traditional loyalty).

The influence of party images is well-established, but the elements in such an image are manifold. Undoubtedly one factor in a party's image is its actual or supposed stand on important issues of the day, and another factor is its record in office as this is supposed to have affected the voter's interests or those of the group with which he identifies. These considerations logically involve careful exercises of judgement but are usually made under conditions of considerable ignorance.

Anthony Downs has argued the rationality of voting according to party images, on the grounds that these images are primarily built up from past or prospective party policies and thus provide a shorthand guide to the sort of results a voter can expect to receive. Since he would need to expend enormous effort in order to acquire enough information for discovering his interest on specific issues, and since it would be quite irrational for him to try to do so (as he only has one vote), the sensible course is to identify with that party which seems to offer the best generalised policy package or which is closest to his position on the one or two issues about which he feels most strongly. There is actually some evidence that voters' party alignments are correlated with the particular issue or issues which concern them most.[2]

Downs gives a plausible account of how rational voters, and parties that responded to such voters, might tend to behave. Even so of course the correlation between the generalised policy preferences of party supporters, the 'image' of that party, and the party's performance when in office will remain a very loose one indeed. It will not guarantee much correlation over the treatment of specific issues unless perhaps an issue is particularly important and figures in an election – and even then there is ample evidence that parties sometimes renege on their electoral promises. Moreover, to the extent that voters are ignorant or apathetic about policy preferences, and vote for such extraneous reasons as a politician's charm or a personal grievance, the correlations will be distorted. Finally the large block of 'traditional' voting hardly seems rational in Downs's sense though it may be rational in terms of certain political theories. Such voting often expresses a shared trust in the capacity of party leaders to 'do their best' for the group or nation, it contains little policy input, and it may not be geared to any calculation of individual advantage.

Even so Downs's point about the high information costs which a voter must incur in order to judge the probable results of party policies still constitutes a rational argument for trusting party leaders (who are presumed to have more information) to decide the detailed policies. Even the large block of traditional voting may seem rational from this standpoint if it reflects an accurate assumption that the leaders will look after their supporters' interests. However, rationality in this context suggests a specific calculation of advantage, even if the advantage being considered by the voter is not simply his own but that of some wider reference group (a class or a nation) with which he identifies. Unless he makes such calculations and is prepared if need be to switch his vote, there is no scope for party competition over policies. Completely traditional voters need not be reckoned with in the *politician's* calculations because their votes are in the bag. On certain normative theories, traditional voting based upon mutual trust between leaders and followers may have the desirable results of increasing political stability and of strengthening political leadership; but this situation hardly squares with a market theory of politics, and has to be explained and defended on other grounds than the instrumental value of achieving policies that are to the voter's liking.

Seemingly an obvious way to improve the rationality of political choice would be to introduce referenda on as many specific issues and decisions as possible. This could apply to public projects such as the Channel Tunnel and to pension and health proposals as well as specifically political issues such as membership of the European Economic Community. In the United States voters are often able to pass a verdict upon public projects through the requirement that they support a bond issue for the purpose in question, although in practice the bond issue is sometimes related to a package of projects which must be endorsed or rejected as a whole. Such devices could be refined and multiplied.

Unfortunately an extensive or indeed almost any use of referenda is subject to severe drawbacks from the criterion here under review, namely improving the precision with which voters' preferences can be registered. Three limitations should be mentioned:

(*a*) Most public decisions *affect* individuals very unequally and often in multiple capacities. For example the nationalisation of the steel industry concerns management and workers in that industry more than it does the public as consumers although it also affects them too. The Channel Tunnel will affect some individuals strongly as travellers or traders, others because they live nearby and will suffer noise and intrusion, others in both these capacities, but many people only slightly or hardly at all. There are also issues which do affect the public in a more general and uniform way. Thus if health or pension plans are designed to give help to all citizens who fall ill or become old, the benefits are non-discriminatory and the costs may also be non-discriminatory in the sense that they come from a general pool of taxation whose equity can be separately evaluated. Such issues would seem more appropriate for referenda on the grounds of a generalised or indeterminate equality of interest – individuals do not know (although they can guess) how the cost–benefit equation will work out personally and can judge the issue to some extent as impartial citizens.

It may be said that proposals which confer benefits or costs on specific groups ought also to be judged by the less-interested or disinterested opinion of the general public. However, this does not seem to be a very efficient way of checking special interests when one allows for the ignorance of the public about the detailed effects of the policy in question. Hence the desirable field for referenda would seem confined to generalised schemes or to basic constitutional or political issues. Whether one actually favours referenda in such cases would hinge upon the old debate about the respective advantages of direct versus representative democracy.

(*b*) Individuals *feel* differentially about public issues and decisions quite apart from how they are affected. A socialist may passionately desire steel nationalisation although he would be little affected by it; an egalitarian may be keen upon eliminating private schools or medical practice even though the results might be indifferent or inimical to his personal welfare; an educationalist might be keen that concerts should be subsidised even though he never goes himself. These 'ideal-regarding wants', as Barry calls them, affect the intensity of individual preferences about public decisions in different, sometimes opposite directions from the factor of personal gain or loss. *They have little parallel in the motivations of economic behaviour as this is normally understood.* Sometimes a consumer will refuse to buy some product from disapproval of its manufacturer or its country of origin, but the effects upon market behaviour seem pretty marginal.

It is hard also to say how far political behaviour is affected by these ideal-regarding wants or preferences, but certainly they exist. Moreover, there is also disagreement as to whether such preferences are the most desirable (some would say the only ethically legitimate) basis for public decisions, or whether, contrariwise, such motives are an undesirable influence which confuses and prevents the more rational over-all results that would flow from personal calculations of gain. There is a difference here between the views and assumptions of many economists and those of one major school of political philosophers.

As far as referenda are concerned, it would seem to be neither practical nor democratically defensible to give individuals extra voting power simply because their motivations are of a certain (ideal) type or because they feel these ideal motivations strongly. (This as we have seen is different from being strongly affected by a decision.) An argument for the use of referenda in such cases would seem to arise, if at all, only where substantial numbers of individuals feel strongly upon a question of moral principle. Interestingly some of the few cases of the use of referenda in Britain are of this type, as when Welsh counties settle the issue of Sunday drinking by a popular vote in which the self-regarding 'wets' are arrayed against the ideal-regarding (if they are so) 'drys'.

(*c*) The very considerable ignorance of the public about the precise nature and consequences of policy decisions is a formidable argument against referenda. There is a sharp contrast here with economic markets. It is true that public information about the quality and performance of products (especially consumer durables) is often inadequate, but at least the consumer has a more direct acquaintance with his own tastes and a clear incentive to find out more. The information required is also much less complicated.

There is another difference of importance. In a market choice the individual's own exercise of choice is decisive for the results which he experiences; he gets what he pays for and if he can pay he is at least sure of getting the product he has chosen. In a political decision, on the other hand, his choice makes only a tiny difference to the result and its effect is decisive in only the rarest of cases; while additionally the results of his preferred policy impinge upon him usually by an indirect route even though they may be important for his want satisfaction. These considerations, particularly the former one, have led some writers to conclude that a rational individual would not bother to vote in an election or referendum; the probability of influencing the result is not worth the personal time and effort.[3] The accuracy of this conclusion would seem to depend upon the meaning of rationality, and upon whether it is indeed rational to be an egoist of this type. (See Chapter 6.)

Of course the mere existence of extensive referenda will constitute *some* incentive to individuals to acquire more information, but the previous analysis suggests that this incentive will not be large and the actual functioning of referenda seems to support this conclusion. It can still be argued that if a majority are apathetic and do not bother to vote, it is only reasonable and not unfair for the issue to be settled by those who do care. In such a situation, however, these individuals are likely to be the ones most obviously or deeply affected by the result, while the more minor and diffused types of interest will be under-represented. In the aggregate, however, these latter interests may be important, and the result of the referendum is liable to be very different from any total summation of costs and benefits to individuals – assuming that were possible.

In fact this picture of wholesale abstentions has to be modified to allow for all those who will cast a vote, not from any clear opinion on the issue in question, but from loyalty to political leaders or interest groups or under the advice and exhortation of the media and of opinion leaders. To some extent this situation merely reproduces features which are anyhow inherent in the making of a political decision, but there are also differences. Instead of pressures being brought to bear upon Ministers or the legislature, they will be transferred to the public arena. In consequence less influence will probably be exerted by administrative officials and experts, by advisory committees and by other organs of specialised or 'inside' opinion, and more influence by party activists, wealthy pressure groups (possibly), and certainly by manipulators of opinion such as the mass media. Whether the results could be judged better, in terms of meeting the wants of individuals, seems at the least to be highly doubtful. Only those with a strong faith in the value of direct democracy are likely to suppose so, and their picture seems often to be derived from a rather unreal world of Greek or Rousseau-esque democracy in which all citizens willingly and intelligently participate in public debate.

This critique has brought out the limitations of referenda and of voting systems generally as devices for ascertaining individual preferences about public decisions. The strongest case for such referenda exists where an issue affects all or most citizens in similar capacities even if (necessarily as a rule) to a varying degree; and possibly in relation to issues of public or social morality where feelings run high; but even in these cases the limitations can be seen to be considerable.

In particular the increased precision of referenda as a means of expressing policy preferences is offset by the still higher information costs to voters, particularly if we accept the argument that a general-purpose vote can rationally be cast on the basis of a very generalised party or policy preference. In relation to referenda, such generalised stances are inadequate, and fuller information is essential *if* the operation is intended to convey the specific preferences of individuals.

It must be remembered that voting is only one element in the total political process, and the other elements must also be introduced in any assessment of the capacity of politics to satisfy the preferences of individuals. But before essaying this task, which will be tackled in successive stages, it should be remarked that the limitations of political voting techniques provide in principle a case for introducing economic techniques as a means of ascertaining individual preferences more accurately. This is where C.B.A. and similar techniques reappear. C.B.A. purports to offer a way of ascertaining the impact on individual wants of possible or alternative public decisions. It does so by calculating the gains and losses that will accrue to affected individuals in terms of their willingness to pay for the results. In this way it offers in principle a much more precise measurement of the direction and intensity of individual preferences for possible results than any system of voting could conceivably manage. It is grounded in the assumption that government should give individuals what they want, subject to the considerable problem of aggregating and combining these preferences in a satisfactory way. In principle then C.B.A., or at any rate the economic-welfare theories which underlie it, are grounded in a democratic philosophy of an individualist kind, and purport to offer a powerful tool for implementing that philosophy.

Although they will receive extended treatment later, some basic difficulties of principle about this economic position need to be noted here. Leaving aside all the difficulties of consistent monetary quantification (which is not an issue here), there is the problem that economic analysis normally concerns itself only with assessable gains and losses accruing to affected individuals and not with the ethical or 'ideal-regarding' considerations which figure in political debate and which the individuals themselves might wish to introduce into a public policy preference. How analysts might deal with this limitation (if it can be dealt with) is for the next chapter.

Also, there is the problem that the economic test appears in one sense to be profoundly undemocratic, in that it is related to the differential wealth and incomes of individuals. The analyst's yardstick of willingness to pay (W.T.P.) is related logically to the concept of capacity to pay (C.T.P.), for example even hypothetically I can only pay to obtain some result within the limits of my actual or assumed income, and the totality of incomes must be consistent with the results demanded.

The economist's conventional response to these problems can take two forms. First, he can argue that W.T.P. is a legitimate test or partial test for certain categories of public decisions – those to which actual or notional market tests can reasonably and rightly be applied. It then becomes a question of arguing, in terms of general social theory, the scope of this proposition. Alternatively or additionally he can introduce the familiar concern of welfare economics with issues of distribution, and seek ways of weighting the analysis so as to recognise the force of ideals of political justice. How effective such a reconciliation could be is again left until later.

There are other possible escape hatches for the economist concerned about the democratic or ethical inadequacy of the W.T.P. principle. One such came up in an earlier chapter when it was noted that certain 'subjective' techniques of valuation seem to shift away from any logical measurement of the individual's economic capacity to pay for his desired result. This may be viewed as sloppy thinking, or it may be viewed as an attempt to register intensity of preferences or desires according to a scale of measurement which has little relationship with economic calculation as normally regarded. Monetary units are used then only as convenient but misleading symbols. Basically this is the old search for a hedonistic calculus of pleasures and pains, dressed up in economic symbols, and the impracticality and illegitimacy of adding up subjective experiences derived in this way need not be further discussed. The approach is also basically anti-rationalist inasmuch as estimates about the intensity of feelings of expected pain or pleasure (and should not individuals also be compensated for lack of such feelings?) are substituted for more objective types of measurement.

A quite different escape hatch is to break the link altogether between measurement of preferences and size of income. Instead one might start from the formally democratic position of giving each individual the same quota of counters which he could then distribute as he chose to promote or to block public decisions. Thus he might distribute his counters equally between various policy proposals which he favours or concentrate them all upon a single measure; and he might use some of the counters for blocking or be given a separate pile for this purpose. One need not of course start with an equal distribution of counters, which could be allocated according to wealth, age, social status, party membership or any criteria. If trading in counters was allowed they would soon acquire a money value; if not there would be ample incentives for side-payments or bribes although secret balloting would restrict such transactions.

This rough model of a sophisticated voting system could of course be expanded and improved upon. Without doubt it would hit on many snags, some of which have already been expounded. Such models are likely to interest economists because of their concern with the logic of individual choice, but any model of this kind (if it were practicable) would register the preferences of individuals in a political not an economic capacity and be subject to all of the political considerations previously touched on. We need not follow this idea further.

B. The Policy Process and Democratic Theories

The ascertainment of individual preferences, whether by C.B.A. or in some other way, has to be slotted into the policy process, within which voting by the electorate constitutes only one element. There is no one consistent and adequate theory of democracy which can either explain or justify political behaviour in modern Westernised states. Rather is democracy a hodge-podge of ideas and theories, sometimes conflicting and sometimes complementary. None the less, economic techniques have to come to terms with democratic politics (or, if practised elsewhere, with other species of politics) in both a factual and normative sense, because of their claim to provide an acceptable and indeed usually a democratic basis for recommended decisions. To explore the political usefulness of such techniques, it will be useful here to set out briefly three democratic theories about how policies should be made. Necessarily this requires a good deal of simplification and cutting of corners, but the usefulness of the exercise can be judged subsequently.

Politics works through a structure of influence. Influence provides for the political scientist a concept somewhat analogous to money for the economist, a measure of the individual's or group's capacity to secured desired results. One can 'buy' a desired policy or decision with influence just as one buys a desired good with money. As Banfield, Schultze and others have pointed out,[4] opportunity cost is as valid a concept in politics as in economics; it refers to the debts which a politician must often incur in order to secure support for his policy, through such ways as supporting other persons' policies in exchange or of modifying his original aims to suit their wishes or of forfeiting some of his influence or 'credibility' among those who dislike the policy in question. Of course there is a major difference – money can be measured and influence cannot.*

Just as normative economics concerns itself with the proper distribution of wealth, normative political theory concerns itself with the proper distribution of influence – who should exercise influence, in what capacity, for what purpose, subject to what controls, and so on. Constitutional theories concern themselves with the procedural rules within which influence should be exercised; they cannot specify the amount or kind of influence† directly but only hedge it around with procedural requirements. Political scientists have always recognised the limitations of this approach – political influence

* Some writers have therefore suggested that in considering a policy its political opportunity cost should somehow be added to its economic opportunity cost. It is quite obscure how this could be done but the point presumably is that one should be asking what alternative policies are being forgone in terms both of resource availability and political feasibility.

† Usually the word 'power' is used in place of influence in all these contexts, but power suggests a degree of determinate ability to secure results which is not realistic or appropriate to the circumstances of modern democracies. Essentially decision-making becomes a collective process, and the final decision is the product of diverse influences even if (as is usually the case) it is formally made by some determinate individual or group such as a Minister or Cabinet. One is reminded of President Truman's remark about his successor, General Eisenhower: 'Poor Ike! He'll sit there and say do this and do that and *nothing will happen*. He'll find it's not like the Army.' The statement both justifies my use of influence and suggests that in some organisations (the army or a dictatorship) *power* might be appropriate.

is too slippery a factor to be controlled very closely or effectively – even though constitutional rules and conventions are important constraints upon its proper usage. Political theorists are also much concerned with the desirable limits of political discretion, initiative, and leadership, which require theories of representation that cannot be absorbed into constitutional law. Inevitably there is much argument and uncertainty about such theories.

Our theories of modern democracy or rather of the elements in a composite theory of democracy might look like this:

A　　Majoritarian Representative Leadership (M.R.L.)
B　　Pluralism (Balance of Interests)
C (i)　Classical Political Populism (C.P.P.)
C (ii)　Modern Consumer Populism (M.C.P.)

We cannot dwell here on the details of Theories *A* and *B* which are standard fare in political-science textbooks. Theory *A* posits that a majority of the citizens (although in practice it is often only a plurality) shall through various routes determine the composition of the political leadership which is then entitled and required to make basic policies and decisions on behalf of the entire society. This right of elected leaders to make policies is usually qualified in certain ways; for example they should accept at least a *prima facie* obligation to try to honour their electoral programmes and promises, and they should pay some attention to the wishes of opponents as well as supporters. Such ideas reflect no more than minimum assumptions to the effect that elections are meaningful, that genuine political competition exists, and that it is possible and not too difficult for the composition of majorities to change. If the underlying conditions are satisfied then the interest of political leaders or parties in achieving re-election will point in the same direction as a minimal set of norms or conventions; in particular they will have an incentive to take the whole nation as a reference group for some purposes since both opponents and supporters may always change their votes. In an intolerant society divided along rigid lines M.R.L. will work very badly indeed as a concept of democracy, because no considerations of interest will come to the rescue of its normative assumptions, which indeed may themselves not be accepted.

Theory *B*, as a normative concept of democracy, purports to remedy the deficiencies as well as the tyrannical tendencies of Theory *A*. It rests upon the right of any group of citizens to organise so as to advance their mutual interests or opinions (unless these are contrary to law or perhaps are repugnant in a moral sense), and it extols the advantages of such action for making government attend to as wide a spectrum of shared wants ('interests') as can be spontaneously organised. In this way the theory serves to fill out the deficiencies of knowledge on the part of elected leaders as regards the actual nature and content of societal wants, as well as correcting through political pressures any tendency of those leaders to act capriciously or selfishly or to impose a crude majoritarian view upon minorities. In its extreme form Theory *B* supersedes Theory *A* almost entirely, just as a full version of Theory *A* allows no or little legitimate scope for pressure from organised interests. In this form Theory *B* reduces the role of elected leaders to brokers who mediate between the claims of sectional groups according to certain rules of the game, imposing no policies of their own which cannot be derived from some aggregation of or compromise between the various sectional interests.*

Theory *C*(i) (Classical Political Populism) has impressive intellectual origins in the writings of the Philosophic Radicals during the early nineteenth century. Essentially it seeks to maximise the direct decision-making capacity of the electorate, thereby limiting the discretion of elected representatives and converting them potentially to no more than mandated delegates. The theory utilises such devices as widespread referenda, frequent elections, and powers for recalling elected delegates who depart from their actual or assumed electoral mandates. The rationale of the system is to get as close as is technically possible to direct democracy, linked sometimes (as in James Mill) with the simple assumption that the electorate as a whole will only be interested in the 'public interest' and their power must be invoked to overcome the 'sinister interests' which will otherwise prevail. The theory also is often linked with distrust of politicians and officials who should be closely watched and checked; in this form it has a bias towards negative or limited government which was indeed the bias of the Philosophic Radicals who believed in the beneficence of economic markets if properly policed. As a theory for ascertaining the wants of individual voters with any degree of precision, it suffers from the sort of problems about referenda already discussed.[5]

Theory *C*(ii) (Modern Consumer Populism) attempts, as was earlier suggested, to fill out the deficiencies of *C*(i) as a way of ascertaining individual wants. It concentrates upon the wishes of those individuals actually affected by a decision, and its direct impact upon their welfare. It utilises such devices as exercises in public participation, social surveys, and cost–benefit analysis.

It has already been stressed that no one of these theories is adequate on its own to provide either an operational definition or perhaps an ethical foundation for modern democracies. The problem is to decide how the various elements should be balanced and weighted. It also would seem that

---

* This extreme version of Theory *B* is more often held as a sociological description of how politics works in certain societies, particularly and perhaps exclusively in the United States; it is not necessarily recommended as a desirable democratic system although it may be and the attitude of most American writers to the theory is favourable. There is a long American literature on political pluralism of which the best empirical statement is probably still David Truman's *The Governmental Process* (New York, 1953). In other modern democracies, and of course also in authoritarian systems, concepts of 'the public interest' (as opposed to sectional interests) still figure too strongly for Theory *B* to win ethical endorsement save on a limited and qualified basis. However, versions of the theory have had a great influence upon academic political sociology in all countries under the influence of American writers and exponents, helped by liberal research and travel grants.

ideas about democracy are changing. In some democracies, certainly in Britain, what I have called the M.R.L. theory held a dominant position about thirty years ago. It was accepted that the function of the political system should be to produce reasonably strong governments which, armed with a general mandate from (hopefully) a majority of the electorate, could then lay down authoritative policies until the test of the next election. As purveyed in the political textbooks of the time, the advantage of disciplined political parties (and especially of a basically two-party system) was their contribution to working the system. There was little scope here for Theories $C(i)$ and $C(ii)$, and Theory B was viewed as more dangerous than beneficial. However, increased legitimacy seems now to be accorded to the political role of organised groups in Britain, perhaps because of their greater number and visibility. More recently populist ideas have gained strength, partly because of dissatisfaction and protests over public policies and perhaps also from suspicion of pressure groups. Pluralism and Populism have entered the lists more definitely and are, in some ways, rival beliefs.

In a formal sense democratic rules are concerned with the mechanics of election and representation, and with the methods for controlling leaders, and say little about either Pluralism or Populism (except for the specifications about periodic elections). Some constitutions give an entrenched position to certain organised interests, for example through the design of a second or upper legislative chamber; but the interests there represented are usually either hereditary or geographic and, in principle at least, geographic interests are no more than a recognition of the case for democratic decentralisation. The influence of organised interests (Theory B) works almost wholly through extra-constitutional influence as exerted by these interests upon elected representations, political parties, elected leaders, and public officials (particularly the last two). Theory $C(ii)$ is almost wholly extra-constitutional in a formal sense and depends upon the initiative or discretion of politicians and public officials. Thus the increased importance of Theories B and $C(ii)$ can also be traced to the expansion of government functions and the rise of the 'administrative state' with a much increased role therein for both elected and appointed officials.[6]

Theory $C(ii)$, because of its affinities with the concept of an economic consumer, might be termed 'economic populism'. As applied to cost–benefit analysis, the term is misleading only because of the historical connexion between populism and the claims of weak economic groups. Thus agrarian populism in the United States was motivated by the wish of farmers and other interested groups to curb the powers of big business and economic monopolies. C.B.A. is *not* populist in this sense, because of its linkage with the spending power of individuals and groups. By contrast $C(i)$, political populism, has often been seen as a vehicle for reducing economic inequalities.

Because of its very pragmatic character, C.B.A. can be slotted into any stage of the policy process. It can be related to authoritative goals set by political leaders or to the aims of particular organisations or interests. However, there are good grounds for saying that, because of its grounding in the welfare of individuals, the proper form of C.B.A. is open-ended. Ideally it should not assume that any policy, plan, or aim is intrinsically desirable, because this assertion ought to be tested against evidence about its probable impact upon the welfare of individuals. Of course this is a counsel of perfection. It would be impossible to start each analysis with a clean sheet of no policy assumptions, and often (although not always) politically impracticable for analysts to find clients who would allow them to do so. This is the analyst's problem of 'no suitable client'. The public is not organised to receive the wisdom of welfare economics.

However, the logically correct position for C.B.A. appears to rest with Theory C(ii). On this basis analysts can test out the impact of possible decisions upon individual welfare untrammelled by political preconceptions. The logical and policy problems of structuring such an analysis are further treated in Chapter 7. Here we should note that the problem of the analyst's client is not insoluble. Political leaders and public officials may well want to find out all they can about the costs and benefits that will flow from a decision even if they already have a policy bias or predilection. They may particularly want to do so if they mistrust or want to check the claim of organised interests. This leads us to the subject of the next section.

Before proceeding it will be useful to look briefly at the alternatives to C.B.A. under Theory C(ii) for ascertaining individual wants with some precision. Public participation exercises are an obvious device for eliciting direct reactions from individuals affected by an impending decision. The limitations, first, are the difficulty of reaching many of those affected and, secondly, the resemblance with pressure-group activity in that the participants are usually drawn from the more active and articulate citizens. Attempts are now made by sensitive officials, such as some planning officers in Britain, to seek out the reactions of more apathetic groups but they have formidable obstacles to overcome even if they understand the 'problems of participation', which does not often appear to be the case.[7]

Social and opinion surveys of various kinds use sampling techniques and can be more systematic. They can unearth a great deal of information about the preferences of consumers of public services which can provide a useful, indeed essential corrective to the beliefs of politicians and experts. For example, the design of public housing projects in Britain could hardly have been so heartily disliked by many residents if social surveys had been used to check the personal tastes and monumental ambitions of architects. Social surveys have the advantage over C.B.A. of being more straightforward and intelligible, and of avoiding all the pitfalls involved in converting diverse data into monetary equations. For the same reasons, of course, they cannot purport to offer so comprehensive a formulation of the incidence of costs and benefits.

C. Political and Economic Concepts of Interest

We can distinguish between an economic (cost–benefit) and a political definition of *interest*. In the former sense an interest consists of a bundle of individual wants measured ideally according to the W.T.P. of each individual to obtain or to avoid some possible change in his circumstances; these individual wants are then aggregated possibly according to some rules of distribution (see pp. 139–45) so as to form the total interest of some defined group of individuals who will be affected by the proposed change in a certain way.

A political definition of interest is more difficult and arguable but it can be viewed as political activity taken by or on behalf of a set of individuals in respect of some shared want or wants. The best-known and most obvious examples are the activities of organised interest or pressure groups.* But in addition politicians and officials can also be said to take action on behalf of the shared wants of individuals, indeed almost all political activity can be viewed in this way. This extension of 'political interest' becomes relevant when we consider the self-regulating properties of the political system.

Both these definitions of interest are derived from the wants of individuals,† but neither, save coincidentally, expresses the net wants or preference of any one individual as he might express this himself if called upon to do so. Thus a cost–benefit analysis of the kind we are considering treats individual wants in categories such as those of pedestrians, air travellers, bird-watchers, and so on. Assuming that *all* relevant wants have been listed and accurately measured, the net want of any individual could, in principle, be derived from the whole equation, but individuals as such are not the unit of measurement.

Similarly political pressure groups do not claim as a rule to speak for fully integrated individuals, but factorise the individual into various capacities: the Automobile Association, for example, speaks for individuals only in their capacity as motorists; the Council for the Preservation of Rural England is confined to those wants which arise from liking the appearance of a particular countryside; and so on. Clearly some kinds of want are more limited than others, and one want may seem dominant to some individuals. Thus some individuals may regard their wants as farmers, as expressed by the National Farmers' Union, as being dominant over any other want in case of conflict, but they will certainly recognise that they *have* other wants which must be catered for by other organisations.

Both economic and political articulations of interest are open to the objection that they factorise the wants of individuals into numerous compartments, and do not offer any scope for an integrated individual judgement. By contrast, a system of direct voting on issues does or could satisfy

* These terms can be distinguished on the basis that an interest group often provides services to its members in addition to (or instead of) putting pressure on government and other organisations to achieve desired results. Pressure group is thus unduly restrictive. However, pressure group is appropriate here because we are concerned with activities directed at public decisions or policy changes.

† This is not in fact true of those pressure groups which are concerned not with the wants of individuals but with their goodness or duties, for example the Lord's Day Observance Society. Since here we are confining ourselves to the calculus of individual wants, we must exclude pressure groups of this type.

this criterion in principle despite its gross limitations in practice. For example a proposed motorway may affect some individual in a variety of roles such as traveller, home-owner, countryside-lover, and so on. A C.B.A. might attempt to put a cash value upon each of these interests, and pressure groups may assert each interest separately; but the individual's own judgement of the issue – whether or not this would accord with the outcome of either the economic or the political test – could bring to bear the considered opinion of a 'whole man' judging for himself the relative importance of each consideration. Moreover, this opinion might also express (at least ideally) an ethical judgement about social welfare which is normally excluded from C.B.A. and is not conspicuously apparent in pressure-group activity (but see below). The rational–liberal tradition of democracy has understandably laid stress upon the value (both for the individual and for society) of such integrated individual judgements. It may be only because this ideal is so greatly vitiated in practice, because of information costs and public apathy, that solutions based upon the factorisation of individual wants have won acceptance as the indispensable alternative. But even so voting remains a part of the political process, and retains importance as a somewhat vague and ultimate check upon the conclusions reached through more specialised procedures.

This is the point at which to introduce the arguments which welfare economists *could* make (although they rarely advance them consistently) in favour of basing policy decisions upon 'economic' rather than 'political' definitions of interest.* Essentially the argument will be that the economic analysis is a much more objective and precise way of discovering how individual wants will be affected by some decision than reliance upon the arguments and interaction of politically defined interests. The analyst can offer in principle a schedule of which interests will gain and which will lose from the decision, and by how much; and he has or should have no motive for political bias. By contrast, pressure groups are biased and partisan almost by definition, and any argument that their biases may cancel each other out so that a general interest will somehow prevail is subject to the objections (*a*) that this must be a matter of luck or chance since the incidence of costs and benefits cannot by this method be properly known and (*b*) that in any case the aggregate political process is intrinsically biased for various reasons in favour of some interests and against others.

To consider these arguments we must first consider more carefully the concept of interest in politics. The partisan conflict of interests is endemic throughout politics and is certainly not in itself condemned, but its exercise is governed by the 'rules of the game' – the laws, conventions, and norms of the society in question. Some political scientists regard proper rules of the game (whereby the exercise of partisanship is governed) as the only

* To avoid possible confusion it should be made clear that what are often called economic groups, such as National Farmers' Union, Confederation of British Industry, etc. rank in this analysis as *political* articulations of interests. The economic definition of interest is here confined to the results that can be produced by C.B.A. and similar economic techniques.

proper meaning to be ascribed to 'public interest', which then becomes procedural and not substantive. However this be there is no doubt about the importance of these conventions for the way that the political process functions.

In political debate individuals and groups do not simply articulate their self-regarding wants, but formulate and refine these wants in accordance with social norms of justice and reasonableness. This consideration leads Plamenatz to conclude that the concept of 'interest' cannot be derived from any utilitarian calculus of personal or private desires but posits a moral view of society which is prior to interest formulations.[8] There is some force in this argument, but it should not be allowed to prove too much. One must at least try to distinguish between the rhetoric and the substance of political arguments, and between the respective contributions of want conflicts and ideas of justice to political debate.

In Britain pressure-group leaders do habitually recognise in debate the importance or even paramountcy of some idea of national or general interest, as well as accepting in principle the need for reasonableness and moderation in relation to competing claims. For example the National Farmers' Union has always tried on paper and in argument to reconcile its view of the agricultural interest with governments' views of the national interest; and has (so it claims) often accepted sacrifices and hardships, which must be sold to its members, in order, for example, to help fight inflation. We must discount a lot for rhetoric here especially by a group which is heavily dependent upon public subsidies and therefore needs to project a favourable image upon politicians and public – although the very importance of projecting this image does at least support part of Plamenatz's case unless we assume that social norms are wholly hypocritical. But we should also beware of supposing that this example disproves the relevance of a utilitarian calculus. After all farmers do have wants which can only be satisfied by government action (such as the control of inflation) and this category of wants is inevitably in conflict to some limited extent with their wants, say, for higher farm prices. Of course it would suit their private schedule of wants better if other groups would take on the whole burden of fighting inflation so that they could press without inhibition for higher prices. Undoubtedly some farmers see the issue wholly in this light, and the main weight of the Union's pressure is probably thrown in this direction. Any moderation which the Union shows over pressing its claims becomes a function of three factors: (a) recognition of some conflict of wants among its members, (b) acceptance of social norms, and (c) strategic or tactical considerations relating to its claims and its 'image'. The three factors interact and seem impossible to weigh separately. Hence the difficulty of saying how much of the Union's rhetoric is *complete* hypocrisy (conscious or unconscious), although undoubtedly much of it is, and hence too the naturalness of the conflict within the Union's leadership and that of other interest groups over the wisdom of relatively moderate versus more extreme strategies. As one would expect this conflict again reflects a mixture of normative and strategic considerations – those farmers who think it is right for the Union to display some degree of moderation also try to argue that it will pay it to do so, and vice versa. Of course moderation can be and often is argued for exclusively on strategic grounds, although even here the speaker may himself choose these grounds strategically – it helps him to avoid the usual reproach against moderates of being soft-headed. These arguments lead into an endless maze, but at least suggest that a completely 'realpolitic' view of political interest groups is unlikely to be true.[9]

These ethical and psychological considerations also suggest the possible desirability of reformulating our concept of interest as a simple aggregation of individual wants. Barry suggest that interest refers to the *opportunity* to satisfy wants, so that a lawyer restraining my angry outburst in court is blocking my immediate want but is doing his best to help me win my case which will be more helpful to my want-satisfaction in the long run; and, as Barry points out, an expert can often look after my interests (in the sense of protecting my income or my health or my legal status) without knowing much about the content of my wants.[10] In politics this trustee notion of interest would not apply to delegates but it does fit the classic theory of representation, since representatives are supposed to take a balanced, prudent, and far-sighted view of the wants of their constituents; and the same idea would apply to pressure groups to the extent that they were constituted and behaved in this kind of way.

The fact that participants in the political process are at least *expected* to relate their claims to the interests of others and to ideas of justice, etc. gives to political debate its peculiar character – a mixture of selfish assertions and moral arguments, of large claims and substantial concessions, of fluid and variable positions. Political statements of this kind may seem foolish or infuriating to a cost–benefit analyst because they completely lack the precision which he seeks. Of course an economist can accept the proposition that the correct value of something (say the 'interest' of the Farmers' Union) lies between x and y depending on certain variables; it is the plotting of the variables that appears to be so hopelessly elusive.

The question here is: which concept of interest (the economic or the political) forms the most suitable basis for the aggregation of individual wants or welfare? How are they to be compared in this respect? If it can be said that some redefinition of individual wants in the light of social norms is essential to social co-operation and all its attendant advantages (see Chapter 6) then political forms of analysis might be judged superior upon utilitarian as well as ideal grounds. But this normative character of political debate is a two-edged sword; it can be used and manipulated in many ways for self-regarding ends and to impose burdens upon individuals inconsistent with *any* detached view of their welfare. This two-headed character of politics and of the state suggests once again the possible *corrective* view of introducing the more cold-blooded and specific measurements of C.B.A. as a test of how individuals *will* actually fare under some decision.

D. Politics as a Self-regulating Market

Our earlier discussion suggested the superiority of economic over political modes of choice for registering the wants of individuals. But it has emerged that voting is only one element in a complex political process, and it may be that the whole process is or could be more rational (in terms of responding to the wishes of individuals) than an analysis of its parts suggests. This is indeed the view of certain economists who have applied the logical–deductive methods of their discipline to the functioning of politics. On this basis a certain analogy can be drawn between the functioning of economic and political markets under conditions of perfect competition.

There is now a large literature by the 'Public Choice' school of political economists[11] and others which utilises economic and logical modes of analysis (such as games theory) to elucidate political behaviour. Almost all these theories tend to start from egoist postulates, which assume that the individual is motivated by self-regarding wants and not by ideal considerations about the social good. The problem of social and political norms about justice, etc. is dealt with in two different ways. One way is to assume that certain basic rules of the game exist in the form of a constitution, which then operates rather like the rules of economic competition; within this framework all participants act in terms of self-interest and ideal motivations are ignored on the grounds that an adequate theory can be constructed without them (presumably therefore these ideals are of small importance or are hypocritical). The alternative approach is to deduce the rules of an ideal or satisfactory constitution (the decision-making rules) from the individual interests of all participants. This second approach introduces problems of justice and distribution which in some ways parallel those of welfare economics, and is best deferred to the next chapter.

The first approach gives us our analogy between economic and political markets. Thus Anthony Downs assumes that politicians will be concerned exclusively with maximising electoral support, irrespective of the contents of their policies, in the same way as a businessman is supposed to seek to maximise his profits irrespective of what he is selling. If we assume now that the constitution favours a two-party system (an exogenous factor) and that the preferences of voters can be ranged along a single continuum, the behaviour of political parties can to some extent be predicted. Both parties will take up their position side by side in the centre of this spectrum of voters' preferences, and if one party moves to left or right the other must move after it to maximise its coverage of the electorate, the assumption being that its flank is secure from the intrusion of a third party (if, however, a third party does appear and the two-party constitutional assumption holds, then the party in the middle must logically be gobbled up).[12]

Downs's aim is predictive and his model can help to explain some features of political behaviour in certain situations. For example when the electorate moved to the left in the 1945 British general election and Labour won a large majority, the Conservative Party (after much internal debate) followed in the same direction, which helped it to regain power in 1952 and initiated the era of 'Butskellism' – competing parties with similar policies. But the theory's assumptions seem usually to be very imperfectly realised; voters' preferences often do not lie along a single axis and some politicians at least care about the content of policies. Even in the above example, what caused Labour to move to the left in its 1945 programme? If it knew or calculated that the electorate was moving leftwards the party (on Downs's hypothesis) had much better have stayed in the centre; but if it thought the electoral continuum was unchanged (or only slightly changed) it had much better have tried to move right in order to eat into the existing Conservative majority. It is much more plausible to posit that party programmes represent a mixture of internally desired policy goals and electoral considerations.

A comparison between political and economic markets might posit that public agencies play the part of business firms in providing desired policy outputs (i.e. economic goods). These operations are 'financed' by politicians (i.e. merchant bankers) who mobilise enough votes (i.e. money) to provide desired outputs and take their pay-offs in the form of electoral success. In a general way the same sort of distorting influences upon competition arise in both systems; excessive concentrations of money power (banking and business monopoly) are matched by excessive concentrations of political influence (dominant parties or powerful pressure groups) and the propaganda of advertisers is matched by that of the mass media. Of course it is obviously difficult to provide for anything like perfect competition in either market; and presumably much harder in the political than the economic context since economic competition can be policed by the state, whereas for political competition one must ask: *quis custodes custodet*?

Closer examination suggests that a theory of economic competition can be internally consistent in a way that does not apply to politics. In the first case the ground-rules and the exclusion of distorting influences can be specified much more clearly than in the second. In the first case the price system provides (at least in principle) a yardstick of values which has no adequate equivalent either in voting or in the broader, vaguer concept of political influence. Additionally the comparison overlooks normative and ethical elements. While a postulate of egoism may not be altogether realistic or logically necessary in economics, at least the postulate makes more sense (and receives more social endorsement) in that context. Politics may also be largely egoistic, but if so it is egoism of a more complicated kind difficult to express in basic axioms. In fact one would surmise that political behaviour is in various ways both *less* and *more* egoistic than is economic behaviour, the variations depending upon the actors, the situations, and the social or cultural norms.

Even if we do accept the existence of some analogy between the functioning of economic markets and of democratic politics, and ascribe in each case a beneficial role to free competition (for markets or for votes) under appropriate rules, it is still far from clear what values would thereby be maximised. Thus it might be claimed that a fully competitive and pluralist system is preferable to other types of political system, although we have given reasons for doubting this conclusion. Alternatively the point might be that a properly competitive political system will maximise the sum of individual welfare in a spontaneous manner without any need for economic analysis. To make this proposition plausible we would have to posit dual markets (economic and political) in which welfare functions are established by separate and parallel processes, each of which is equally rational in its own way; and we would have to describe the permitted boundaries of and interactions between the two systems.

Without entering upon such formidable speculations, it has been established that a major barrier to the rationality of a competitive political system is the lack of information available to participants. If techniques such as C.B.A. can improve the flow of relevant information about policy outcomes, then it can assist the ability of the system to satisfy individual wants. Even if C.B.A. cannot cope adequately with 'political factors', these factors could be introduced (as in fact they are) as corrections to the analyst's conclusions. Thus we return to the question of the suitability of the information provided by C.B.A. for policy decisions, noting here the value of any tolerably relevant data in a low-information situation.

It may be more useful to wrestle with empirical problems about political interests. One would expect that in any society the structure of political influence will be biased towards the politically active and articulate, and that rich and educated individuals will have advantages in these respects. Thus privileged groups will be more likely to form organised pressure groups, and these organised interests will be at an advantage over interests which are only weakly articulated. In the latter category one would expect to find: (*a*) the special wants of poor or underprivileged groups, (*b*) widely shared but weakly felt interests (for example those of consumers generally as opposed to groups of producers), (*c*) potential or diffused interests that cannot be attributed to a specific group of individuals (for example those who will benefit from a public project such as a new town not as yet constructed). There are other ways of organising this list.

Empirical evidence supports this analysis. For example, in Britain environmental pressure groups flourish in middle-class areas but are rarely found in working-class areas where the environment is actually worse. (It can of course be said that the poorer groups care less for their environment in their order of priorities and have less to care about; even so they cannot be supposed to want the *deterioration* of conditions which often takes place, for example through traffic schemes; yet they rarely organise to protest.)

The bias of the system towards the more organised, visible, and privileged groups will be corrected to some extent by other elements in the political process. Political decision-making brings in successively broader constituencies, so that the narrow base of a pressure group is corrected by the broader one of a political party and by the still wider one of an elected government. Through this process the influence of latent or weakly organised interests can be introduced into the final outputs of government via the intervention of political entrepreneurs. David Truman gives the example of the 'charismatic' leadership of President F. D. Roosevelt who won the support of a concurrent majority of poor and underprivileged Americans through his New Deal programme which catered for the unorganised interests of poor farmers, unemployed workers, and new immigrants.[13] However, Roosevelt did not abolish the existing agencies which were already helping more privileged groups such as the wealthier farmers, he merely gave their weaker brethren some share of the cake. Moreover, the possibility of organising such a coalition of the underprivileged depends upon circumstances – it does not seem to apply to the United States in the 1970s.

Political ideals or norms of justice also figure in this process. Promotional pressure groups may give unsolicited support to the needs of the underdog, as with the fairly influential activities of the Poverty Action Group in Britain; but of course many such groups are concerned primarily with middle-class aims or ideals. Again impartial officials may try to introduce group needs which have low visibility into a policy equation and be backed up by open-minded or conscientious politicians, although the politicians' conscience will often be somewhat mixed – after all there may be latent votes in considering such interests, if not among the affected group then among other citizens with consciences. We cannot say what such structures of altruistic influence are worth in hard decisions, although cynics will say not very much. At any rate the weight of such influences will turn upon political traditions and culture, although nowhere are these factors very strong.

It should also be stressed that latent interests are not equivalent with those of poor or underprivileged people. The phenomenon will arise in all circumstances where one interest is politically visible and the other less so. For example, when a new town is proposed on some site in Britain, the only pressure groups on the scene are likely to consist of local residents or farmers who do not want the new town. The beneficiaries of the new town consist of an unknown list of individuals who have not at this stage decided to move there. This latent group is not necessarily underprivileged – the median income of New Town residents is actually around the national median while some local protestors will be poor people. Once again an entrepreneur exists to represent this latent interest in the form of the government department or local authority which is promoting the town (in a free market the same function will be performed by private developers). How effectively the visible and latent interests are balanced in this *political* confrontation cannot easily be stated;* this is just the sort of issue that

---

* The fact that hardly any New Town proposal has been dropped because of local objections is not conclusive here, inasmuch as some proposals have not been carried to formal designation and enquiry because of known objections (e.g. Mobberley and Lymn in Cheshire). However, it should be added that after an initial period of uncertainty in which local objections nearly scuppered the first New Town (Stevenage), the New Town programme acquired considerable political weight and respectability on a generally bipartisan basis, not least through the campaigning of a cause group (the Town and Country Planning Association) which advanced the latent interests of New Town residents. Thus the example does mainly seem to show the capacity of some latent interests to succeed against more visible interests in Britain.

C.B.A. attempts to illuminate. This frequently occurring type of situation also confirms the difficulties of public participation as a means of ascertaining individual wants since the future New Town residents are not at the public enquiry.

These questions about the balance of political interests can only be answered in political terms through some mix of the elements of democratic theory already discussed. Theories *A* and *B* can also be called theories of power concentration and of power diffusion between which some balance is needed. One's preference will probably depend upon whether one is more concerned about the biased character of interest-group activity, or about the dangers of discretionary rule by leaders (and officials under their supervision) who claim to represent a democratic majority. Either way there can be no ideal solution.

But this problem offers, as was suggested earlier, considerable leverage for cost–benefit analysis. If it be true that some interests in the form of shared wants are discounted politically at the expense of other interests, for no reasons other than the structure of political influence (that is to say the difference is not attributable to any divergence between political and economic evaluations of the *content* of wants, but solely to power factors that apply irrespective of this content) the analyst has indeed the opportunity to offer a truer accounting. The more diffused, latent, and under-privileged types of interest will then show up more fairly upon the analyst's balance-sheet – in terms that is of the extent to which they actually do represent wants of the individuals concerned and for which in principle they would be willing to pay.

But the discussion has also revealed two problems for consideration. First, the structure of interests in a C.B.A. is artificially designed whereas political activity is spontaneous. The advantages of giving full rein to spontaneity are stressed by Lindblom and Braybrooke in another version on the theme of a self-regulating political system. On this view partisanship in decision-making far from distorting results is essential to ensure that relevant factors and viewpoints receive attention. 'Partisan mutual adjustment' is a process whereby affected individuals or organisations react to each other's viewpoints or decisions; coupled with a sufficient diffusion of influence and dispersal of decision-points, the result will be a series of sequential and limited policy changes – 'marginal incrementalism' – which represents both the actual and the desirable tendencies of democratic systems.[14]

Part of Lindblom's argument here and elsewhere[15] concerns the *intellectual* difficulties of taking a comprehensive view of any policy issue – so that partisan mutual adjustment, though theoretically second-best, is practically superior to any attempt to set up an objective synoptic view. This intellectual problem of decision models belongs primarily to Chapter 7. Relevant here is the political argument, which turns out again to be a generalised argument for some kind of pluralism. Lindblom and his colleagues do not say *how* diffused or dispersed the decision structure should be (there must be limits to the process somewhere) but their general intention is clear. The objections to this argument are again familiar; it would be the better organised interests that would gain most from this process and even if the totality of political participation was widened *other* interests would suffer.

It remains true that the spontaneous generation of interests which occurs in modern democracies is a vital factor in policy-making, simply because the number of *possible* interests is enormously large (compare the discussion of externalities) and the most intelligent analyst or planner will not spot all those groups that consider themselves to be affected by a decision. He may also come unstuck on the *direction* of an interest through mistaken assumptions. Thus the Roskill Commission, assuming that a monster airport in a rural area would be an unmitigated disaster (a somewhat middle-class assumption) seemed surprised to discover that an active group in one such area were claiming that the airport would be a net benefit to local inhabitants.

The second problem is whether it is in fact realistic or right to isolate C.B.A. from the political influences which will surround its employment. In other words, should the analyst concentrate upon measuring those interests which are evoked by the political process? Such a position would clearly be self-defeating, because the whole rationale of C.B.A. as a counterweight to a check upon politically expressed interests would be lost. Still it should be allowed that, because of the intrinsic difficulties of structuring interests artificially, economic analysis should be prepared to investigate all politically transmitted claims.

It will be helpful at this point to consider more closely the relationship between *economic* and *political* opportunity costs (and benefits). The theoretical analogy between these two concepts is, as already noted, a persuasive one. A politician has to 'buy' support for *his* goals by supporting, or not opposing, the goals of other politicians. Doubtless the most fruitful bargains of this kind occur when politicians at least share the same set of goals although wanting them in varying degrees, and this is the situation which party conferences and programmes attempt to establish; but in practice goals diverge for institutional, ideological, and personal reasons so that (to achieve *his* ends) a politician must sometimes at least support goals to which he is indifferent or acquiesce in ones to which he is opposed. Moreover, the politician's goals are diverse and usually include some mixture of the *procedural* goal of maintaining or increasing power (of the politician or of his party) and the *substantive* goal of achieving certain policies favoured by the politician or his party. Thus there will be trade-offs between procedural goals (for example appointments) and substantive ones (for example policies) as well as within each category. Political systems vary considerably in respect of the structuring of these transactions and of their normative constraints – for example in some societies politicians' goals normally include the acquisition of personal wealth, while in others such behaviour is morally taboo and may be rare.

Now the diverse nature of these political 'costs' and 'benefits' is in principle no different from the diversity of factors which the welfare economist wants to include in *his* analysis. The significant difference seems to lie in the possibility of measurement, since it is difficult (although attempts are being made) to measure inputs and outputs of political influence in the same way as resource flows. If measurement *were* possible, then political values could be given the same schematic representation as those of economic welfare.

It seems inevitable that political and economic opportunity costs will diverge and conflict, often sharply. Thus politicians personally experience only a tiny part (or none) of the economic-welfare effects of their decisions, whereas they suffer directly the political consequences. Of course an increase in economic welfare is also as a rule desired by politicians, sometimes passionately so, and the economist's advice is therefore quite likely to be taken *if* it is believed and does not conflict with political demands and pressures; but very often it does. Again, even if many politicians are public-spirited seekers after a S.W.F., they must still reckon with the need to maintain political structures of support, a requirement that must sometimes at least conflict with the economist's definition of welfare goals.

How are such conflicts to be viewed and if possible resolved? Aaron Wildavsky is emphatic that

> the political problem is always basic and prior to the others. . . . This means that any suggested course of action must be evaluated first by its effects on the political structure. A course of action which corrects economic or social deficiencies but increases political difficulties must be rejected, while an action which contributes to political improvement is desirable even if it is not entirely sound from an economic or social standpoint.[16]

Wildavsky seems here to incorporate two different notions. One is the idea that political considerations always *will* triumph over economic-welfare factors in the event of conflict. This is merely a tautology if 'political' refers to the ultimate and effective power to make decisions. (Thus the point will still apply even if politicians are no more than the mouthpiece of a dominant class.) The interesting positive question to ask is how much influence cost–benefit analysis has or might have upon the ultimate decisions. The answer may be 'quite a lot', at any rate in some political systems and under some circumstances.

The second and (I judge) dominant idea in Wildavsky's argument is that the support of a political structure is *normatively* more important than welfare goals, because the maintenance of a satisfactory political system is basic to the pursuit of all other goals. Hence the need to reject 'political difficulties' and choose actions which contribute to 'political improvement'. But how to define political difficulties and improvement? These cannot be equated with the net product of the political costs and benefits as identified by politicians *unless* one assumes that the political system is already automatically functioning as well as is possible. Once this improbable hypothesis is dropped, it would seem that Wildavsky is calling for a political analyst who can maximise political values in the same way as the economic analyst seeks to maximise welfare values. The actual calculations of politicians will then bear much the same relationship to this ideal, as do the calculations of businessmen to the ideal of a S.W.F.

This viewpoint of Wildavsky's suggests some kind of tug-of-war between the requirements of an ideal political system (presumably some kind of democracy) and those of welfare maximisation. But does so olympian a conflict make sense? After all, in principle the two goals appeal to the same basic authority – the wants or needs of individuals – and it is their interpretative routes which differ. In terms of methodology also it is difficult to see the priests of political rationality and of economic efficiency sticking to separate compartments; rather such theories are intrinsically expansionist and incapable of formal limitations. One cannot easily understand the basis on which conflicts between the political and economic analysts could be settled. It may be because 'political rationality' seems the vaguer of these two criteria that Wildavsky is keen to assert its claims against those of the cost–benefit analyst. But his logical position ought not to be in the stressing of the importance of political opportunity costs, which are apparent enough in practical terms to the participants and no answer at all at the theoretical level to welfare economics, but to *explain* the relationship of a satisfactory political system to the goal of economic welfare.

E. Conclusion

At this point we should ask, and certainly the economist will want to ask: what values precisely are being maximised by these or any theories of political democracy? The question is a difficult one. The values of democracy are procedural ones, and we cannot logically deduce from them any consequences about the content of public policies. There may be an empirical connexion between more democracy and more public welfare schemes but there is no necessary one. Still more obviously, as much recent history testifies, the goal of economic growth may be pursued much more effectively by a dictatorship than by a democracy.

The only ultimate rationale of a democracy lies in the equity of its rules and norms for reaching public decisions, not in the content of those decisions. But, in practice, the acceptability of rules and norms depends also upon their results, and the individual often finds it difficult (although it is certainly possible) to distinguish between the justice with which his claim has been treated and the satisfaction that he has received. Democracy is often judged by the degree of social harmony which it produces; but the harmony produced by any system is related empirically to expectations about its performance. Thus when most people had relatively low political-economic expectations, and accepted a considerable degree of hierarchy and inequality to be inevitable, political institutions attracted less criticism. With rising individual expectations, claims, and assertions, the same institutions have come under increasing attack – even if, as is possibly the case, the system has become *more* democratic in a procedural sense.

The zeal of democratic politicians over recent decades in pressing for (and claiming to achieve) faster economic growth can be seen as their response to widespread individual wants or demands. But economic growth is also needed to meet the ideas of justice which individuals hold (possibly quite illogically) about the proper functioning of the democratic system. This entanglement of performance with procedures might be avoided to some extent if politicians would refrain from excessive promises and criticisms, and remind citizens that duties are the correlatives of rights – but that is another story.

In another sense though, performance *is* relevant to the procedural values of democracy, because the system can be claimed to work well when it conveys individual wants as precisely and as accurately as possible to the providers of public services. This is where economic ideas and theories offer a choice of routes. Cost–benefit analysis would look to the disinterested assessment of these wants as measured in monetary terms as a means of at least supplementing and/or correcting the information provided by the political process. By contrast, the economic theories of politics touched on in the last section would look to the improvement of the democratic process itself as a transmission belt for the conveyance of these individual wants. This aim could take the form either of recommending or of endorsing (if the system is already adequate) the sort of diffused decision-making procedures suggested by marginal incrementalism; or it could take the much more radical form of proposing sets of decision-making rules which are as consistent as is possible with the egoistic interests of every citizen – which is basically the approach of the U.S. 'Public Choice' economists.

These economic-type theories can be linked with the classic political debate over the meaning of the 'public interest'. It is not clear that an increase of political pluralism, for example of the number of organised groups or agencies that can influence decisions, will of itself improve the 'transmission belt' function of democracy. This is not only because the groups in question may be relatively wealthy or privileged (which would add to the inequalities of political influence) but also because more specialised 'wants' may be achieved in this way at the expense of more generalised wants. There are reasons for supposing that this will be so in modern pluralist democracies, so that while the whole system may be gaining in terms of the number and variety of shared wants that are effectively articulated, and also in terms of the total quantum of political participation, the net effect could still be adverse upon the total sum of want-satisfactions assuming we find this concept meaningful. In theory majoritarian representative leadership provides more leverage for the recognition of generalised wants through the necessarily broad basis of its electoral appeal and through the implied mandate for leaders to override special interests, although spontaneous political activity is lower and the elected leaders have more power to ignore wants. Thus we are left with the earlier formula of preferring some mixture of democratic theories. The complexity of institutions precludes any clear or neat solution.

Some of the 'Public Choice' economists, on the other hand, would wish each public agency to be directly responsible and responsive to that particular section of the public supposed to be served or benefited.[17] The 'Public' would then be dissolved, formally and not just indirectly, into a series of specialised publics. This would have the apparent advantage of organising the demands for public services more efficiently, in terms of relating them to the specific wants of determinate groups. One difficulty about the proposal is the large volume of political participation required which would be a particular burden upon the egoists that these writers suppose citizens to be. The burden would be still greater if one brings in the need for extensive bargaining between the public agencies involved if services are to be adequately co-ordinated – otherwise there would again be a loss of efficiency on the supply side.

Once again one has to ask how diffused or potential interests would be covered. Especially high bargaining costs would be involved in their organisation, if indeed that were possible at all. The relevance of this problem becomes plain when one recalls that many public agencies *control* specialised interests on behalf of the diffused interests of a general public. Who, for this purpose, is to be the controlling political clientele – those who benefit ultimately from the regulations or those directly affected by them? One doubts that such action would be organised at all in the absence of a dominant political structure that could channel, however imperfectly, the interests of weak or latent majorities.

The economists who see an actual or potential rationality in the political system regarded as a whole seem either to make too much out of some generalised tendencies (such as incrementalism) or else to rear their constructions upon narrow assumptions or beliefs of an egoistic kind. Some of the 'Public Choice' economists might be said unkindly to be applying discredited forms of economic reasoning to the less-tractable and suitable arena of politics. Theorists of democracy are left, as has been said, with no more than a set of basic elements which can be mixed and argued about pragmatically. If these theories satisfy any rationale, this can only be grounded in certain minimal notions of justice; although it does not follow of course that democratically made decisions cannot be unjust, nor that they should not themselves be resisted on occasion in the name of some higher principle of justice.

Any idea that democracies should be judged by their capacity to equalise the distribution of political *influence* (as opposed to equalising formal *rights* such as voting at a general election) would seem to be even more utopian than judging economic systems by their capacity to equalise wealth. The most that the theorist might suggest is that certain tendencies towards concentration of political influence should be corrected. Moreover, the political process appears to be less open to basic change than the economic process save perhaps by revolution. Political authority can be and has been brought in to reduce inequalities of economic wealth; but could economic authority truly be invoked to assist the converse effect?

What is the relevance of these issues to cost–benefit analysis specifically? Of course if it be accepted that the political system is or could be fully satisfactory, or that the system as a whole reveals a 'higher rationality' than is apparent from the functioning of its parts, there would seem to be little need for C.B.A. Some economists, bemused by the analogy with perfectly functioning markets, view this as a tenable position.* This seems merely mystical however. Democratic theories themselves offer no tests about the desirability of public decisions beyond the procedural norms which they invoke.

The analyst may take up one of three positions. He may reject democracy as offering *any* justification for decisions which conflict with his own interpretation of welfare economics. Thus Mishan states that majority decisions in politics are often wrong and should be repudiated by economists on the basis of their own more enlightened standards – although he seems to forget that welfare economists are anything but agreed about these standards. Mishan's own position rests upon a few ethical principles of distribution, discussed in the next chapter, with which few of his colleagues would agree. Layard stresses that C.B.A. is rooted in morality not democracy and that it should confront democratic decisions where necessary on this basis, although the source for his *ad hoc* ethical interpretations of C.B.A. seems to be only himself.[18]

Secondly, analysts may rest upon the 'efficiency' principle for maximising wealth or the sum of individual satisfactions, and accept that their advice is relevant only to the extent that this test is politically acceptable. This has the advantage of appealing to a principle which to many people will seem satisfactory and even self-evident, while allowing politicians to bring in other factors as they wish. The adequacy of the efficiency principle as a basis for public policy decisions is discussed later (pp. 139–42).

Finally, C.B.A. might be assigned a specific role within the policy process where it can be viewed as a *corrective* element within the framework of general democratic theory. This position, although not usually explicitly adopted by economists, is fully congruent with the view that their techniques should and can serve democratic purposes because of their basis in individual wants. This position implies a willingness to use economic techniques in order to amend the interpretations of individual wants provided by any participants in the political process; but the techniques can most realistically be used as an aid to political leaders and impartial officials for

---

* Margolis suggests that if the budget has been optimally allocated by government, then 'the ratio of marginal cost of two public outputs will be the same as the ratio of their social values, and therefore the marginal costs figures will have the *same interpretation as we give to competitive market prices*' (my italics). Margolis does not necessarily subscribe to this interpretation, but it is a curious example of the attempt to translate a perfect political ordering of social values into economic language. If the proposition were true, then the problems of 'implicit prices' discussed in Chapter 4 would also be solved; governments, however inconsistent they might seem, would always be achieving somehow the right cost–benefit ratios. In fact few political theorists would believe in the possibility of such a theorem. See Julius Margolis on Shadow Prices in R. H. Haveman and J. Margolis (eds), *Public Expenditure and Policy Analysis* (New York, 1970) pp. 327–8.

ascertaining and evaluating shared groups of wants (interests). As such this economic approach is in conflict with all those (including other economists) who posit that a sufficiently pluralistic political system will be adequately self-regulating, and that spontaneous political adjustment is always to be preferred to *ad hoc* interventions by experts such as cost–benefit analysts.

Of course this is only a *possible* view about the uses of C.B.A.; it does not correspond closely to how the technique is *actually* used. None the less, this viewpoint has received some degree of respect and support in this chapter because it gropes towards a conception of public interest that is not dependent upon the assumed beneficence of political pluralism, and which does not assume either that elected leaders or officials have adequate political sources of information about the structure of individual wants. But this tentative theory will only make sense if in fact the leaders and officials are sufficiently open-minded and public-spirited to want more information of this type and *if* the techniques of C.B.A. can in fact provide it.

6

Techniques and Values

A. The Problem of Egoism

Economists normally hold that the only relevant costs and benefits are those that accrue to individuals, and which are a function of the preferences of individuals, which leads to the problem of reckoning these preferences. Preferences are logical constructs and must conform with certain logical rules (including transitivity and a number of others) if they are to be consistently stated.[1] They imply a reasoning mind, but what if an individual is capricious or unreasoning and lacks consistent preferences? The short answer of course is that one can only give a man his preferences to the extent that he has any, and the analyst must do his best with the data available.

There is another problem. Suppose that individual preferences vary fairly consistently in different situations? Suppose for example that A's preference ordering of a set of possible results will differ significantly in a political context and in a market context. Which reading is the analyst to adopt? If public policy is the subject the political ordering might be supposed the appropriate one; but the difficulty may be that the individual himself may view the issue differently depending upon how it is presented to him. In any event if the economist simply accepts the preference orderings implicit in political decision-making, he has abandoned his claim to possessing an independent standard of welfare. To sustain this position he must look behind a purely logical construction of individual preferences at the wants and motivations which underlie them. He must dig up a philosophy.

For various reasons this is an embarrassing problem for cost–benefit analysts, as the fudgy treatment in their textbooks testifies. Classical economics (like much of the utilitarian treatment of politics) was built upon a foundation of egoism. The individual was presumed in his economic transactions to be maximising his own satisfactions, and the egoism of each was then supposed to produce the maximum possible total satisfaction. This particular approach is now quite unacceptable to the school of purely logical economics, but the limitations of a theory of 'revealed preference' still cause economists, a bit uneasily and equivocally, to peep into people's heads and distinguish between those sorts of wants which are or are not to count for the purpose of their analysis. The Theory of Egoism is not yet dead.

Here is a typical textbook view. Remarking that 'philosophers might be slightly surprised to find the economist treating all wants as selfish', the authors explain that 'some actions are executed out of a sense of duty or altruism which does not fit easily into the economist's use of the term "preference"' (but they do not say why not). They continue later:

> Of course an individual may reveal different preferences when acting in his self-interest compared to his preferences when acting 'in the community's interest': i.e. the individual adopts different roles in different contexts. The question is: which preference is the relevant one for C.B.A.? Since C.B.A. purports to act 'in the public interest' it should perhaps record the preferences of persons thinking of the community's best interest. In practice it does not do this; it records preferences in the selfish category.[2]

The riddle is not explained here and 'selfishness' is not defined. A few analysts revolt against this self-regarding approach. Layard continually brings in *ad hoc* moral judgements in his account of C.B.A., observing that 'it seems absurd to argue that one should always regard people's present preferences as decisive' (a strange statement because decisive is not a moral category), and that C.B.A. 'is not in itself a "democratic" process. It is a thought process which attempts to throw light on what is right given our knowledge of the consequences of certain actions.'[3] But who is to say 'what is right' other than Layard himself? On this point Mishan is at least more logical in his appeal to basic ethical rules (pp. 142–4).

If we seek a more coherent view of egoism, we must turn to the American political economists of the 'Public Choice' school. Here we find a most surprising paradox. Egoism having been largely expelled from modern theoretical economics has been reintroduced by some economists themselves into the study of politics which has long been a much less hospitable field (and most ordinary people would think a less suitable one) for the espousal of this doctrine. Still the resulting theories are interesting and may be fruitful in some ways, and they offer a refreshing contrast also to the obsession with pure logic in economics itself. Some of these new political economists simply start from crude egoistic axioms or postulates, like Anthony Downs in his theories of bureaucracy, who starts with the proposition that every official will act for his own advantage,[4] but James Buchanan and Gordon Tullock in *The Calculus of Consent* (though not Tullock in his other writings) are more cautious and reflective. They therefore qualify 'egoism' in various ways.

Indeed initially they deny it. 'The representative individual in our models may be egoist or altruist or any combination thereof.' But the explanation is introduced that in exchanges of an economic type the vital assumption for theory – which is not as they admit always realised in practice – is that the interests of other parties to the exchange can be neglected. In other words, an actor may be personally altruistic or idealistic, but such motives are 'assumed away' in exchange relationships. Then the 'behavioural assumption' is introduced that in political exchanges like economic ones men seek to maximise individual utilities which vary. We are urged to set aside possible moral censure of 'such individual self-seeking action', not on the grounds that morality is irrelevant but that the chosen assumptions are reasonably realistic to work with; and that we should reserve our limited store of morality for those cases where egoistic behaviour by individuals cannot be reasonably reconciled through agreed decision-making rules.[5]

Why does egoism crop up so frequently in economics? Is it true that economics (including welfare economics) is in some sense 'selfish', and if so does this affect the uses and acceptability of economic techniques? Is there a sense in which political orderings of preferences are 'ethical' and unselfish, and is this an important cause of their divergence from economic orderings?

Two ideas seem to me to connect economics with egoism, one of which has a very long history. This is the search for a psychological and/or ethical principle which can underpin the economist's methodology. The problem here is often misunderstood, anyhow as it presents itself in modern economics. One cannot say that altruism or social norms have no place in economic behaviour because clearly they do. One can say, as in the quotation from Buchanan, that economics predicates exchange relationships in which the participants are assumed to consider only their individual economic gains. This assumption will not always hold in practice by any means, but the point is that it appears to be sufficiently true to serve as a basis for reliable predictions under appropriate conditions. Moreover, the proposition is to some extent *ethically* legitimised in modern societies, although continuously under attack for example by socialists. It is not thought wrong however (even by democratic socialists) for consumers to seek to maximise their own satisfactions even though firms go bankrupt as a consequence of changes in consumers' tactics; or for firms to maximise profits at the expense of other firms.

Now there is no real need for a general theory of egoism to explain this 'institutionalised selfishness' of the market. It requires no more than that individuals be expected and allowed to take an instrumental and non-ethical view of certain exchange relationships, and it can be accepted that some individuals, from ethical or religious beliefs, will refuse to do so however socially legitimised the practice is. The practice is basically legitimised, not necessarily because 'selfishness' is supposed to be universal or desirable but because it is reasonable and consistent with a general balance of individual advantages to ignore the interests of other parties in some kinds of relationships.

Moreover, similar instrumental exchange relationships can exist and can also win some measure of social acceptance in other fields such as politics. The difference here is that politics is directly concerned with the 'authoritative allocation of values' for society, including the higher-order rules which are required to regulate and monitor the market or economic system. This institutionalised concern of politics with social norms creates (as Chapter 5 pointed out) the special character of political dialogue, including its ambivalence between egoistic and altruistic (public interest, social good, etc.) types of argument. Consequently instrumental exchange relationships are viewed with a good deal of moral suspicion – they appear to be violating the politicians' own language – although sophisticated students of the subject realise that they play a necessary part even in the pursuit of idealistic goals.

Political culture makes a lot of difference to the acceptability of an instrumental approach, which is much more acceptable in the United States than in Western Europe, for example, and more acceptable (that is in terms of prevailing social norms) in Western Europe than in the Soviet Union. Where politics has itself been brought closer, in image and in practice, to a model of bargaining and compromise between diverse interests, it is not surprising to find that the idea of 'institutionalised selfishness' also takes root. As with economic markets, the view can be held that if the basic rules and conventions are good ones then instrumental behaviour in politics may also (at least sometimes) be to the general advantage, this proviso about rules and conventions being of course still more vital today in politics than in economics.*

Egoism is a curious theory to predicate specifically of economic behaviour, because the ultimately dominant and coercive character of politics provides more blatant and brutal opportunities for self-seeking, although because of the nature of politics it is often group interests that are aggressively pursued. In properly functioning economic markets (admittedly a tall order) egoism *is* at least consistent with honesty and is favourable for productive work and saving; but politics must have very satisfactory rules and conventions for egoism to be as fruitful or as harmless. Economic interests have always turned to politics in order to shift the rules of economic bargaining in their own favour; this was true of landowners and capitalists in the last century and it is true of trade unions and capitalists in the 1970s. Of course, ideas of justice also figure prominently in political debate, and to a lesser extent influence political action, because we must always allow for the two-headed nature of politics; but such normative influences can hardly be described as dominant.

Indeed political egoism or group assertion tends to be more blatantly and hypocritically successful in those very societies where 'public interest' is most loudly proclaimed. At least the pluralism as displayed in the U.S. literature, for all its weaknesses, does manage to achieve some sort of a balance of selfish interests.

However, there is another relevant difference between economics and politics. In economic behaviour an individual can normally make his own private calculus of advantage, and the gains and losses from economic activity are usually tangible, divisible, and accrue to determinate individuals. In politics the individual calculus of gain and loss is to a large extent snapped. The citizen is required to make various contributions (taxes

---

* When the scope of government was small and that of economic markets was large, individual welfare depended very strongly indeed upon the exchange relationships of the economic system, and this was the time when 'classical egoism' flourished as a theory in economics; but even then political rule-making was fundamental for the functioning of the economic system, although Marx may have been right in thinking that the rules were made in the interests of a dominant economic group (actually there were two groups – landowners and capitalists).

compliance with numerous rules, perhaps military service, etc.) which are not directly related to the benefits he receives. This requires a normative input of support for the political system which may be related empirically to its general performance but which cannot possibly be reduced (as much economic behaviour can be) to a specific calculation of private gain. The political system therefore displays a pervasive concern with the existence and legitimacy of social norms.

The significance of egoism for welfare economics is rather curious. On the one hand, welfare economics aspire to alter, potentially quite drastically, the basis of economic calculations through introducing a long list of externalities which are not normally priced. Since these externalities are to be measured in terms of individual gain or loss wherever possible, a welfare-based price system should *reduce* the scope of political rule-making. Instead of having to rely upon social norms or public laws or both in conjunction to deal with such nuisances as loud noise, polluted air, or congested roads, the economist would give them all an appropriate price (related to individual preferences) and the nuisances would abate themselves to the full extent that was logically desirable. Any remainder of the nuisance would have been compensated for in the pricing system, and would therefore be worth incurring for its associated advantages (again as individually tested). Economists would of course agree that this is a counsel of perfection and that, in practice, welfare pricing could not achieve so much nor cover many externalities that are of social or political concern. Still the tendency of these economic theories is clear – and points towards the enlargement of an egoistic as opposed to social basis for decisions.

But in another sense welfare economics points *away from* egoism, because of the new factors which have to be allowed for in the concept of individual preference. How is an individual to put a price upon consequences which he is accustomed partly to consider (or at least to accept that he should consider) in socially-normative terms? It will not do to say that the analyst's results will show where the net balance of advantage lies because this will depend upon how individual preferences are expressed. Take the case of 'merit goods' which are goods that individuals suppose to be ethically and socially more valuable than the sums that they are privately prepared to pay for them. If this social element is ignored in the integrated 'welfare' preferences of individuals, as it is in their present market preferences, then the existence of 'merit goods' must be dismissed by economists as a political error or folly although this is actually quite implausible (see next section). If this element can be somehow included in the integrated preferences then welfare economics will be aspiring to measure directly the weight of social as well as self-regarding types of preference.

Egoism also interests economists because of its apparent but misleading connexion with the idea of rationality. Rational calculation is most efficient when there is an unambiguous value to be maximised. This fact explains the appeal of games theory, where an artificial goal is clearly specified for all participants and any amount of mathematical ingenuity can then be devoted to the choice of an optimum strategy. But real life is not a game even though some real-life situations (elections or international conflicts for example) contain some features that are analogous to games.

If we assume a narrow egoist who is concerned only with the equation of his direct personal costs and benefits, then it appears easier to define rational behaviour. This is because the value to be maximised has (at least apparently) been carefully restricted. Such an individual *is* being assumed in such examples as the 'irrationality' of voting when this is deduced from the proposition that the possibility of one vote influencing the result is so small as not to be worth the individual's effort.

But the example assumes that the act of voting is viewed as a burden and not as a pleasure, privilege, or duty. (It is curious that economists should so often regard as costs forms of political participation which were fought for as highly desirable benefits.) Of course, however voting is viewed, the rational voter will *still*, it could be argued, be deterred by the minute size of his influence on the result. Some features of voting behaviour could be explained in this way, such as higher turn-outs in marginal constituencies, but this result by no means always occurs.* The evidence suggests that quasi-rational calculations of this kind play a rather small and uncertain part in voting behaviour because of the influence of other factors, such as intensity of feeling and sense of duty, upon willingness to vote.[6] These influences are only 'irrational' if one assumes that voters should be egoists, and why should one assume this?

The paradoxes of egoism as a maximising principle are fairly well known, for example in the very familiar case of the 'prisoner's dilemma'.[7] The logical egoist has a motive to take the benefit and avoid the cost of any co-operative venture, so long as he goes undetected and avoids social or legal sanctions and so long as his action does not appreciably influence those of others. If, however, most people act in this way the results will often not accord with the preferences of egoists themselves because they will lose the advantages of social co-operation and be placed in a situation of mutual conflict and suspicion. Therefore, as Sen points out, the best *available* strategy for a logical egoist will often be to act co-operatively so long as he has some element of assurance that others will do the same.[8] Egoism, through abstracting from social norms and their co-operative advantages, becomes an unpromising value for a welfare economist to use as the basis for his calculus.

Of course the idea of egoism can be extended to include 'psychic satisfactions' such as the satisfaction of helping others or doing one's duty. But then it easily becomes vacuous as a theory or as a maximising principle because it becomes entangled with the whole diverse structure of individual

---

* In a marginal constituency the probability of a single vote being decisive is still extraordinarily minute but it *is* higher than elsewhere. The difficulty with any theory of probability is that it cannot explain what odds will seem to the individual to be worth acting on, especially if the cost is very low, so that the idea of rationality is much vaguer than it sounds. Thus one might argue that it is *irrational* to vote in a marginal constituency because the meaning of marginality has been misunderstood by the voter.

motivations. This extended sense of egoism usually rests upon the classical theory of psychological hedonism, which holds that an individual always *does* seek to maximise his pleasure subject to the constraints of his situation. We now have to say that someone who incurs much personal pain and deprivation for the sake of duty is motivated by the fear of much greater pains (of conscience or of retribution) if he defaults. Actually this is no longer convincing as a psychological explanation, but if we water down the theory (for example so as to exclude duty but include benevolence) its meaning becomes no clearer and it no longer has the apparent logic of a circular proposition. It does seem that even today, when some economists want to posit a maximising principle, they draw tacitly upon old ideas of psychological hedonism because the idea of rationality is always meaningless unless relevant values have been specified. Then the idea of egoism can be used to gloss over the failure to state those values, or to suggest plausible axioms of behaviour whose roots are not revealed.

B. Individual and Social Preference

I have suggested that economists hanker after some theory of egoism for two separate reasons. One is the wish to have some specific value to maximise, but egoism patently will not do for this purpose as indeed most economists now realise. At the most egoism furnishes some loosely stated postulate or axiom which (as in the theories of Anthony Downs) provides the basis for some partial exploration of human behaviour in certain contexts.* Secondly, the economist has a need to fill out the very generalised logical concept of individual preference. As Chapter 2 suggested the theory of 'revealed preference' is difficult enough to apply even for the purpose of macro predictions under the specific conditions of economic exchange. Treated as a much broader notion so as to encompass, in principle, *all* the manifold preferences of individuals, and stripped (as it must then be) of any restriction to egoistic behaviour, 'revealed preference' becomes a thin basis indeed for a cost–benefit analysis.

The problem may be looked at this way. Individual preferences, to the extent that they can be logically ascertained, come in a variety of shapes and sizes. One possible distinction is between individual preferences in a narrower and broader context, and in the short and the long run. Now logically of course, if the individual is completely consistent, these prefer-

---

* The plausibility and partial truth of these explanations, as demonstrated by Parkinson's Law, Downs and Olsen on political behaviour, and other examples, seems to derive from some psychological tendency to maximise the relationship of personal benefit to personal effort in situations where the individual does not identify his own interest with the relevant social or organisational goal. The explanations are only partial because they ignore the influence of personal or social norms upon reducing this 'identification gap'. Bureaucracy is a favourite subject for this kind of study because the weakness of personal work incentives increases the weight placed upon appeals to duty or social norms and some of those norms amount to mutual rationalisations of egoistic convenience.

ences will be wholly congruent. But it seems to be an empirical fact that this congruence is lacking. Thus one might add up the set of revealed preferences of some individual about the use of his leisure time, and find that the result conflicted with the integrated judgement held by that individual as to how he wished to spend his leisure.

Now the analyst might say that only the set of revealed preferences were to count because the integrated judgement had made no practical difference to the results. But the individual's plan of life may at least make some difference to his future behaviour, and *he* may wish account to be taken of this in public policies which affect his use of leisure. Moreover, his preferences are revealed under a given structure of opportunities and he has no easy means of showing (or perhaps of knowing) how he would respond in a different situation. There is no great psychological puzzle here, but the methodology of C.B.A. has a certain inbuilt tendency to overlook or underrate the more purposive and imaginative aspects of human behaviour. Of course, it can be said that C.B.A. makes no pretence to deal with consolidated judgements but only with specific preferences revealed in specific situations; but this defence would also suggest that individual cases ought to be checked against general judgements.

Also, one can distinguish between egoistic and social types of preference so long as one recognises that these are 'ideal types' not fully realised in practice. In the former case an individual makes a separate calculation of his own advantage; in the latter case he subsumes this calculation (which may or may not also be separately made) into a more generalised calculation of the advantage of some broader reference group, which may be a social organisation or group, a nation, or even all of humanity. Because of the tendency to shift between reference groups, and back to a separate private calculus, these social judgements are intrinsically fluid and difficult to tap but this does not make them less real. Again social norms will influence both types of preference (an individual will not be blind to social approval or fashion in calculating his personal gain) but in the social context these norms are the specific subject of the individual's preference. In deciding what is best for his reference group the individual will either be moved by or be seeking to influence the norms of other members of his reference group.

Expressions of individual preferences are shaped by the institutional structures through which they pass. Egoist-type preferences get freer rein under the institutional conditions of economic exchange, and social preferences get much more play under those of politics. We must not assume that social preferences have some intrinsically superior moral status, since they are often tyrannical and assertive especially where the advantage of a limited reference group is aggressively pursued. I am not espousing any idealistic theory of the state, but only pointing out the logical form which social preferences take.

Economics and C.B.A. is methodologically biased towards the calculation of egoistic-type preferences. This does not logically commit economists to a general belief in egoism, but it does produce problems about the status of an individual's social preferences and their reconciliation with his egoistic ones. As we have seen this distinction can be made either conceptually or in terms of institutional structures, and the latter distinction is perhaps easier to analyse. Though fairly familiar territory to many readers I investigate this question in the next section.

However, there is a long tradition of economic thought which is better described as 'individualist' than egoist. This is not just a matter of 'methodological individualism' which posits quite correctly that consciousness and choice belong exclusively to individuals. It is an ethical doctrine which stresses the value of individual autonomy as opposed to susceptibility to the pressure of social norms. This is relevant to the way in which social preferences are formed but it is not a denial of their existence. Historically, ethical individualism was linked with egoism (or 'enlightened self-interest') on the premise that in certain circumstances a prudent and far-sighted calculation of individual interest would work also to the general advantage. But enlightened egoism cannot be discovered from (although it might not be inconsistent with) an analysis of revealed preferences. As an integrated ethical judgement it is irrelevant to logical economic analysis and to C.B.A. as this is usually practised. But it *is* relevant to the scope of public policy.

C. Wants and Welfare

Economists are, in principle, indifferent about the content of individual preferences, their measures of value being based upon willingness to pay. Social norms influence personal expenditures, and can be studied as a part of economic sociology, but the economist does not pretend to sit in judgement upon the results. His ethical stance is either completely neutral – he is merely studying how people behave in an economic context – or else it is favourable towards the results of the institutions he is studying if they are working properly. Then his position will be the familiar one that there is no better way of deciding which wants should be satisfied, and to what extent, than the freely chosen preferences of individuals. He will accept that this rule cannot be universalised, that for example some wants should be legally prohibited and others perhaps discouraged by political action and/or social norms; he may also accept an ethical case for income redistribution; and he may think that it would be better if some people spent their money in different ways. But all such judgements are made as a citizen or moral being, and they are consistent with a favourable verdict upon the principle of 'consumers' sovereignty' within the limits that they suggest.

Now welfare economics, as we have seen, is in a curious position on these issues. Its neutrality over the context of wants combined with its enlargement of the scope of individual preference leads, as Chapter 2 suggested, to the paradox that 'welfare economics' produces a quite different view about the meaning of welfare from that held by ordinary opinion and conveyed through frequently made ethical and political judgements.

As already noted economic and political orderings of preferences often appear to differ. How does this come about? Is it the result of the same raw data about individual preferences being processed through different systems? (In other words the inconsistency resides in the systems not in the individuals themselves.) If this is so which system is perverting or confusing the raw data? Alternatively is it that individuals themselves vary their preference orderings in different social contexts? If so is this a case of irrationality or unresolved ambivalence, or does it represent a factorisation of preferences which, in principle, is quite reasonable? In either event which ordering should be dominant in cases of conflict, or is the answer to this already given by the fact that (almost by definition) the political ordering will *prove* dominant? (At any rate in a legal sense; in practice there may be a rejection of political authority and a substitution of economically settled priorities, for example by 'black markets'.) Such questions deserve to be more frequently asked than they are in either economics or politics.

Economists talk of 'merit goods' (and merit bads) to refer to individual wants which are stimulated or depressed by political action. Prominent in such an analysis would be the actions of modern democratic governments in subsidising 'necessities' (such as housing and sometimes food or clothing) and in heavily taxing 'luxuries' (such as tobacco, liquor, and gambling). Such actions undoubtedly form part of the political conception of welfare, but are quite contrary to the economic idea of welfare which would logically hold that (subject to any rules of distribution) all types of expenditure should be equally taxed or subsidised.

This familiar example is chosen because it cannot be plausibly interpreted as representing to any appreciable extent, if at all, a redistribution of welfare from rich to poor, and so could not possibly be justified by any general rules of distribution. In Britain, for example a large majority of people get a substantial subsidy or tax rebate in respect of their housing (it is in fact often argued that rich owner-occupiers come out best from the arrangements). Conversely, taxes on drink or gambling bear if anything more heavily upon the poor than the rich. Nor can the results be plausibly explained by the leverage of political interests. Pressure groups certainly abound in the housing field, to some extent balancing each other but probably boosting the total of public support; on the other hand, why are there no pressure groups campaigning against the swingeing taxes on 'luxuries'?

The only plausible explanation will therefore refer to some dualism or ambivalence in the preference orderings of individuals themselves. These political orderings might be explained by at least three considerations. One would be a prudential motive leading individuals to approve or at least accept intervention with their want patterns so as to protect their own longer-term satisfactions against their immediate desires. This would be a version of Barry's trustee concept of interest – the government is safeguarding the individual's capacity to satisfy his own wants in the long run for reasons of his frailty, ignorance, or convenience.[9] A second motive would apply the same reasoning *altruistically* on behalf of other individuals (or more probably their dependents) who were too frail to look after themselves. A third motive would be simply ethical: whatever my wants may happen to be, I may recognise that some wants are morally superior. As we have seen, ethical arguments of this kind (whether they are individually-held or imposed by social pressures) become relevant in political argument in a way which does not apply to market situations. Finally all these motivations can be supported by utilitarian arguments about favourable consequences; through discouraging gambling and encouraging better housing, social disorders will be reduced and economic efficiency will be improved.

Almost certainly all these motives are involved, although it would be enormously difficult (even with the help of opinion surveys) to estimate their respective cogency. The third motive is not logically relevant unless an individual also believes that it is right for governments to enforce moral duties in contexts such as this one, in which case he might logically support very strong measures of government intervention. Some combination of these four arguments seems quite sufficient to explain popular support for welfare interventions. Moreover, it will not do to contend that a large majority are indifferent to these considerations because enough people must be concerned in order to explain the political orderings.*

How could welfare economics deal with these various motives or arguments for state intervention? The fourth argument is a possible example of favourable externalities (e.g. savings in the crime rate, etc.) brought about by public intervention, although these could not be isolated and measured. Beyond this point the economist might stretch the notion of utility to include prudential or altruistic motives which give assurance or satisfaction to individuals, and therefore form part of a possible schedule of personal wants, although duty could less easily be accommodated. He might perhaps agree that such wants would have more impact upon the price system if they had not been pre-empted by political action. More simply he could drop any lame extensions of 'utility' and contend that an integrated preference structure for all wants is conceivable and desirable. But the argument is not convincing and few economists would explicitly make it.

If the economist falls back upon a normative ideal such as that individuals *should* order their preferences sensibly and farsightedly instead of leaning upon the state, his position is more tenable and can allow of exceptions. But this position is useless to the welfare economist and to C.B.A., because they base their measurements upon a concept of welfare and not upon an ethical principle of responsible freedom. Thus they cannot explain, nor do they usually try to do so, *why* political orderings of welfare differ so markedly from economic ones. It is worth noting, though, that the

* Nor can one accept the familiar argument that patterns of taxation (though hardly of subsidies) are to be explained simply by 'fiscal convenience'. Governments certainly have an incentive to tax products with a high elasticity of demand, as liquor and tobacco do have, but in a pre-welfare situation any differences in elasticity of demand between these products and various 'necessities' would be either insufficient or adverse for this line of reasoning. Of course, once a convenient fiscal system has been introduced there is a motive to continue with it, but this fact does not explain why the system was introduced in the first place nor why it continues to receive popular support or acquiescence.

higher-level normative debate over the claims of individualism and of collectivism provides the actual basis on which reflective people attempt to arbitrate between the claims of economic and political preference orderings.

Let us briefly consider another example of merit goods, namely public provision or subsidies for arts and recreation. Here again there is no question of redistribution in favour of the poor since the beneficiaries almost certainly have above-average incomes. There are plenty of pressure groups at work, but these could hardly succeed if there were not a background of favourable public opinion – although in this case, more obviously than in the last, there are people who oppose subsidies on the economist's grounds of sticking to the evidence about individual preferences. The favourable opinion again rests upon several arguments which this time turn not upon prudence but upon the development of individual capacities and of communal life.

There appear to be two somewhat conflicting strands of thought here. One argument sees an intrinsic desirability in the development of certain individual capacities (intellectual, artistic, or physical); and because this development requires training and effort it can also be said that individuals will not be aware of the eventual benefits to themselves. (This is akin to J. S. Mill's idea of 'higher pleasures'.) A second belief recognises a special value in the 'common enjoyment' of such cultural experiences, which can also be held to advance such specifically political values as civic participation or the integration of classes or races. Individualists may support the first goal but be dubious about the second one, especially the political values which might as easily be authoritarian as democratic. The value of 'common enjoyment' (which in cost–benefit terms means simply that A enjoys some experience more if B, C, etc. are enjoying it also – although at some point diminishing returns set in, for example if one gets crushed) need not turn upon specifically *civic* provision although subsidies to private organisations may be necessary. However, the supporters of civic culture can also argue that, if a society *is* adequately democratic, their approach will reinforce and publicly demonstrate democratic values.

A C.B.A. might attempt to deal with the relative advantage of increasing the size of individual gardens or of creating a public park. (This has actually been an issue in British New Towns.) Efficiency of supply is all on the side of the park which also can be supported by the value of common or civic enjoyment; but the development of individual capacities favours the private gardens which probably would do better on an analysis of W.T.P. The irony perhaps is that since amateur gardeners rarely stop to look at their roses, the cost in this case *is* the benefit.

These individualist and communal goals, in whatever mix they occur, can again be supported, as welfare interventions, by altruistic and utilitarian arguments such as that 'healthy recreation' keeps people from mischief and improves work performance. Once again it is difficult for welfare economics to deal with these questions. As I have suggested part of the problem is that if one takes a snap-shot view of individual preferences, one can allow little for factors of human development;* but political preferences do deal with the factors, sometimes of course in a pernicious way. (One thinks of the Hitler Youth Movement which also would have got nowhere on the basis of cost–benefit analysis.)

But, it may be asked, do economists *pretend* to have much to say about these subjects? I admit that usually they do not, but it seemed worthwhile to explore a little the basis of political preference orderings to see if they were reconcilable with the economist's welfare calculus. This is the more necessary because it can be shown that similar factors, in a paler way, much influence individual opinions about the kind of externalities which economists do claim to measure objectively.

At the extensive Roskill Commission hearings many critics alleged a discrepancy in the research team's valuations over the relative importance attached to noise nuisance and to travellers' time. The latter factor proved a much more significant factor than the former one in the results of the analysis. Now, whatever its factual basis, it seems clear that this criticism was much influenced by cultural and ethical attitudes. Public opinion has been increasingly sensitive to the 'bads' (e.g. noise) as opposed to the 'goods' (e.g. mobility) of technological developments. (If the Commission had sat ten years earlier the criticism would certainly have been much less.) In addition it could be said that, ethically speaking, loud noise represents an involuntary nuisance imposed upon individuals whereas (at least to some extent) faster travel is only an extra bonus accruing to a voluntary choice. These criticisms caused the Commission to amend the figures of its research team. As regards noise nuisance it decided to assume 'that the value placed by the community on residential quiet will increase by 5 per cent a year compared with 3 per cent a year (previously assumed)...This is an important change of principle which has the effect of increasing house depreciation values and noise endurance costs by about one-third.'[10]

This 'important change of principle' is a curious one. Logically it ought to have been based upon evidence: not that the research team's valuations of the current nuisance of noise were false, but that people's willingness to pay to avoid the noise nuisance would accelerate at a much faster rate in the future – at 5 per cent instead of 3 per cent. But how could this be known when the only evidence at the hearings concerned the distaste for noise that people *already* felt? It seems more likely that the increase from a 3 to 5 per cent acceleration rate was simply a technical method (and a quite illogical one) for coping with a cultural or ethical attitude which had not been properly allowed for in the original cost–benefit figures.

Why in that case were the original research team figures accepted by implication to be wrong? An answer can of course be sought in the inconsistencies of valuation techniques (pp. 76–89). It would be wrong to suppose either that these techniques had managed to *exclude* cultural and ethical influences altogether or that they had treated these influences in a *logically*

---

* It may be said that cost–benefit studies of education and of the development of 'human resources' contradict this statement, but they concentrate upon income or production effects which are not being discussed here.

consistent and impartial manner. Thus the basis of valuing the time costs of businessmen in terms of lost earnings or production represented a 'social efficiency' test which *was* in intention culturally neutral, for example it excluded any feelings that individuals might have about the 'goodness' or 'badness' of travel (more specifically of air travel) as such. Conversely, some of the techniques used for measuring noise nuisance, for example the enquiries about the value placed by home-owners upon their existing amenities, *did* introduce normative influences although in an erratic way (because the owners would certainly incorporate some view about the 'bad-ness' of noise in addition to tangible economic loss into their replies; indeed the theory of 'consumers' surplus' seemingly allows them to do so). It would seem that the inconsistency of techniques was tacitly accepted by the Com-mission itself in a purely *ad hoc* way, because it chose to 'write down' the time figures, just as it wrote up the noise figures, in an apparent effort to allow again for cultural and ethical opinions (expressed extensively at the public hearings) which regarded the time costs as excessive.

In point of fact the Commission increasingly moved towards a stance of 'even if...then still' which is the staple form of policy argument. Thus its *ad hoc* adjustments for noise and time valuations seem to have been influ-enced by the wish to argue that, even if substantial concessions (on the original figures) were made to meet the objectors' case, the Commission's preference for an airport site could still be validated. In the same way, the Commission finally decided to put a generous figure upon the nuisance suffered by churches from noise (this was increased by £10,000 per church to allow for the insulation of the roofs in addition to double-glazing of windows), while removing those churches which would be rendered more or less unusable by the airport from its calculations altogether and treating them as an 'intangible loss'.[11] Here of course one sees a complete departure from the principle of individuals' W.T.P., and retreat into a familiar defen-sive stance of suggesting generous compensation for those deprivations which can be alleviated, and a sigh and a shake of the head for those that cannot be. The position *is* ethically defensible – it is on a par with the argu-ment about submerged Welsh valleys (see p. 84) – but it rests upon propositions that have nothing in common with those of welfare economics.

Suppose we decide that economic measurements even of such 'obvious' externalities as time and noise must somehow be corrected for these norma-tive factors, how is the operation to be done? One familiar way is to 'weight' the original data in various ways so as to allow for either (*a*) impartial evidence about the missing elements of individual preferences or (*b*) partisan political judgements about the weight that should be accorded to such factors. Either way, but particularly on the second option, the weightings will logically be somewhat indeterminate so that a range of possible values should be given. The Roskill Commission was concerned with the first (impartial) sort of weighting, and this position corresponded to a familiar distinction between an impartial investigating commission and a partisan political viewpoint. Thus logically we could envisage a two-stage process in which two sets of separate weightings were adduced, with presumably more evidence being attached by disinterested opinion to the first of these exercises.

This weighting could be done more logically and systematically than it was by Roskill, who produced such weightings for time values only. However, as we have seen, one latent reason for their procedure was that the original data did not deal consistently with cultural and ethical factors in preferences; and where this is so the logic of weighting breaks down (if *some* allowance for these factors has already been made, what *further* allowance will be reasonable?). Thus the weighting theory breaks down *unless* the meaning of individual preference is clear and consistent in the first place – which it does not appear to be.

This example has showed the difficulties of catching certain elements in individual preferences which are usually met through normative or political orderings, rather than an economic calculus (of any kind). This omission is much more serious in relation to the measurement even of allegedly 'obvious' externalities than in relation to marketable goods because in the latter case the meaning of individual preference *can* be restricted to the motives and circumstances of an economic exchange and corrected if need be by a separately articulated political judgement. In contrast welfare economics and C.B.A. seem unable to cope with the issues about the relative desirability of individual wants which form a staple of social and political argument. The two sets of preference orderings that we started by positing (and which is itself a considerable simplification) become confused rather than integrated.

D. The Issue of Distribution

This issue is the *pons asinorum* of welfare economics and of C.B.A. There are two main schools among economists. The orthodox view holds that C.B.A. rests upon the 'efficiency' principle of maximising total welfare, and that only limited deductions (if any) about distribution of welfare can be reached from this principle itself (see pp. 20–3). The less orthodox view holds that welfare economics itself must incorporate or rest upon certain ethical principles which then become fundamental to the practice of C.B.A.

The words 'orthodox' and 'less orthodox' refer here primarily to the pragmatic assumptions of economists when they give advice, rather than to the volume of theoretical literature. On the latter basis the less-orthodox view would be at least as well represented as the orthodox one, or rather one would find a middle spectrum of contributions which used a mishmash of both approaches. The 'saddle point' of this spectrum is of course the Pareto principle which neatly appears to combine the wish to be 'scientific' and also to recognise some ethical rule which can be squared with the first consideration. The Pareto principle fails completely because the efficiency principle is not itself genuinely scientific, and the Pareto modification is a narrow and (to ordinary opinion) unacceptable rule of justice.

These issues were treated to some extent in Chapter 2, where it was pointed out that, *if* it is meaningful to add together the welfare of individuals, then it is also meaningful (and indeed logically necessary) to settle the distribution of welfare among those individuals – otherwise total welfare cannot be maximised. The welfare maximisation principle has distributional implications of a mixed kind; in principle these are egalitarian (because observation *does* support the idea of diminishing satisfaction from rising levels of income or welfare) but practically they are also inegalitarian because of the undoubted though variable influence of 'incentives' upon increasing the totality of economic welfare that is to be shared out. The efficiency principle is therefore indeterminate on this point, which has to be settled empirically. This awkward fact gives another motive to the 'ortho-dox' school for shying away from the issue of distribution because they cannot talk about it as reliable pundits.

However, all the arguments that they can logically allow on distribution must ignore the question of social justice, because the efficiency principle itself ignores this subject. It is logically neutral as to how pains and pleasures are distributed, and as to whether some people are poor and wretched, so long as the sheer totality of welfare is the maximum possible. Distributional weightings though necessarily implicit in the principle are wholly dependent upon it.* Once this point is understood it becomes evident that the efficiency principle is *not* acceptable to most people as a basis of social policy. Rawls identifies it with the principle of 'classical utilitarianism' which supposes that the world is being viewed by a sympathetic spectator who enters into the experiences of each individual and then disinterestedly adds up the results. As a consequence the differences between individuals are not taken seriously and there is no attention to individual rights as such. Few people and few economists too can really swallow this rejection of justice as ordinarily understood.[12]

Subtle economic theorists understand these points perfectly well but practical analysts often do not, and neither curiously does 'ordinary opinion', including the beliefs of many politicians and officials. The explanation seems to be that economists are still trading, unconsciously one hopes, upon the respect given to the maximisation of economic gain as a respectable but limited goal under conditions of economic exchange. Economists in other words are viewed as authorities upon 'efficiency' because they know how to increase productivity and profits (so opinion assumes: businessmen are more sceptical). The same idea can be extended to the operations of government on the assumption that the economist will know how to maximise some national goal such as economic growth (this task is harder, but the scepticism of the business world is now conveniently at arm's length). At this point the economist can substitute a broader goal of

---

* An illustration which often crops up in economic textbooks is the question of whether the marginal productivity of an individual gives his contribution to society and hence is an acceptable principle in relation to the maximisation of welfare. Few welfare economists can accept this argument anyhow because of market imperfections, but their disposition still to think of it as a 'scientific' (as opposed to an 'ethical') argument shows the hidden hand of the efficiency principle.

'welfare maximisation', and broader and looser theories about what he is doing, without this extension of thought being clearly realised; and to the extent that it *is* noticed, the goal of welfare seems sensible and even self-evident until closely inspected. Thus the 'efficiency principle' which can command public support in limited contexts and subject to constraints subtly gets transformed into an all-embracing principle of social policy. Once these things are understood, the contingency of the efficiency principle itself upon the broader social goals or values becomes quite apparent. Indeed the name of the principle gives the game away since efficiency is an *instrumental* value. This is what suggests its 'scientific' status until attention is directed to the goal that is to be maximised.

How then are 'orthodox' analysts to deal with the distributional effects of their proposals which *logically* they cannot ignore? It is here that a certain dualism comes into their arguments. Thinking as citizens, so to speak, they may concede or be aware of the ethical and social inadequacy of their efficiency principle; and they will be disposed to the same conclusion by the difficulty of finding adequate 'scientific' rules of distribution – they may even doubt (again as citizens) the sort of rules which their basic theory would seem to suggest.* Their safest course therefore is to find some socially legitimised yardstick to appeal to – to throw themselves upon the social conscience so to speak. But the social conscience speaks with many voices (because ideas of justice are complex and partly conflicting) and, after all, economists like some measure of precision. In this situation there seems to be two courses available:

(*a*) The analyst can recommend that the distribution of capital and income (more precisely the capacity to purchase units of welfare) be established and maintained at some 'optimum' level without saying what that optimum shall be. The matter is remitted to politics and public opinion. The analyst will then do his work without any consideration of the distributional effects of his maximising principle. This is logically unsatisfactory for the results of each analysis; he can only console himself that any deleterious consequences will be remedied in a rough-and-ready way by automatic rules of redistribution. This approach enables the economist to separate his roles as economist and citizen though not in a very satisfactory way. He is not being a logical economist; and as a citizen he must have an uneasy conscience that the assumptions of his work will *not* be generally understood (and perhaps a suspicion that if they were understood he would get less work) and that for this and other reasons the distribution problem will *not* be adequately solved by political means.

(*b*) Alternatively the economist can build distributional rules into each C.B.A. Taking out his social yardstick he can hit on the old idea of 'implicit prices' as revealed in the differential weights accorded to individual welfare by public policies and decisions. This could be done by

---

* Although some analysts do so, it cannot be *logical* for them to shrug their shoulders at the whole problem as too messy. If they really confine themselves to the efficiency principle, they must do their best to deduce the relevant distributional rules, however difficult or socially unacceptable these may prove to be.

assigning welfare coefficients to groups based upon the differential benefits assigned to them by past public decisions or by taking the marginal rate of taxation as an indication of the amount of welfare due to any individual.[13] (Thus a rich man's benefits would be very substantially written down to meet the low public valuation placed upon his increase of welfare and the poor man's as a consequence written up; these exercises would be on paper only – the point would not be to tax the rich man several times over but to make sure that the policy adopted was biased towards the interests of the relatively poor.) Such devices invite the old objection that they are merely projecting and hence exaggerating the consequences of past public policies but, assuming these policies change regularly and ignoring the time-lag, the objection is hardly decisive if some social yardstick has to be found. A possibly more formidable objection is that the method abstracts public decisions from their specific contexts and gives them a general application that had not been intended; no ingenious 'averaging' of relevant measurements can altogether overcome this defect.

Again alternatively one can seek a broader approach such as Foster's proposal that a C.B.A. should be weighted by the ratio of average national personal income to the personal income of each affected individual[14] (in practice perhaps of groups of such individuals). This has the result of favouring those policies which are beneficial to individuals below the national average, and vice versa. However, the method requires acceptance of a general rule of justice which has not been legitimised by any social practice. It may be no worse for that philosophically speaking but it would be enormously difficult – impossible surely – to get the idea accepted.

Indeed the practical problem with any of these proposals is to get agreement between economists and politicians (and within both of these groups) about the relevant rules to write into C.B.A.s. One might seek a solution through propounding a variety of rules from among which the final decision-maker can select, thus making the analysis more indeterminate, but still the problem seems insuperable. Issues of justice simply cannot be settled in this way, and probably the more an economist argues that they should be the lower (quite unfairly perhaps) his credibility becomes. One might perhaps have rules of this kind introduced into some C.B.A.s but unless the conventions are universalised the results will be extremely inconsistent.

If the orthodox school of economists cannot resolve the issue of distribution the less-orthodox school have problems of a different kind. There is first the baleful influence of the Pareto principle. This principle can either be presented as an ethical constraint upon the maximising principle *or* as a basic ethical rule which allows increases in total welfare to be realised only in certain restrictive circumstances. The first view, which receives some credence from the orthodox school of 'maximisers', is in fact logically untenable on the efficiency principle as we have seen; and moreover, its practical application usually ignores the requirement that losers must literally be fully compensated thus dishing its ethical context altogether. In the hands of the 'less-orthodox school' the Pareto principle can figure more logically as a basic ethical rule which *must* be satisfied before any increase of welfare can take place. But then one has the problem as to why exactly this principle should command acceptance simply as a basic ethical rule. As such it is no more than a doctrine that everyone should be entitled to keep what he possesses at a given point in time and to use these assets to his *further* advantage, subject to not actually worsening the position of others (which may of course and often will be much inferior). A general bias or sentiment in favour of respecting existing rights has often been argued for by political philosophers, but rarely indeed in such an absolute and Procrustean way.

Mishan assures us that welfare economics rests not upon the utility principle, but upon certain basic ethical rules. These rules 'appear to be too obvious to warrant mention in actual constitutions' but can 'be said to form part of a virtual constitution'. Two rules are then described, the first upholding the legitimacy of a Pareto improvement, the second sanctioning distributional changes 'if there is near-unanimity that the distribution resulting from the economic rearrangement is an improvement'. As he says, the rules sound modest enough, indeed they hardly take us beyond Pareto. His second rule is apparently introduced to meet the argument that there are cases where a Pareto improvement made by reference to utility alone would affront 'the moral sense of society'. But it is quite unclear what impact this second rule of justice is supposed to have; since 'near-unanimity' is required (and what exactly is that?) one imagines that the impact would be pretty negligible. Mishan presumably postulates 'near-unanimity' because of his frequently stressed distrust of majority rule, which he curiously shares with political economists like Buchanan and Tullock who reason from wholly different premises to quite different conclusions. It is a case of extremes meeting with very worldly and unworldly (Mishan) economists disliking majorities for opposite reasons.[15]

Mishan's idea that Pareto is enshrined in the hearts of men and in the 'virtual constitutions' of states can only be risible. If one wants to found welfare economics and C.B.A. on principles of justice, it is necessary to go to such basic arguments as those deployed by John Rawls. Rawls urges that some principle of 'justice as fairness' is serially superior to other principles, for example its conditions ought to be satisfied before proceeding to other considerations. Rawls's argument requires every person to place himself behind a veil of ignorance so that he does not know his historical and social position or his particular desires and tastes, but considers only the ideas which would strike him as fair under the necessary conditions of social co-operation and continuity. The distributional rule, he suggests, would then be that any social arrangements should be of advantage to the worst-placed members of society; which means that any institutional inequalities should be defensible in these terms. Similarly, a rule of fairness must be applied as far as it can be (for there cannot be equality) to the prospects for each generation. Principles of this type are surely more suitable as the basis of a 'virtual constitution', and make better sense of the proposition that economics should be based upon distributive rather than maximising rules. However, Rawls's principle is rather too general to serve as an adequate basis for the critique of particular institutions or of second-order rules of distribution.[16]

Philosophically speaking, the economist's dilemmas over rules of distribution can only be settled through an appeal to higher-order principles. These principles will then have to determine whether the relationship between rules of justice and some concept of welfare maximisation is to be a serial or concurrent one, for example whether one principle is to have absolute priority or whether they are to be balanced in some way. If the former approach is adopted, for which there are weighty arguments, then one has to reckon with the complexity of ideas of justice. Rules of justice have their first and clearer application, as Rawls points out, to liberty rather than welfare. Some rules of liberty, for example the prohibition of slavery, can be applied whatever the material circumstances of society. But when we apply rules of justice to welfare, we cannot gainsay the fact that a society should try to produce enough to provide its members with a reasonable standard of life.

This circumstance produces the familiar dilemmas of economic justice: what weight should be given to criteria of desert (such as natural or acquired abilities) as against criteria of need? As Sen argues, the former criteria depend largely upon contingent considerations of the individual's service to society since there is not much of an intrinsic case for rewarding him for his abilities according to a principle of fairness; but there is a clearer case for recognising on these grounds the basic needs that are common to humanity.[17] Equity now reappears to support the old adage that man should not expect to eat if he will not work. These ideas are expressed in the communist principle (though hardly the practice) of 'from each according to his ability, to each according to his needs'; or in Bernard Shaw's pithy saying that every man should be paid £1000 (it might now need to be £5000) and as a necessary corollary be required to earn it. Whether these requirements should be satisfied through exhortation and social norms, or through compulsion, or through a qualified system of market incentives, is a further issue and one that has much relevance to the concept of liberty. Here it is sufficient to sketch the philosophic relationship of justice to distributive welfare rules.

This philosophic digression has been introduced as a corrective to the rather narrow notions of welfare economists about rules of distribution. It has served to support the proposition that such rules, suitably conceived, are indeed more important or at the very least as important as a maximising principle which in any case cannot be logically applied in isolation from them. Moreover, the economist's welfare criterion must also be redefined if it is to serve as a criterion of public policy. It must be purged, not of its 'methodological individualism' which *is* logically correct, but of its assumption that individual preferences can be articulated and aggregated independently of ethical rules of distribution.

At a much more pragmatic level, one device for minimising these distributive pitfalls in C.B.A. is the 'planning balance sheet' developed in England by Nathanial Lichfield.[18] This is not a maximising technique since no attempt is made to reach a total of net welfare, and there is no assumption that all items should be quantified. In principle all relevant costs and benefits are supposed to be listed, and are allocated to the different groups who will be affected by each decision or plan that is being evaluated. The balance-sheet thus reveals the uncorrected incidence of welfare effects which decision-makers and observers can use in their own verdicts. Thus the methodology remits normative judgements about both maximisation and distribution to the political realm where they institutionally belong, subject of course to the inevitable intrusion of these factors into techniques of valuation. This method's relative modesty of approach has been influenced by the intrinsic difficulties of applying C.B.A. to urban and regional planning but could be followed in other exercises. (However, Lichfield is anything but modest in other claims for this methodology. See Chapter 7.)

E. Social Ideals and C.B.A.

As we have seen C.B.A. cannot allow adequately for the expression of integrated individual judgements about desirable social goals (we need not specify here whether these goals are more individualist or more collectivist in character; they will usually be both these things in varying degrees). Put more simply C.B.A. lacks any imaginative or developmental perspective upon desirable future states either of individuals or of society, except as these can be derived from the present compartmentalised desires of individuals, assuming that these can be separately discovered. This lack of integrated vision could be reckoned as a blessing. If economic techniques are inhospitable to building a new Jerusalem, neither will they give much countenance to grand designs of evil or destruction.

Yet this defence of C.B.A. overlooks its inability to cope properly with the normative and cultural components of public policy. A systematic treatment of such components will result in a social goal or ideal, and if further systematised we can arrive at a set of such goals which can form the basis of a public plan. Now C.B.A. certainly need not be silent over the value of such goals or plans. It can play the critical role of testing them against what it can discover about individual preferences as these currently exist; and it can play a constructive role in plotting the relationship of goals to available resources. Many people would claim no more for C.B.A. than these two points, and in principle there is nothing to quarrel with in this position. The problem is that the very severe limitations of this position receive inadequate recognition, both from the analysts themselves and from those who commission them.

A public policy usually incorporates many considerations of a kind which cannot be reduced (save in a very notional and unreal way) to forecasts of individual gain or loss. These considerations assume complex causal chains whose results (and even existence) cannot be properly foreseen, and which are individually judged from a wide spectrum of viewpoints. In this situation systematic social and political beliefs provide an essential element of simplification. Almost everyone recognises in practice that most public policies *cannot* be adequately judged from a specific calculus of individual gain, but must be tested against general ideas about its balance of advantage to the individual himself, his family, social groups, and society generally. The values that are implicit in social goals are too elusive to be pinned down, let alone measured, by economic techniques.

The danger with this situation is that C.B.A. will appear to be promising more than it can possibly perform. It can criticise some aspects of social goals from its chosen position but it cannot produce proper alternatives, because its own view of 'welfare' is inadequate for this purpose. It can analyse the resource elements in a policy equation, although often speculatively, but this analysis must either be applied to goals which are (to a large extent) independently supplied or else the limitations of a C.B.A. must be filled in with a generous measure of assumed objectives. Because C.B.A. deals with those factors in a policy problem which *appear* to be relatively tangible and hard-headed, its results may be treated with respect, especially in a society which is highly uncertain about values and (partly for this very reason) deferential towards techniques. Quantification is a palliative or soporific for the malaise of uncertainty about values. This conclusion is not altered by the fact that C.B.A. attempts to plot a wider range of values than do more conventional forms of economic analysis. Its explorations are welcomed for this very reason, and the weak light with which dark places are illuminated escapes attention.

Consider an analyst called in to advise upon the case for keeping open a branch railway line which runs through beautiful but remote countryside. By definition the branch line is commercially unprofitable. He might start by positing that people who rarely or even never use the line may nevertheless value it as a standby facility; in principle such people might be willing to pay something to keep it open although there seems no way for the railway to tap this revenue. Equally some regular customers might be willing to pay higher fares. Because of the practical difficulties and unpopularity (or illegality) of differential pricing on railways, these forms of 'consumers' surplus' cannot be tapped but they could be written into an analysis – subject to the obvious points that they cannot really be calculated and any implicit losses of 'producers' surplus' elsewhere will be ignored.[19]

More promising perhaps will be the tourist potential of the region and its beauties as observed from an old railway line. The railway company (or a possible purchaser) should have made these calculations itself, and the analyst can add nothing new in principle unless through another use of the 'standby' concept. Then there are the road congestion and accident costs which will be consequent upon the branch line's closure, although these may well be small in the circumstances envisaged. (A lot will depend though upon how road accidents and environmental damage even on a small scale are valued, and also upon the tourist estimates.) Finally, it is probable that if public services, of which the railway is an example, are withdrawn or reduced, more local people will quit. This situation will impose higher overhead costs and worse conditions upon those who remain, and it might in certain circumstances reduce the supply of food or other products. To pay some small premium against the latter contingency would be yet another version of the 'standby' argument.

In this example the analyst will partly be checking the commercial estimates of the railway company (he may extend this to such factors as the linked economies of branch and main lines), but will mainly be introducing factors that cannot figure in the company's accounts. The most specific of these factors will be road congestion costs simply because of the existing conventions of measurement, and the analyst may therefore stress this point whether or not it is important. The other factors he can adduce – such as the environmental damage of road traffic, various versions of the 'standby' or insurance concept, and the increased burdens of local inhabitants – are in varying degrees beyond the realm of meaningful calculations. His main function in practice will probably be to produce some empirical data on these matters without (if he is wise) pressing them into the service of a single equation or estimate of net welfare.

But even so the more basic social judgements will elude the analyst's grasp. First, are local inhabitants *entitled* to some minimum standard of public services? (If so which services and to what standard?) This is a distributive problem. Secondly, is it intrinsically undesirable that rural areas should be gradually depopulated? In the nineteenth century, some political economists and many politicians would have answered *this* question by pointing to favourable 'externalities' of a rural population, such as a high birth rate, a reservoir for military service, and a forcing ground for useful social virtues such as thrift and hard work. In the modern world these alleged social gains from rural life are much less believed in or approved, which represents a substantial shift in cultural values, and the case against rural depopulation is more likely to be argued as an aesthetic or cultural preference. Still there is a lingering belief that a rural way of life contains some sort of unmeasurable bonus, which may perhaps include favourable effects upon individual character and social behaviour.

As has been pointed out these general arguments about social fabric and social behaviour do enter into individual preferences in some sense, but cannot be tapped by a calculus of individual gains and losses. The rights of local inhabitants can be introduced through the Pareto principle in the form either of compensating them for a loss of welfare or assisting them to move out. This point, should it be accepted, will not settle the type of compensation or the policy problem. Moreover, until these issues are explored and social goals are clarified, one cannot always be sure what question the analyst is attempting to answer. For example, if there *is* any case for checking rural depopulation, then the relationship between population size and infrastructure or service costs is clearly important. A railway subsidy could then be looked at as one (but not perhaps the best) way of subsidising a minimal package of local services.

Let us take a broader example of the relationship between social goals and C.B.A. which starts from the goals. In a famous book,[20] Ebenezer Howard preached the value of 'garden cities', that is to say medium-sized, low-density settlements surrounded by a green belt. Howard had two relevant beliefs or assumptions: (1) that all men had similar likes and dislikes about certain things; for example they wanted a 'reasonable' range of social facilities and job opportunities close at hand, but they disliked crowded areas or long journeys; (2) that men needed or anyhow benefited from certain opportunities such as frequent access to the countryside, and participation in community life. On both tests he claimed that garden cities were preferable to either big cities or rural areas because they achieved most of the virtues of each of these alternatives without the drawbacks.

A cost–benefit analyst would regard this as naive. He would not start from the assumption that men had similar tastes, since they might be very different, and he would probably reject the Aristotelian character of Howard's second assumption. He would be more sympathetic, however, to Howard's contention about increasing returns following upon economies of scale and diminishing returns resulting from indirect congestion costs. This would be a way of saying that, to the extent that similar individual likes and dislikes can be posited, these can best be realised under given technological and other conditions in settlements of a given size.

Howard's ideas proved influential in Britain and eventually the New Towns Act was passed in 1946 to facilitate the movement of population and industry to new medium-sized settlements. In 1944 eight New Towns were proposed in Abercrombie's Greater London Plan and were linked with the proposal for an extensive green belt to restrict the growth of the capital itself. Surplus population and industry were to be steered away from London to the New Towns. It is interesting that Abercrombie's Plan, although it was uncosted and untimed and was presented with hardly any economic analysis, was nevertheless largely implemented by the various public authorities. Moreover, the results won a good deal of political approval, and the New Town and green belt programmes have been maintained, although the actual New Towns have by no means fully met Howard's original aspirations (partly of course because tastes have changed). This brief history shows the persuasive influence that social ideals can exert upon policy formation.[21]

How would an analyst have viewed the Abercrombie Plan if he had been consulted? He would have factorised and analysed the specific demands for housing, industrial growth, and so on. He would certainly have pointed out the high opportunity cost of the Plan for meeting these demands, which could have been satisfied more quickly and economically through locating new development close to London (for example by utilising spare capacity in roads and services, tapping the existing labour pool for new industries, avoiding the movement of construction workers, and so on). He might have paid attention to traffic congestion costs, although in 1944 that would have been less likely. What he would have missed out was the imaginative synthesis of individual wants that Howard provided and his normative ideas about community life. His assumptions about time preference would also have been crucial because even a very modest discount rate would have told heavily against the Abercrombie Plan. Actually the Plan was much helped by very low government-controlled interest rates whose rationale at a time of very scarce resources would now puzzle economists (and did so at the time).

The use made of economic techniques in subsequent regional plans tends to confirm this hypothetical example. These techniques have been especially applied, as one would expect, to transportation models based upon travel forecasts which themselves are derived from forecasts or assumptions about the distribution of population and facilities, car ownership, and the 'modal split' between public and private types of movement. These often sophisticated techniques reverse Howard's approach; instead of treating travel as a function of a satisfactory settlement pattern and 'way of life', they judge settlement patterns for their consistency with forecasted travel requirements. This reverse test can be useful, but the dangers of specifying the conditions for meeting one specific want, without much attention to a possible synthesis of wants, should also be apparent.[22]

Economic analysis has also been used on occasion to support the argument for new developments which are large enough to achieve economies of scale without running into the diseconomies of congestion. This was the cost–benefit element in Howard's own thought. But in the hands of economists the argument, if used at all (and not all economists agree with it) becomes necessarily generalised and vague. There is, for example, no real way of measuring an individual's W.T.P. for access to one packet of facilities rather than another. Thus the 'growth areas' proposed in the Strategic Plan for the South-East of England would range in size from under 250,000 to two million or more people and the proposal lacks the clarity of Howard's ideas.[23] I am not arguing that Howard's ideas are indisputably desirable, but only showing that economic techniques cannot derive any adequate alternatives from their chosen ground of 'individual preferences'. Also their difficulties over mapping much of the territory covered by social goals or ideals leads to a biased attention upon those specific demands which seem most capable of technical analysis and measurement; in this example, the demand for transportation.

7
Planning and Cost-Benefit

A. Rational Decision-making

A rational decision implies, at a minimum, a model or form of analysis for structuring the problem. It is plainly insufficient just to open an accounts book and enter 'costs' on one side and 'benefits' on the other, save perhaps for simple financial transactions. Policy problems can be and are structured in a great variety of ways which I do not intend to discuss fully. It will prove helpful, however, to start this chapter by setting out two very general models of decision-making. These are no more than loose logical frameworks, but they help to illustrate some basic problems about the choice of different methodologies for reaching decisions.*

The most familiar decision model is the ends–means one whereby a goal is first set and the most efficient means for achieving it is then sought subject to constraints. The single-goal model represents an obvious simplification of problem-solving which only makes sense where a single purpose (such as winning a war) can be treated as dominant over a wide range of issues; or where an administrative system is so closely and perfectly co-ordinated that each unit can concentrate upon a single task. (In this latter example, however, co-ordinators have to determine, combine, and allocate the various goals.) If, as is usually the case, there are multiple goals to consider, then logically a 'goals matrix' is required which will settle the trade-off functions between the various goals. There is the further problem that constraints upon the choice of means can be treated either as absolute (in which case they represent the negative counterparts of a completely dominant goal) or

* The words 'policy' and 'decision' are to some extent interchangeable here, and the choice between them depends upon the context. A decision is a single act whereas a policy is a general directive which, if consistently applied, will determine a number of different acts. (These acts are no longer 'decisions' because the policy is the decision.) In practice no such clear-cut distinction exists. Major individual decisions, like policies though to a lesser extent, have to be filled in with further decisions which are not in practice closely determined by, and indeed may be inconsistent with, the original 'decision'. The policy process can be thought of as a decision tree with higher-level choices determining, to a very variable degree, lower-level choices, and to some extent vice versa. There is the further point that 'policy' is a vaguer word than 'decision' and does not carry the same implication of a definite commitment. It is a familiar feature of political behaviour that policies 'float' in an aura of vagueness, and are very imperfectly and often reluctantly applied to particular situations. For further discussion see Peter Self, *Administrative Theories and Politics* (London, 1972) pp. 64–72.

qualified. To treat them as absolute is another simplification which invites obvious difficulties, but qualified constraints logically should be weighted in relation to goals. Finally, *if* goals and constraints have been adequately specified, the choice of means can be treated as a technical or efficiency issue. Even this is really a simplification because no choice of means is wholly technical or value-free, but only relatively so within a given context. The decision model is therefore set out according to the decision-maker's judgement and convenience; it can provide no adequate counterpart to the complexity of reality but renders the problem more manageable through allocating those factors judged relevant to the decision into three flexible compartments (goals, constraints and means).

Herbert Simon criticised the ends–means model for its inflexibility and its alleged confusion of facts with values. His 'behaviour alternative model' starts with the specification not of goals but of a given situation in which the decision-maker has various alternative courses of action open to him. He should examine as many of these possible lines of action as possible, trace out the factual consequences of each one, and then evaluate each set of consequences. The best decision is that which scores highest on the evaluation. Despite his claims Simon's model in fact involves the same elements and problems as the ends–means one. The decision-maker's search cannot be boundless or it would be infinite and must therefore be guided by constraints and by his standards of evaluation. The idea that factual consequences can be traced and then subsequently evaluated is also false, because only those consequences should be traced by the decision-maker which are relevant to his standards of evaluation.[1]

If we now equate 'standards of evaluation' with 'goals' the process has come full circle, and Simon's model is the same as the ends–means model turned upside down. The same three elements are present, have the same logical relations to each other, and have the same dependence upon the decision-maker's value judgements and practical convenience. None the less, this reversal of the original model is not without practical significance. In effect Simon's model *recommends* to the decision-maker a more open-ended approach, so that instead of first specifying his values and then applying them to the situation, he will first look at possible courses of action and judge which one is the best. In practice neither will be used in a logically pure way and probably the models will be mixed. But the difference of approach does make some difference to how an issue is treated.

For example, architects or town planners may first state their goals and then produce the design which seems best to accord with them; or they may produce several alternative designs and then ask themselves (or the public) which is the best one. Logically speaking this is a loaded example because the determinateness of the design should be a function of the specificity of the goals or of the evaluation criteria; thus the architect could produce several alternative designs which accorded with his goals unless these were highly specific. Equally the public could be asked to contribute to the architect's statement of goals just as (in the second case) they can be asked which design they prefer. The real point is that Simon's model puts more weight upon value judgements at the end rather than at the beginning of the process and thus makes it easier for laymen to participate in a public decision because they can observe its implications.[2]

In some forms of C.B.A. it is a familiar question whether the analyst is to maximise some prescribed set of goals, or whether he is to supply his own criteria of evaluation. In the former case politicians or administrators supply the social-welfare function, in the latter case the function is (theoretically) more objectively provided by welfare economics. The first approach is akin to the ends–means model, the second to the 'behaviour alternative model' of Simon. Simon himself appreciated this affinity because his ideal was to make the behaviour of 'administrative man' (about whom he was writing) as similar as possible to that of 'economic man'. Welfare economics supplies in fact the ideal evaluative criteria for Simon's model. If it is possible to convert the factual consequences of each alternative choice into a numerical scale of net aggregated welfare then the best decision can be scientifically determined. In this case one substitutes for the package of goals a system of measurement which can read off the consequences of choice in the same way as a cash-register reads off the goods in a shopper's bag. Simon himself did not draw this full conclusion – perhaps he was too canny – but it is implicit in his ideas.

However, economists cannot just rest upon their ideal methodology but have to fit in with the policy process. As was pointed out in Chapter 5, a familiar feature of this process is the right of elected leaders (subject to certain political or ethical constraints) to specify authoritative goals on behalf of society. The practical economist has to work with such goals, and if he believes in representative democracy he may want to do so. He may even have sufficient reservations about the theories of welfare economics to accept these political goals as reasonable approximations to the social-welfare function which he wants to maximise.

But another difficulty now enters. The goals of politicians are frequently vague and ambivalent. Many economists can testify to the frustrations they suffer through being unable to get policies specified closely enough for their purpose. Precision is as necessary to economic analysis as vagueness is to politicians. The analyst can now interpret or fill out the goals himself, and some do so, but there is no legitimacy (either political or economic) about this proceeding. This situation increases the extent to which the analyst can introduce and rely upon his own ideal methodology. This is naturally not the end of the matter since the politician, unless he likes the analyst's conclusions, will correct these according to his own criteria of evaluation. In fact it will often seem easier to politicians and officials, just like the public, to make *post hoc* judgements of this kind than to formulate consistent goals, as the example of architectural designs has already suggested. But these final corrections are often made without much understanding of the economist's methodology, so that the result may in fact be less rational than if political preferences were more clearly indicated to the economist in the first place.

These practical problems of decision-making may seem to have little to do with the adequacy of theoretical models. However, the basic theoretical models are intrinsically so limited and so flexible that their application cannot be separated from the policy process. In practice the use of C.B.A. does not usually conform to any ideal-type model, but entails some mixture of prescribed or assumed policy goals and constraints, interpretations (by analysts, officials, or others) of these goals and constraints, economic-welfare criteria, and final political evaluations. However, it *does* make a difference how these elements are mixed and related, and this point will be illustrated in the next section.

We can also look at the theory of decision-making in a different way. Because the elements that *could be* treated as relevant to any decision are so numerous and various, the issue has to be simplified in order to be manageable. Banfield draws a distinction between the 'active' and the 'contextual' elements surrounding any decision; it is the former which occupy the decision-maker's attention, although what items should be placed in this category can only be a matter of opinion or judgement as exercised by the decision-maker himself or conveyed to him by others.[3] Often the decision-maker will find subsequently that he has cast his net too narrowly, and he will be compelled by the intervention of others to introduce additional elements. (This is a well-known feature of public policy-making; the initial political or administrative statement of an issue is much simpler than it subsequently becomes, especially in pluralist societies.)

Another approach to this subject is to analyse the evaluative lens through which a decision-maker perceives reality. In Vickers's phraseology he makes 'appreciative judgements' which are configurations of factual and normative perceptions of the outside world, and these 'judgements' (sometimes partly unconscious assumptions) guide his view as to what can or should be done in a given situation.[4] These judgements vary with the position of the observer and also with the evolution of social ideas. Thus an administrative official will usually make a much narrower appreciative judgement about some situation than would an idealist or reformer. Through the evolution of ideas many issues change their apparent character, as when the existence of traffic congestion ceases to be viewed as a case for building more roads and gets viewed as a case for restricting traffic and promoting public transport. Thus any decision will be a product of diverse and often conflicting appreciative judgements. Any attempt at a logical division into 'facts' and 'values' encounters the difficulty that appreciative judgements unite both elements.

The extraordinary complexity of decision-making in both theory and practice has led Charles Lindblom and others to criticise the notion of a 'synoptic' approach to decision-making such as C.B.A. ideally represents. The comprehensive planner or analyst cannot know and manipulate all or even most of the relevant factors in his equations. Better results will therefore be obtained if responsibilities are factorised and widely dispersed so that each decision-making agent has a limited ground to cover. Moreover, 'partisan mutual adjustment' (see p. 117) is the best practical way of securing adequate attention for each factor affected by a decision. Partisans can both assert and mutually correct their various viewpoints, whereas the comprehensive planner lacks motivation and knowledge to take proper account of all these factors.[5]

Lindblom's case is a mixture of political and intellectual reasoning. However, the argument that a 'broader' decision must be *intellectually* harder than a 'narrower' one is not altogether convincing, because appreciative judgements may sometimes achieve more leverage upon the problem in the former case. This point links in with the inadequacy of a *political* bias towards dispersed decision-making. Societal decisions have to be related to the scale of perceived societal problems, and even an indifferent 'synoptic' viewpoint may be preferable to a series of partial viewpoints if the latter cannot cope with the relevant scale of societal problems. Moreover, whatever its virtues, 'partisan mutual adjustment' can often be modified to good effect, as when contending expert viewpoints are merged in the work of a joint team which is required to view some problem from a broader perspective.[6]

But while defences can be found for 'synoptic' techniques of analysis, C.B.A. still has formidable problems indeed over structuring the elements in its equations. As was pointed out in Chapter 3, the further an analysis is extended into the consequences of a possible decision, the greater the number of interests that will be affected. There is no *a priori* method available for defining these interests, although C.B.A. has a logical bias towards disaggregation because, thereby, greater precision should be obtained. But more significant still are the 'appreciative judgements' which influence how an issue is viewed and hence how far the effects of a decision are traced through space and time. Since (as Chapter 3 also showed) there are differences also in the use and appropriateness of valuation techniques which depend upon the selected perspective, this choice becomes crucial for the results. Loosely speaking, the more limited the perspective the more determinate the results, but their relevance to the decision then depends upon a careful understanding of the limitations of the chosen perspective. More comprehensive perspectives tend to produce results of increasing indeterminancy.

These problems of methodology are very weakly recognised in the relevant literature. Lichfield's use of ten criteria for the evaluation of alternative plans illustrates this point. Five of these criteria (Numbers 2 to 6) specify that the coverage should be comprehensive (e.g. Number 5 'Take account of all benefits to all sectors, including externalities') and he cheerfully argues that his own methodology, the Planning Balance Sheet, fully satisfies these requirements. This is plainly absurd. Criterion Number 7 requires complete quantification in money terms, which he admits is sometimes not possible, and Number 8 shows the incidence of costs and benefits on all sectors of the community, which is the specific (and useful) contribution of his own methodology. Criterion Number 1 requires evaluation to 'have regard to the stated or implied objectives (ends, values) of the decision-makers (which may or may not be the objectives of those for whom they are planning)'. This sounds like political realism, but the relation of this criterion to Number 10 – 'be usable as an optimising tool with a view to ensuring the best solution' – is simply passed over. The economist's idea of optimisation is not normally consistent with the stated or implied objectives of decision-makers, but problems over their reconciliation have not been faced. Lichfield's remaining criterion need not concern us here.[7]

Given the intrinsic *intellectual* difficulties and indeterminacies of structuring a comprehensive analysis, it is only to be expected that some special biases will occur in the appreciative judgements that analysts must make. They may of course share, and often do so, the policy and organisational biases of their employers or sponsors. This simplifies the work of structuring an analysis. If such partisanship is absent altogether, then the tendencies to a 'subject' bias or a 'technical' bias will be correspondingly greater. The former bias projects techniques that have been developed in one subject-field into other areas of policy-making (which may of course sometimes be fruitful), the latter bias elevates the significance of the techniques themselves and in particular those of quantification.

B. The Airport Controversy

The work of the Roskill Commission in Britain has been quoted already and its history also provides a good illustration of some issues of decision-making. Our interest here is not in airport controversies as such, or in the more technical aspects of the Commission's work which have attracted a considerable literature.[8] Some of these matters are already dated and will prove ephemeral.

From our standpoint the interest of the Commission is twofold. In the first place it offers a unique example of the attempt to combine a judicial and an economic treatment of a complex problem. Because of the powerful local objections that could be expected to be raised against *any* site for a major airport in the London region and which had already successfully defeated the Government's first choice for an airport (Stansted, in Essex), it became politically important to satisfy public opinion that the choice of site would be made upon fair and impartial grounds. Hence the appointment of the Commission itself as an impartial investigating body when the Stansted proposal was suddenly shelved by the Government in 1968 under considerable political pressure and hence also the appointment of a judge (Mr Justice Roskill) to be its chairman. The chosen instrument for selecting the best site was a comprehensive cost–benefit analysis prepared by the Commission's research team. This analysis was then extensively discussed and criticised at a long series of public hearings held in front of the Commission. These proceedings were judicial in form, most of the interested parties and also the Commission itself being represented by legal counsel although some objectors conducted their own case. Additionally a member of the Commission (a planning inspector) had earlier conducted a series of more limited hearings into local objections to possible sites.

It was clearly the hope of most members of the Commission, and particularly of its chairman, to utilise C.B.A. to find a decision that would be publicly regarded as satisfying the tests of both equity and efficiency. This wish was demonstrated by the Commission's attempts (prior to the hearings themselves) to get the maximum possible agreement among interested parties over the meaning and validity of its research team's figures; evidently it supposed such agreement to be possible, and initially it was not wholly disappointed. The weight placed upon C.B.A. was then confirmed by the spectacle of the flower of the English planning bar gargling gingerly and reverently with the cost–benefit figures, including more than a day spent by the Commission's own counsel upon explaining, a bit pontifically and dogmatically, the relevant methodology. The same point was shown by the Commission's patent preference for 'objective' economic figures as against the claims of pressure groups or even professional planning organisations whose views are recorded but not given much weight in its final report. (In the terminology of Chapter 5, it much preferred an 'economic' to a 'political' articulation of interests.) The weight which the Commission placed upon a comprehensive C.B.A., including the structuring of its extensive research work to suit this aim, provided a unique test of the practical use or value of this type of technique. It apparently assumed (and the Commission's counsel stated) that this analysis would represent the 'objective' part of its work, with 'subjective' opinions to be added later if needed.

Thus there are reasons enough to find interest in the Commission's cost–benefit methodology. But also, and secondly, the Commission encountered in their work the claims of what appeared to be an alternative methodology for settling issues of this type, namely comprehensive physical planning on a regional scale. Committed to and believing in the superior claims of C.B.A. as a comprehensive methodology, most of the Commission were unable to accept and perhaps to comprehend the alternative claims that could be made for 'planning', which was treated in their Report as partly an indeterminate factor (for which they had indeed evidence) and partly as a question of 'intangible' environmental factors that could not be satisfactorily measured. However, one member, the planner Professor Buchanan, took the opposite view in favour of the primacy of 'planning' and eventually dissented from his colleagues over the choice of airport site.

Our particular interest is to consider how the cost–benefit methodology fitted into the Commission's proceedings and conclusions, and what were the principal factors which lay (contingently or necessarily) outside its scope. I have therefore tried to isolate the principal factors in this decision process, following the Commission's own work as closely as possible. Naturally one cannot expect to get proof on these matters, especially in a short summary, but the evidence is at least suggestive of some conclusions. To tackle this programme I will deal in turn with (i) the structuring of the problem; (ii) the cost–benefit methodology; (iii) problems of weighting; (iv) regional planning; and (v) a general assessment. To repeat, many points must be left out but I do not believe that they would affect my conclusions.

(i) *Structuring of the Problem*

The goals and constraints prescribed by the Government to the Commission seemed specific enough. It was to enquire into 'the timing of the need for a four-runway airport to cater for the growth of traffic at existing airports serving the London area, to consider the various alternative sites, and to recommend which site should be selected'.[9] None the less, this statement contained some important appreciative judgements which shaped the character of the C.B.A. It assumed that another airport should be built to serve the London area and that this should be a four-runway one. It is true that the instruction to consider *timing* might logically have allowed the Commission to consider whether the selection of a new airport should be postponed, or whether a smaller airport or several airports should be constructed instead. Some critics later contended that the Commission ought first to have undertaken an analysis to settle whether the benefits of a new airport would justify its costs, when allowance was made for noise, pollution, and public subsidies for aviation; but this criticism was not heard initially or at the extensive public hearings. One organisation (the Town and Country Planning Association) did question the four-runway concept at the hearings, on the grounds that increasing population dispersal within the region constituted a case also for airport dispersal rather than for one great concentrated facility.

However, the Commission conducted its C.B.A. on the assumption that the *benefits* of a new major airport need not be proven, although a slight uneasiness about this assumption led it to include some loose arguments about the general benefits of air travel which were wholly out of line with the intended rigour of its economic techniques. The Planning Association's argument was also dismissed on the grounds that the chosen site ought to be at least capable of taking four runways as and when these were needed (also the treatment of planning issues was generally weak; see below). But in taking these positions, particularly the first one, the Commission was only accepting an appreciative judgement which was at that time held by much the greater part of 'informed opinion' as well as by the Government. Perhaps with its substantial resources the Commission ought to have probed further, but a common-sense interpretation of the word 'timing' did not give it much leverage, and investigatory bodies are notoriously anxious not to add to their work or to risk having to report that their task is unnecessary. None the less, these were fundamental assumptions.

The terms of reference did not specify how near to London the airport had to be or how it should relate to airports in other regions. England is small. Some 18 million people live in the South-East economic planning region within a maximum of 80 miles from the capital, but north of this region are other populous regions containing another 16 million people located mainly within a range of 80 to 180 miles. Because of the dominance of the existing London airports and internal rail and road communications, a high proportion of air travellers in other regions use the airports around London. What was the Commission to assume about this traffic? Frequent arguments were heard that better regional airports should, and eventually would, be provided for this Midlands population, and prospects for such airports would inevitably be much affected by the Commission's choice. If the new 'London' airport were located well to the north, between London and Birmingham, then a much larger proportion of this traffic would be pulled southwards whereas a new London airport east or south of London would have a converse effect.

A proper answer to this problem would require a national airports strategy or a concurrent set of regional strategies, but these were not available. Once again the Commission had to interpret its mandate. It made the simple but significant assumption of a stand-put situation whereby Midlands traffic would continue to be attracted southwards according to the capacity of the London airport system. However, this play-safe position heavily tilted the advantages of airport accessibility in favour of an inland site towards the Midlands, and this advantage was further confirmed by the C.B.A. methodology which credited 'generated traffic' to the more accessible sites on a model which allocated traffic to only one airport (Manchester) located in other regions.

Finally, the Commission itself made an appreciative judgement to the effect that the new airport ought not to be located close to London or to any major urbanised area (technically expressed by the exclusion of any site subjecting more than 50,000 people to excessive noise as defined by the Commission).[10] This absolute constraint somewhat confused the logic of noise valuations, because it suggested that a reduction of the existing nuisance around Heathrow Airport (which by this standard was intolerable) ought to be an explicit major objective. And yet Heathrow would have done so well upon the Commission's surface-access criterion as easily to have topped any list of sites. This suggests a basic contradiction in the criteria of evaluation. The same reliance upon simplified assumptions came in the final report with the argument that since so much had initially been conceded to the environmentalist's case, it was now reasonable to lay correspondingly greater stress upon picking the economically most efficient of the short-listed sites.[11]

(ii) *The C.B.A. Methodology*

This followed Simon's ideal type of 'behaviour alternative model'. A large number of possible airport sites were sieved according to various constraints, goals and selection criteria. Four sites were eventually selected; all were about 40 or so miles from central London (reflecting the already noted judgement about public opinion as well as air-control constraints); three were to the north of London (reflecting the locational pull towards the Midlands), and one was a coastal or off-shore site to the east (reflecting the need to canvass an adequate range of alternatives). For each site a long list of items was costed, including airport, road and rail construction; passenger and freight user costs; interference with defence establishments; losses to agriculture, to various types of property and to recreation; deterioration in residential conditions; airspace movements, airport services, and meteorology. The aim being to reveal the least-cost site, differential and not total costs were shown for each item with the best site marked as zero (total costs were initially published but were withdrawn from the final analysis as misleading). The items were then simply aggregated.[12]

Although perhaps too little time was given to the initial elimination of sites, this method coincided well with Simon's model for a rational decision. There was a wide search for alternatives, a detailed analysis of the consequences of each choice, and a single standard of evaluation which expressed all items on the same numerical scale. The obvious queries relate to the methods of listing items and of quantification. The items were rather miscellaneously assembled according to 'subject' and not group categories. Lichfield's adjusted version of the analysis so as to show the incidence of costs among various groups of producers and consumers provides useful additional information,[13] as of course might other ways of structuring the data.

The issues of quantification will not again be reviewed beyond noting that this is an extreme case of adding together items derived in a variety of ways. Here we are more concerned with any methodological causes of the intersite differences. Clearly many general techniques of analysis (such as the choice of a discount rate of 10 per cent, with coverage of 25 years from a base year of 1982) must affect the *size* of the intersite differences but will affect their relative placing only to the extent that costs at any site would be differentially spread over time. It seems doubtful whether a different discount rate would have much affected the placings unless applied discriminately between types of cost. Many specific methods both of forecasting and evaluation could have affected the intersite differences, but undoubtedly the most important was the forecasting of traffic flows under different airport systems. This was derived from a gravity model that was used to predict both passengers' choice of airports and also the amount of new traffic that was presumed to be generated by the relatively greater accessibility of some sites (more strictly of some airport systems). Gravity models as used by geographers are not impressively reliable, and this particular model (and still more the deductions about 'generated traffic') has been cogently criticised by other writers.[14]

The importance of this point can be demonstrated. 'Passenger user costs', in other words the costs of surface access to the airport, were finally listed as between £167 and £207 million higher for the worst site (Foulness) compared with the best site (Cublington). This difference was a little larger than the over-all cost difference between worst and best sites which were the same two places. Moreover, no other item showed up nearly so strongly, the next largest being a debit of £61 millions to Thurleigh for Defence costs with most items showing only small cost differences. Thus the site preference was based very heavily indeed upon the costing of surface accessibility, but this costing depended upon a very speculative chain of reasoning. First traffic had to be allocated according to the gravity model and *its* assumptions about population distribution, propensity to fly, road and rail networks, etc. at a future date. Then 'generated traffic' had to be credited to certain sites, on the assumption of some statistical relationship between proximity to an airport and propensity to fly. Then these figures were converted into travel costs (making assumptions about petrol and rail charges), to which the arguable factor of time costs was added. Finally, although this is a different item, the capital costs of Foulness were 'written up' to allow for the fact that it would be handling less traffic, hence conferring fewer benefits. The analysis also assumed that government would not intervene to direct traffic between airports, but this assumption might be justified on the argument that such intervention would be a cost to air travellers.

Of course highly speculative assumptions are an unavoidable feature of this kind of analysis, and whether they were well or badly done is not our main concern. If weightings for uncertainty had been included, as they surely should have been, the range of possible figures would have become very wide indeed, although the relative positions of the sites would not have changed. (On the other hand, if a different accessibility model had been used or tested, relative positions would also be affected.) But the criticism that the Commission mixed together relatively 'hard' and very 'soft' figures within a single equation was certainly true. In its final report it attempted to meet this criticism with an additional table that distinguished between capital costs, operating costs, and subjectively felt costs (such as time costs). This was closer to conventional economic analysis, and more logically defensible. It showed the coastal site of Foulness to be a mere £78 million worse than the best site on current and operating costs.[15]

One other significant methodological problem was the treatment of environmental 'intangibles'. At each of the three inland sites an airport would have had an enormous impact upon the local environment, including the community life of villages, churches and historic country houses, rural landscapes, and so on. At Foulness there would be few similar losses but wildlife would be seriously affected and a lonely coastline (currently used by the Army) would go for ever. The Commission could and did acquire a great deal of factual information on these matters but its problem was evaluation. Residential costs and noise costs and some recreational items were calculated, and initially values were put on churches and historic buildings (later withdrawn), but the valuation of landscape or wildlife was not attempted. The upshot was a special variety of 'horse and rabbit stew'. The Commission, having valued some environmental losses in its analysis, where they showed up very weakly, had to judge the remainder 'subjectively' at the end of the day.

(iii) *The Problem of Weighting*

Arguments for 'weighting' the figures in various ways, in relation both to the context of wants and to the distribution of costs and benefits, cropped up at the public hearings. One group of objectors argued that the desire to travel by air was in some sense intrinsically inferior to other desires such as eating food or enjoying the countryside. The Commission could not of course accept this argument which not only seemed contrary to the theory of C.B.A. (although supported in evidence by an economist), but was flatly contrary to their stated belief that air travel was as valid a want as any other. They were more impressed by the case for 'weighting for posterity' because a 10 per cent discount rate hardly seemed to do justice to the preservation of cultural treasures, of rural landscape, or of simple peace and quiet. But believing (quite correctly on a normal C.B.A. view) that the only grounds for weighting here would be inferences about the wishes of future generations, and confessing to a proper scepticism as to whether posterity would value a Norman church or Brent geese the more highly,[16] they shifted posterity to the realm of their subjective judgements except for crediting the future with a rising demand for peace and quiet (see pp. 137–9).

Other objectors argued the familiar case for giving the poor man's £ a greater weight, or at the least for showing the incidence of costs upon a group and income basis. One practical implication would be to devalue the travel costs of business men and foreigners. The Pareto principle also made its mark with the idea that some weighting should be attached to uncompensated losses, and the Commission reflected that only in one area (a part of Kent affected by the Foulness site) would the airport cause losses but no gains. Although their relevance was conceded, the Commission rejected these distributive arguments[17] partly on the grounds that the marginal income utilities of individuals were inadequately known.*

(iv) *Regional Planning*

A great airport not only has an enormous direct effect upon the local economy, but has further vast but variable effects upon the growth of industry and services, upon economic and social opportunities, and upon the nature of urban development. The airport will also have a differential impact in various locations, even within an already much developed urban region. For example, in a more rural area the airport will remain for a long time a highly dominant employer of labour, whereas in a more urbanised area there will be diversification of employment. There will also be differences over the availability of local services, transport and labour, and variable effects upon the possible scale and density of new development and the system of service centres. These factors, including the nature of the terrain, will affect the general attractiveness or appeal of the chosen area as a location for living and working.

These differential effects should constitute a substantial part of total benefits or costs attributable to an airport site, but would be most difficult to isolate and to measure. The Commission did not attempt to do this beyond an assessment of the costs of associated urban development which showed little difference between its four sites, but which did not attempt to

---

* Report, ch. 12, paras 65–6. It is surprising to find an old economic argument used here which is only relevant on the basis of an exclusive adherence to the 'efficiency principle' whereas most people at the enquiry clearly supposed that distribution was an ethical issue. In this and many other contexts (but not quite consistently) the Commission stuck close to the orthodox school of efficiency maximisers (see Chapter 6(D)). But the Commission added that 'even if we had such knowledge (about income utilities) we would be reluctant to recommend that government should use such a formula in public decisions'. They do not say why.

cover further growth effects, changes in the structure of local opportunities, general attractiveness of the area, and so on.[18] On these matters the Commission hoped for guidance from regional planners.

Political coincidence frustrated this hope. It happened that an expert team commissioned by government and local authorities was simultaneously preparing an 'authoritative' regional plan. The regional planners, though urged to do so by the Commission, were wary of getting embroiled in the airport controversy, the more so as the head of the team was also chief planner at one of the government departments (Environment) which would have to pass on Roskill's recommendation. Doubtless the planners reasoned that they would have to live with whatever airport site was finally selected, and that they would need to put much research into the interface between regional and airport planning. At any rate the opportunity was missed. The chief planner would say no more than that three of the Commission's sites would be consistent with the new regional plan and that one inland site (being in a proposed 'green sector') was inconsistent, although the planner did not regard even this point as an absolute objection. This opinion hardly offered blinding illumination to the Commission.

Subsequently, and only partially at the time, the importance of regional planning was apparent to some observers. The Foulness site, although fairly insulated in respect of noise, was close to several towns in South Essex, and this zone was designated by the regional plan as a 'growth area'. Since there was already substantial commuting from this area into London, and since industrial growth was uncertain, the airport would provide a valuable stimulus for the employment growth which was much wanted by the planners and the larger local authorities. Conversely, however, such a big airport might 'overheat' the local economy in relation to the rather limited capacity of the terrain, unless development went into an intended conservation zone. The issue was indeterminate and the long-term 'regional' benefits of this location and of the alternative inland sites were not carefully assessed. The Commission returned an agnostic verdict upon regional planning considerations.[19]

(v) *The Decision and its Evaluation*

The end of the Roskill story can be quickly told. The Commission set aside regional planning as neutral (except as an argument against one site) and largely disregarded the broad considerations that had been technically expressed as problems of weighting. Primarily therefore it had to balance the quantified intersite differences over costs against the unquantified intersite differences over environmental damage. Somewhat reluctantly and sceptically it made an ordinal ranking for the second difference which showed Foulness as fairly definitely the best site and Cublington more doubtfully as the worst one, which was a reversal of the cost comparison; but it then decided on general grounds that the cost difference was the more important one and recommended a Cublington site. The one dissentient, Professor Buchanan, concluded from factual evidence and personal observation that to put an airport on any of the inland sites, and most of all at Cublington, would be 'an environmental disaster', and argued for the coastal site of Foulness on both local and regional planning grounds. The Government quickly overturned the Commission's recommendation and chose Foulness (then rechristened Maplin).

The fact that, after such extensive work, the Commission's recommendation was promptly overturned by the Government in favour of its *worst* site (in C.B.A. terms), does not of course show the Commission's methodology to have been mistaken. Conversely, the argument that this was a highly rational report overturned by very biased pressure groups will not pass muster either. While the local anti-Cublington lobby *was* vociferous and influential, nearly all the local authorities and planning bodies in the region (who were at least more detached) favoured Foulness, while much of political opinion seemed to share Buchanan's environmental judgement about inland sites.

If one seeks to explain this brief history of a public decision (itself quite soon to be abandoned) the significance of general appreciative judgements stands out. The assumed necessity of a four-runway airport was derived from traffic forecasts, and yet only a few years later downward revisions of these forecasts provided a respectable argument for abandoning Maplin or any new airport for the time being.* The Commission's and Buchanan's views on the environmental acceptability of inland sites rested upon the same quite detailed (but not economically quantified) set of factual data which led them to opposite conclusions. An interesting point here is that the traffic forecasts are more determinate – *if* they are true it is widely, though not universally, assumed that they should be met; but since they are actually very speculative and erroneous they became merged with other considerations to produce erratic swings of opinion. By contrast, data about the local environmental effects of a project can be fairly reliable and will change only slowly; but its evaluation (and the evaluation of how *others* will evaluate it, i.e. public opinion) is very variable although opinion seems to be moving in a straight line towards more environmental protection.

Contingent political or administrative circumstances are also shown to have been influential. Thus, *if* there had been some attempt at national (or concurrent regional) airport strategies, still more *if* regional and airport planning had been positively co-ordinated, then the structuring of the problem of airport location would have been different and the Commission's solution might also have changed. These errors were not inevitable and they were irrational in the sense of a failure to co-ordinate closely interrelated policies. They could have been avoided by political and administrative fore-

* The Maplin project was scrapped by the Labour Government in 1974, as a result of (1) the need for national economy, (2) changed traffic forecasts, (3) doubts that Labour Ministers always had about Maplin. The oil crisis also influenced the climate of opinion. Curiously the Government's analysis introduced new planning arguments about the drawbacks of relying upon further expansion of Heathrow airport, which suggested that the whole issue might be far from resolved. See *Maplin: Review of Airport Project* (London: H.M.S.O., 1974).

sight. The fact that they were *not* foreseen seems to support, at a theoretical level, Lindblom's belief in the inevitability of 'disjointed incrementalism' and possibly (though not certainly) his conclusion that it is better to view all problems from a limited perspective. Equally, at a pragmatic level, this situation encouraged the Roskill Commission to pin its faith in one type of solution (comprehensive C.B.A.) because a proper alternative framework – the insights of physical planning – could not in fact be harnessed to the problem in hand.

Within these very considerable assumptions or constraints, what actual difference did the C.B.A. make to the Commission's conclusions or to their rationality? Let us suppose, for the sake of argument, that the research team did correctly measure those costs that could be meaningfully quantified, subject to the reservations belatedly introduced about the relative 'hardness' or 'softness' of the various calculations. The Commission could then argue that there was, as some commentators rather dubiously put it, a difference of perhaps £100 million in 'hard cash' between Foulness and Cublington. But what does this figure mean? If treated as a percentage of total airport costs or of total air revenues it seems rather negligible (which is why the Commission withdrew their figures of total costs as misleading and stuck to the intersite differences). Moreover, the Commission seems to have agreed, although doubtfully, that the difference would not prevent the airport from being *financially* viable.[20] This conclusion is hardly surprising because the 'real cost' of Foulness was a marginal increase in the price of surface travel, and though this would allegedly reduce air travel somewhat it would not preclude an adequate turnover or profit margin. However, the Commission argued that the significance of the figure was the alternative use of resources which would be forgone. (Actually if Cublington was built a part of these resources would go on increased air travel.) But the problem still remained of comparing this opportunity cost with the analysis of environmental damage and other 'intangible' factors. On this point the only meaning of rationality could be that evidence was fully researched and presented in as many meaningful comparisons as could be achieved. The Commission's analysis did not comply with this desideratum at all well, because the meaning of resource costs was not adequately explained. Although not economically quantified, the evidence about environmental damage was actually clearer. But in any case informed people could still logically reach opposite evaluations. 'Rationality' was here inadequate for reaching agreement.

If, however, one allows for all the uncertainties about the C.B.A. figures, it would seem plausible to claim no more than that the sites had been correctly ranked *ordinally* on the costed items. In that case one has the problem, at a minimum, of relating two different sets of ordinal rankings. Alternatively, if the factors in the C.B.A. are treated as separate ordinal rankings, according either to the Commission's analysis or to Lichfield's 'planning balance sheet', and if unquantified items are separated in the same way, one has a series of different rankings to co-ordinate. The trade-off operations become harder, but there is a gain in the specificity and intelligibility of each series. Or one could partially break away from the C.B.A.

framework and set up an alternative or complementary 'planning' analysis. In that event one might break away from the difficulties of ordinal comparisons in favour of looking for some empirical convergence between two different planes of analysis. This promising approach was not considered.

The C.B.A. also had indirect effects upon the Commission's proceedings. Whether or not it created a bias in favour of 'quantifiable' items, it certainly directed research efforts towards the production of data that could be converted into money terms. The urge to quantify had an obvious feedback effect upon the character and form of the research undertaken. This aim was quite consistent with the production of useful empirical material – for example, the analysis of Defence problems and costs showed that Foulness, which prior to Roskill had been ruled out on Defence grounds, was actually the most suitable of the sites from this standpoint.[21] But the C.B.A. methodology (as well of course as other considerations) did deflect the research team from the rougher empirical studies which could have illuminated the growth effects and the long-term environmental implications of the choice of a site for the new airport. Because these things were hard to quantify and belonged to 'planning' they were largely ignored.

At the beginning of an enquiry when a problem is structured, and at its end when a conclusion is reached, great importance attaches to the general appreciative judgements then made and to the simplifying assumptions that are introduced. To a large extent these conditions seem to be unavoidable because problems must be made manageable and no amount of evidence is conclusive unless relevant values are completely agreed. In the middle of the process there is more scope for rational analysis over the collection and organisation of data, and C.B.A. offers one technique for this purpose. But there are other possible techniques, as well as various forms of C.B.A., and none has any clear title to 'rationality' as such. The techniques work within the initial structuring of the problem and reinforce its latent tendencies.

C. Planning *versus* C.B.A.

In the last section the idea was introduced that 'planning' offers a methodology for decision-making which is as comprehensive as C.B.A. although very different from it. No real effort was made to judge the airport issue systematically from a planning approach, despite many suggestions that this ought to be done. Buchanan alone of the Commission members held that the issue was basically one of land-use planning, but even he did not object to the original reliance upon a C.B.A. methodology perhaps because (as he subsequently confessed) he did not fully understand its implications. To ordinary opinion the issue became simply a conflict between airport efficiency and environmental protection, and the Commission, Buchanan and the Government all drew up their positions on this basis. Yet it would be wrong to regard the methodologies of C.B.A. and planning as necessarily supporting these opposite positions. C.B.A. should in principle have costed all the elements in a planning analysis if the data had been there and capable of quantification; and planning was not just concerned with protecting the environment but with a wide range of effects that were relevant to human welfare, positively as well as negatively.

Comprehensive planning assumes that certain physical patterns of development will be conducive to human welfare. This sounds more abstract than it should. There need be no relief in an ideal morphology, although many planners have traditionally inclined to such a belief. In any event planning is contingently bounded by a complex existing pattern of land uses, activities, and relationships. It seeks to mould this pattern so as to improve the functional relationships between various activities, and thereby and in other ways to satisfy the assumed wishes or needs (economic, social and aesthetic) which individuals have about their environment. In modern democracies at any rate planning is a trial-and-error process trying to cope with perceived problems (such as traffic congestion, long journeys to work, and so on) and of promoting apparently beneficial relationships (such as towns with a 'good range' of jobs and facilities, or segregation of pedestrians and road traffic).

It is a nice question how far the welfare criteria of planners are compatible with those of economists or analysts. It can be argued that the main difference is not one of principle but of the practicability of testing results. Take for example the green belt 5 miles wide which has been used to prevent building all around the perimeter of Greater London. The green belt has protected the 'amenities' and house values (though not land values) of local residents; it has kept golf courses and country walks, for example, more accessible to Londoners; it has also frustrated many demands for building, displaced some development to more distant sites, increased housing costs and (to the extent that planners will allow) housing densities in London itself; and much else besides. In such a situation the analyst feels a natural and perhaps beneficial itch to try and find out who has gained and lost what from this formidable green belt. But the difficulties of separating out and tracing the effects of planning even with much research are obvious enough. One can produce some interesting evidence and make informed speculations, but hardly produce close calculations. This is even more the case if the planner asserts (as he will) that, for example, the benefits of a 'balanced' set of job opportunities in the New Towns, itself hard enough to assess, should partly be credited to the London green belt. Comprehensive planning produces a closely interlinked mesh of results which cannot be unscrambled for pricing purposes.

Problems of analysis and calculation apart, it seems improbable that the meaning of welfare is the same in these two cases. The planner may bow to 'individual preference' and make use of social surveys and even cost–benefit techniques, but his value assumptions are inevitably in large part cultural and normative for reasons discussed in Chapter 6. He is concerned with types of social judgement or opinion which cannot be reduced to sets of individual preferences unless 'preference' is understood in a sense too broad and too loose to be economically calculable. As Chapter 6 also conceded, the analyst may play a useful iconoclastic function in this situation by showing on occasion how far removed from any calculus of individual advantages the planner's criteria appear to be. This is useful because while the two standards of value are necessarily inconsistent, it can reasonably be held that wide deviations between them ought at least to be explained and justified.

The methodologies are different in other interesting respects. Planning works to some extent at least through reliance upon previous plans and policies which can claim to have achieved social and political acceptability; C.B.A. is in principle quite open-ended, and previous plans are no more than necessary or tiresome constraints. Planning ideally attempts a synthesis of elements through imaginative constructions; C.B.A. ideally factorises elements into their smallest components, measures, and makes a computation. Planning is a rather woolly profession concerned with authoritative but often vague interpretations of public interest; economics is precise and concerned with a calculus of private interests which *together* constitute its definition of 'public interest'. Conversely though, planning lays great store by empirical factual data of diverse kinds, whereas C.B.A. only seeks such data (sometimes rather impatiently) in order to convert it into economic equations. In the terms used in Chapter 5, planning tends to be 'authoritarian–democratic', that is to say it turns upon a partnership between elected leaders and professional planners; whereas C.B.A. is inclined to be 'populist–democratic'.

Of course, these are no more than the *tendencies* of two different methodologies as they seem to occur in practice, and they are subject to many exceptions and contradictions. Also the use of 'planning' here could refer not only to physical planning but to a general style of policy-making which can be contrasted with the style of economic techniques. To illustrate one can return to the conflict between the Roskill Commission and the dissentient Buchanan. He argued that the history of planning in the London region since 1945 revealed a steady development of policies for protecting the settled life of the countryside and for accommodating desirable developments on suitable sites (such as New Towns). The Commission's evidence and his own direct observations now demonstrated that the suggested inland sites for the airport (particularly Cublington) would be quite inconsistent with these established policies. The argument was perhaps not convincing because the government chief planner did not seem to share these opinions at all in his evidence to the Commission, although he did not of course have Buchanan's specific evidence. It would probably be more correct to say that this was the first dramatic confrontation of viewpoints over airport location, and that much public opinion veered towards Buchanan's position (as he did himself) during the hearings. The point here is his appeal to previous legislation, plans and precedents.[22]

It may be useful to draw up a table of these *tendencies* of the two methodologies (see overleaf).

But we have not answered the question of *which* methodology is best suited to tackle a problem such as airport location. Clearly it is no use asking whether this is a land-use or an economic-welfare issue because it is both, and either methodology could in theory be comprehensive.

		Planning	C.B.A.
(1)	MAIN CRITERION	Goals and policies	Effect on Interests
(2)	POLITICAL BASE	Authoritarian–democratic	Populist–democratic
(3)	POLITICAL STYLE	Consensus building	Partisan or arbitrative
(4)	TECHNIQUES	General–synthetic	Detailed–disaggregative
(5)	RESEARCH	Empirical studies	Economic quantification
(6)	PROFESSIONAL INPUT	Imaginative synthesis	Analysis and measurement
(7)	EVALUATION	General physical-cum-social effects	Economic tests of welfare maximisation
(8)	TIME SCALE	Medium or long term	*Ad hoc* and repetitive

Whatever the theory each technique in practice proves to be very much less than comprehensive because its methods can grapple with some parts of the problem much better than with others. To this limitation is added an inevitable professional bias over how the problem is perceived. Thus physical planning is not *necessarily* biased against the wants of air travellers, airlines, or airport authorities, but its practitioners see these wants as only pieces of a more complex jigsaw. For this reason they are prone, when they get round to it, to stress the indirect consequences of the airport for the location of other activities, for functional relations between these activities, and for environmental effects. They are the more prone to do so since their custodianship of generalised (environmental) values causes collisions with specialised interests, and indeed conflicts with the more specialised branches of physical planning itself, as shown in frequent conflicts between specialised transportation planners and general planners. The latter may also have a special concern with aesthetics or with the improvement of urban living conditions which does not fit with the assumption that all wants are theoretically equal; they may itch to substitute 'need' for 'want'.

C.B.A. is conversely biased towards those articulations of individual wants which can be isolated, observed, and measured, and its mathematical approach is congenial to elaborate forecasting exercises using statistical probabilities. The specialised aspects of airport location can therefore be much better covered than the generalised aspects where the analyst is at sea for lack of data. His interest in the quantifiable will make him dubious about the planner's general aims, and behind these doubts will be a quite justified suspicion of incongruent social (and logically also of political) philosophies along lines which were explored in the last two chapters.

The best pragmatic solution might seem to be the fusion of these methodologies in a team effort. This would require both that an investigating committee (such as Roskill) comprised individuals with a proper mix of different approaches to the problem, and that research was conducted by a mixed technical team. Alternatively, where two distinctive methodologies appear intrinsically difficult to blend, one could use the expedient of separate studies by two teams. This would then enable the investigating Committee to utilise the 'mixed scanning' of alternative perspectives recommended by Etzioni.[23] The Roskill Commission and its research activities were not set up according to either of these models but there is no intrinsic reason why they should not have been.*

At a theoretical level this chapter has confirmed the enormous intrinsic limitations upon 'rational decision-making' if rational is supposed to mean some objective or scientific basis for a decision which would command general acceptance if it were explained (see also next chapter). These limitations can be described as:

(*a*) The inevitable existence and interplay of partisan interests (a political factor).

(*b*) The pervasiveness and fluidity of 'appreciative judgements' which combine factual and value judgements into specific ways of viewing situations and problems (an intellectual factor).

(*c*) The large role of such judgements and of simplifying logical or political assumptions over the structuring of problems and over final decisions (an intellectual and a political factor).

(*d*) The intrinsic logical and professional biases associated with possible methodologies of problem-solving and their frequent linkage with the bias of political or organisational sponsorship (a professional factor).

This list is a mixed bag of intellectual and political influences upon the treatment of decision problems. The linkage between these influences has not been adequately explored here, but is of course crucial for the role of 'policy sciences' in decision-making. These 'policy sciences', which include C.B.A. and physical planning, certainly have intrinsic intellectual and methodological biases over the structuring of problems. The position of economics, as has been indicated elsewhere, is a curious one because it combines a considerable intellectual rigour at the theoretical level with a great deal of open-endedness in its practical applications. This is because the idea of 'optimisation' stands for a set of total conditions (themselves the subject of curious intellectual speculations) which can never be specifically identified so that the economic adviser or analyst is dealing in a practical world not of second-best but of *n*-best solutions, which circumstance allows and indeed compels him to make many simplifying value assumptions which are theoretically indefensible. The planner, however, has much less

* The Commission's membership was one judge, two engineers, one businessman, one planning inspector (to hold the local inquiries), one economist, one physical planner. It was instructed to conduct a C.B.A., but not told that all of its research and its public hearings must be geared to this exercise. It seems that there can have been no meeting of minds between the planner and the economist, and that the technically minded members supported the general faith in C.B.A. The Minister and his officials would at least have been wise to have thought harder about these methodological points.

rigorous intellectual theories* if he uses any at all (which is why economists often despise him), and he utilises a rag-bag of applied sciences and empirical knowledge.

The practical result is that both economics and town planning are intrinsically flexible enough for their applications to be structured by the 'policy situation'. This comes about in different ways. The economist descends from on high, so to speak, to give policy advice and, while intellectually free from organisational bias, is organisationally or politically constrained by the circumstances of giving that advice. The planner has no such empyrean to come from, or rather he has an impossibly vast and misty empyrean, and his policy advice is much more directly structured by his institutional position and duties. When nearly all professional planners worked in government offices, there was a great deal more consensus about the aims of planning (resting upon a political–professional 'partnership') than is now the case. Today an extensive use of public enquiries has led planners (and also economists) to disagree fundamentally and frequently in public with apparent intellectual ease.

But the conclusion should not be simply cynical. Accepting political and organisational partisanship as a basic fact of policy-making, and accepting that the intellectual biases of policy experts become subtly linked with their organisational positions or interests, there is still an important distinction to be made between political and professional contributions towards problem-solving. The latter approach is, in principle, more intellectually disciplined and rigorous, more research-minded, more respectful of 'the facts' as its chosen methodology sifts and tests these. A fruitful partnership is possible. Only the guiding 'appreciative judgements' which may cause new problems to be viewed through old lenses, or alternatively may introduce new intellectual and social perspectives, cannot be similarly differentiated. Innovation here may come from any participant in the policy process, and the most technically proficient expert may never be able to change his spectacles.

Also the organisational framework through which policy problems are tackled is of obvious importance. On this point there is no sufficient reason for backing Lindblom's faith in the 'hidden hand' of marginal incrementalism. His theories may serve as a useful warning against rationalist excesses, just like Burke's warnings to the French revolutionaries against a wholesale destruction of established institutions. But purely conservative theorising, though it may be elegant and persuasive, is ultimately not convincing and certainly not fruitful. The problem is to know *which* issues should be lifted to a more comprehensive viewpoint within the organisational scale, or alternatively should be partially detached from partisan pressures and farmed out to an independent agency of inquiry. As suggested earlier, a comprehensive approach can often bring about a synthesis of conflicting interests

---

* Traditionally physical planners have been prone to holistic theorising of a mystical kind, but modern theories of planning seem primarily to deal with the policy process itself which is a significant adaptation to the institutional problems of this activity. For an attempt to set out such theories see A. Faludi, *A Reader in Planning Theory* (Oxford, 1973).

in ways that do not remove but only modify partisan pressures. The attempt will be fruitful if the problem can be structured so that genuinely new perspectives and new data can be introduced at a more comprehensive or detached organisational level. The mutual discussion and attempted integration of expert views plays an essential part in this process and requires a choice of methodology.

The Roskill Commission is a disappointing example of this process, not because political and organisational detachment was lacking or because new perspectives and knowledge were not achieved, but because its methodological approach proved unrewarding. This is not in itself a demonstration of the inadequacy of C.B.A. as a comprehensive decision-making technique. A main reason for this failure was the unfortunate mixture of both dogmatic and confused 'appreciative judgements' about the nature of the problem that were held by the main participants and were embedded in the research team's work. In any case this is only one example and many would be necessary to test-out general hypotheses about the decision-making process. All the same the difficulties of a heavy reliance upon C.B.A., and the case for a broader 'mixed scanning' type of approach, have been demonstrated by this case history.

D. Postscript: 'Nonsense on stilts' and 'Roskillitis'

At the time of the Roskill hearings I wrote a polemical article which borrowed a phrase of Bentham to describe the methodology of the Commission as 'nonsense on stilts'. In a rejoinder Professor Alan Williams analysed the disease of 'Roskillitis', defined by him as the state of being inflamed by Roskill, and argued (1) that my criticisms were mainly mistaken or exaggerated and (2) that my alternative prescription of a planning methodology was substantively void and a recipe for obscurantist intuitionism.[24] Now that the dust has settled on this particular controversy it may be worthwhile reconsidering these arguments in a more detached mood as an appendix to the discussion of methodologies in this chapter. This aim requires some repetition, but may help to clarify further the comparison between C.B.A. and planning. Those sated with this subject should turn to the next chapter.

Williams summarises and seeks to rebut four of my criticisms of the Commission's use of C.B.A.

(*a*) I said

C.B.A. gets its plausibility from the use of a common monetary standard, but the common value of the pound derives from exchange structures. Outside such situations, common values cannot be presumed. . . .The greater part of the figures used. . .represent notional values which will never adequately be tested or validated by actual exchanges, and which are highly arbitrary in the sense that a very wide range of values can plausibly be predicted, depending upon innumerable opinions and assumptions.

Against this position Williams urges that market values are no more and no less 'objective' than any other consistent method of ascribing values, that is their acceptability depends upon the acceptability of the normative assumptions which underlie market behaviour. He then goes on to distinguish between the *method* of valuation which is used and the *precision* with which any particular factor can be calculated by means of that method. If a consistent method yields imprecise results, these results (he claims) cannot be described as 'highly arbitrary' since the value judgements which underlie them should be clear and consistent. The problem is only that these judgements cannot be precisely applied for technical reasons – but that (we are to infer) is a poor reason for not trying.

Williams's logic is correct, but it does not accord with the practice of Roskill or indeed of most C.B.A. exercises. In the Roskill case the basis of valuation was not adequately explained and seemed to shift in different parts of the analysis for reasons that also were not explained. (This point has already been developed in Chapter 4.) However a considerable use *was* made of inferred or hypothesised market values for measuring intangibles; while the imprecision of such data admittedly does not make it worthless or just 'arbitrary', its use does downgrade the significance of monetary symbols because (as I said) the figures cannot be adequately tested against exchange situations which (on this chosen basis) represent the only way that they can be validated. It is in this sense that the strictly limited credence which is conceded to monetary symbols as a standard of value gets very stretched in an exercise such as Roskill's.

> (*b*) the framework of analysis becomes distorted by the grotesque attempt to place all factors on the same monetary basis...such diverse items as 'capital construction costs'...which can be estimated within tolerable limits...and passenger surface travelling costs...which ...far outweigh differences in capital costs...and are based upon an enormous chain of speculative analysis.

My criticism here is admittedly an exaggerated way of arguing that Roskill should have distinguished much more clearly between the relative 'hardness' or 'softness' of their figures according to (i) the immediacy and (ii) the probability of the postulated effects. Williams rightly points out that any rational analysis necessitates the incorporation of such speculative elements and is not thereby vitiated, but he agrees that likely margins of error ought to be indicated. However Roskill did not sufficiently show or admit these margins of error.

> (*c*) The cost–benefit figures are incredible, not only because of the disparate basis of the items included, but because of the important items excluded. Of course, important factors often are excluded from policy judgements, but the appropriate remedy...is to point out the missing factor with the aid of as much supporting evidence as possible. . . . Instead of...being argued upon its broad merits...such an element

...has to be translated into yet more items within a cost–benefit equation....The limits of the financially quantifiable have to be stretched past absurdity, or the logic of the exercise will collapse. And once again more limited types of judgement – which ultimately in fact cannot be avoided – become confused and displaced.

Williams rightly claims that this is somewhat confused. The problem of missing factors arises with any type of policy analysis and is a criticism of C.B.A. only if the results are claimed as being more comprehensive and more scientific than could be the case. It was however the advancement of this claim on behalf of Roskill's methods which stimulated my outburst.

(*d*) The ultimate absurdity of the whole exercise is revealed, paradoxically, through efforts to increase its rationality. Following classical welfare economics, Professor Lichfield has argued...that distributional values should be included in the exercise....But is it in any way sensible to express such factors in monetary terms? Clearly there are almost as many views upon the precise weight that is to be attached to these 'distributional'...values as there are people in Britain. How is the Roskill Commission to proceed? Conduct a Gallup Poll of popular valuations in circumstances in which nobody will have to pay for the figure he hits upon with actual costs? Or ask the Government for directives? One only has to pose the questions to see the absurdity of such proceedings.

Williams sees nothing absurd in seeking evidence about distributional values, so long as the sources for such judgements, such as authoritative guidance from the public sector or evidence about individual preferences, is listed and applied consistently. Once again we are in the area of specifying a range of variability in the figures depending (this time) both upon differences in the sources of value judgements and also upon differences in their interpretation.

Taking these four points together I would concede that my criticisms of C.B.A. as exemplified by Roskill were somewhat exaggerated; but one must remember that during the long hearings nobody besides myself even questioned the principles of the Commission's methodology. It could not so happen today. *Sic transit gloria* C.B.A.

Accepting much of Williams's argument, my criticism of Roskill can now be revised as follows. In the first place the principles for selecting and for valuing the listed items were not explicit or consistent in the way that Williams himself requires. This is not actually a harsh criticism if one accepts the argument of this book (which need not be laboured further) that welfare economics cannot yield coherent principles of valuation. Secondly, and even if one rejects the first criticism, Williams's points would themselves suggest that wide 'margins of error' must be inserted at many points of the analysis in the interests of objectivity.

First, margins of error (in the proper sense of that term) must be included to allow for the varying probabilities of the postulated outcomes of a decision. This in itself is a non-economic constraint which cannot be debited against the use of C.B.A. It becomes a relevant criticism only if the omission of relevant margins of this kind leads anyone to suppose that quantified methods of evaluation are in some sense 'harder' (more reliable) than qualitative ones. This is not so at all, particularly of course when one is dealing (as is often the case) with some kind of joint product. For example, if a large highway is driven along the front of a seaside resort, tourists will benefit from the improved road access but simultaneously their wish to come and/or their satisfaction from their visit may decline because the 'character' of the resort has changed. (For some visitors of course the reverse may be true.) Now while techniques are available for measuring the inferred satisfactions of faster car journeys, they are *not* available for measuring the satisfactions/dissatisfactions caused by the changed character of the seaside resort. Yet the latter effects can be predicted in a general way quite as confidently as the former, and in this example must substantially affect the predictions both of car usage and also (when viewed as part of a joint product) of the inferred satisfactions of their owners.

Secondly, 'margins of error' are to be inserted to allow for the imprecision of valuation techniques over the measurement of externalities. If the valuation theory used is genuinely consistent and coherent then it is correct to use this language; but if this very exigent condition is not satisfied, then one is in the realm not of margins of error at all but of differences of value judgement. In practice both reasons for using a range of figures have to be allowed for here, and it is hard indeed to disentangle them.

Thirdly, there are the quantitative variations which follow logically from different value judgements about issues of distribution and which also can be inferred (if one follows the arguments of Chapter 6) from variations in the value premises underlying economic and political behaviour. Williams boldly ventures on this treacherous ground so far as distributive issues are concerned and accepts the need for a range of figures.

The only realistic conclusion that I can draw is that, if these prescriptions were in fact followed faithfully in a comprehensive C.B.A., then the results – while admittedly more objective – would in all likelihood be completely indeterminate. This simply confirms the conclusion reached in Chapter 4. It would then indeed be a question of paying your money and taking your choice, depending upon what combinations in the possible range of figures one chose to adopt.

The rationalist defenders of C.B.A. would still argue that, even if my conclusion is true, it is a clear gain to make the grounds of an opinion or a decision as full and as explicit as possible. Certainly this is a respectable rationalist viewpoint that ought not to be dismissed through laughing it out of court on the alas, all too true grounds that virtually no one save a cost–benefit analyst (and by no means all of them) would in practice go through the requisite intellectual contortions. A rationalist position deserves rational rejoinders and two may be suggested:

(1) As noted there are two reasons for what economists call 'sensitivity

analysis', represented by technical difficulties of forecasting or measurement, and by differences in value judgements. Now it is clearly to the advantage of analysts to stress and to concentrate upon the former set of difficulties since these might in principle be reduced by improved techniques, thus expanding the range of their art or capacity. It may also be advantageous, since the value issues clearly cannot be dodged, to shuffle these off to the realm of fundamental conflicts of principle where they can be discussed abstractly without overburdening the working world of techniques. Williams's arguments exhibit both tendencies, notably in his misuse of 'margins of *error*' to refer also to value judgements, although he is prepared to take the distributive bull by the horns. The difficulty, to repeat, is that the nature of welfare economics does *not* permit the tidy separation of techniques and values which would suit the analyst. Thus the conditions under which 'sensitivity analysis' is conducted are replete with unsolved problems about facts and values.

(2) Secondly, however, one must ask whether it is in any sense fruitful or realistic to try to pin down the whole elastic realm of social and political debate about values within a range of postulated figures. Since individual valuations are *intrinsically* elastic and related to the differentiated roles and situations experienced by any one individual, it looks like naive empiricism to suppose that the individual can be pinned to any figure, except in a somewhat arbitrary and casual way, unless (as was suggested earlier) what he regards as his economic interests are specifically engaged in an exchange situation. This does not mean that individuals are all impervious to rational analysis and debate, but that the form which this debate usually takes is one of listening and sometimes responding to claims and counter-claims. Of course such debate *might* logically lead an individual to express an integrated verdict in the form of some figure or range of figures, although (as Chapter 6 said) it is just this 'integrated verdict' which the techniques of C.B.A. seem to miss. If the analyst wishes to match this range of debate as honestly as he can with a range of figures, plainly no harm is done – although it will be done if the analyst uses this appearance of democratic sensitivity to buttress his own concoctions. But whether in fact sufficient good is done to set against the risks of abuse seems to me to be very doubtful. At any rate, I would not wish to decry the rationalist aspirations of some cost–benefit theorists, but only to suggest that it is mistaken of them to suggest that the elastic processes of 'qualitative' debate are intrinsically less rational than quantitative techniques. In terms of the possibilities of the human condition the reverse seems to me to be true, and the analyst's position rests upon a kind of utopian search for certainty which in the nature of things cannot be satisfied – and which hence can become *less* rational than humbler devices.

Williams's second line of argument is that the methodology of planning cannot (as I contended that it could) offer any substantive alternative to the use of C.B.A. He is right in suggesting that the concept of public interest as used by planners and indeed by all policy-makers is inherently vague and imprecise. These no doubt regrettable attributes are inherent in the nature of the policy process, at any rate in any type of system that can claim to be democratic. This is because the democratic decisions derive from a diverse range of opinions and influences that are conveyed by various routes to the decision points, and whose contributions are sieved and limited according to certain controlling concepts of legitimacy. This picture, as has already been made abundantly clear, is not at all equivalent with a *real-politik* view of the conflict of interest groups. On the contrary, it calls for some kind of balance between the sources of democratic authority that were sketched in Chapter 5; and it allows too for the concept of some measure of professional authority working within a context of democratic influences and constraints. Thus the professional planner is not a mere technical auxiliary of political forces, he is or should be an individual whose understanding of his chosen field enables him to make *some* positive (and hopefully imaginative) contribution to policy-making.

Now clearly any concept of public interest which recognises a plurality of contributions whose respective degrees of legitimacy are themselves (within limits) a subject for debate, and whose actual force must vary greatly with circumstances and abilities, cannot but be a vague one. Public interest as used by a planner can legitimately refer to no more than his attempt to offer an integrated professional interpretation of the requirements of public opinion as derived from a complex and balanced policy process, and as modified by his own understanding of the relations between causes and effects, and between social challenges and responses, within his chosen field.

But this undeniably vague and tentative view of a democratic planning process needs to be compared, in respect both of its legitimacy and of credibility, with the process of C.B.A. Now C.B.A. in its ideal form, as has already been argued, shines with the clear white light of a populist democratic science which purports to offer no more and no less than the precise aggregated sum of individual wants. But what if individual wants cannot intrinsically be articulated in this one-dimensional way (quite apart from the problems of monetary quantification), but necessarily depend upon a more complex structuring of influences, including therein the roles of political leadership and of professional guidance? What if this more complex view is itself legitimised by social and political beliefs? In that event the legitimacy of C.B.A. is confined at best to being one acceptable source of policy influence rather than to meeting its cherished aspiration of intellectually authoritative guidance to policy-makers.

Precisely the same limitation and constraint can of course be placed upon the role of the planner with the difference that, lacking a coherent body of intellectual beliefs, he is less likely to deny this restriction. Admittedly many professional planners are not, as they should be, intellectually humble. But if they can achieve humility, planners have the intrinsic opportunity to make a more substantive contribution to decision-making than C.B.A. because they have less reason to dispute the complex methods of precedent and adjustment whereby the policy process works. Indeed their position is anchored within the history of the policy process. In contrast C.B.A., through seeking to give a snap-shot view of the gains and losses of each specific decision, lacks any basis for policy continuity other than the very variable applications of its own intellectual foundations. The principal substantive value of C.B.A. is in fact as an occasionally potent critic of sacred cows, not as a workable or acceptable basis for continuous policy-making.

Williams also argues that I bring in the planning process to override those very market values to which I have ascribed objectivity. This is true, but the 'objectivity' of market prices is limited and relative – it refers only to the capacity of individuals to register meaningful indices of their economic preferences under appropriate conditions, and it does not suppose that such indications are the only or sufficient grounds of public policy-making. Williams, of course, equally accepts that market indicators cannot express such social values as (for example) the interests of future generations in environmental protection but contends that 'unless such valuations are expressed directly (or indirectly) in money terms they are bound to be vacuous (and therefore useless operationally)'. But here surely he confuses the intellectual possibility of expressing a policy decision in monetary terms with the grounds for and even the fact of the decision itself. Some of our ancestors made a very effective job of conserving their rural estates for further generations; but they did not need the concept of the marginal rate of social time preference in order to make or to justify their decision on this matter.

8
Economics, Government and Society

A. Introduction

This chapter takes a look at some of the implications of economic techniques for modern governments and societies. The first part deals with a now familiar theme; how far can the new budgetary techniques which seem to promise so much actually change or 'reform' the processes of bargaining over resource allocation? The next section offers some speculations – they are no more – about the influence of economic ideas and techniques upon the organisation of government. The final section reverts once more to the theme of rational decision-making, relates this to certain ideals of welfare economics, and asks where these ideals are pointing and why they are influential in the modern world. Again the tone is speculative, and the verdict though critical is not intended to be dogmatic.

B. The Budgetary Game and Resource Efficiency

To render the allocation of resources more 'rational' and 'efficient' has become a major concern, almost an obsession, of modern governments. Various techniques and methods have been tried out for this purpose, with bewildering changes of nomenclature. The most comprehensive package of techniques to date comes under the name of P.P.B.S. (planning, programming and budgeting systems), although doubtless a differently styled package will have been launched before this book appears. After its initial use in the Defense Department in the United States, President Johnson ordered in 1965 that P.P.B.S. should be introduced into as many branches of the Federal Government (initially 20) as possible. The full medicine of P.P.B.S. proved too powerful or unpleasant to be swallowed by the agencies and Johnson himself lost interest so the dose was cut down and made 'selective'. Similarly, partial versions of P.P.B.S. have been adopted, under various titles, by the governments of Britain, France, Germany, and indeed most Western countries.

The subject is slippery because the techniques in question can be packaged in so many different styles and combinations. There is now a large literature on the subject, despite or perhaps because of Aaron Wildavsky's crack that 'no one' (in practice) 'knows how to do P.P.B.S.'[1] It is not my aim to explore the subject in depth, but to consider some issues about the scope for improving the 'rationality' of the budgetary process. But it should be said first that Wildavsky is at least right in the sense that everyone presents the aims and connexions of these techniques in his own special way, and a selective summary necessarily overlooks some claims that could be made about their utility.

The general purpose of P.P.B.S. and its variants is to improve through systematic planning the ways in which governments use economic resources that are under their control or influence. This task is plainly enormous, being almost equivalent to managing the entire economy so as to maximise social values. However, the focal point and leverage of P.P.B.S. is government budgets, which even so make enormous *direct* claims upon resources. When one introduces also (as one must) the intended and actual effects of public programmes upon economic, social, and political behaviour, the analytic net must be cast extraordinarily wide. In practice such broad reviews, if attempted at all, have to be very selective, and the main thrust of the programme has to rest content with more limited tests of resource efficiency. Still it is worth noting that intelligent commentators, in the United States particularly, see such issues as the incentive effects of public programmes upon private behaviour as being among the more important tests that might be applied to the effectiveness of public spending.[2] Whether such investigations are best done through the comprehensive and somewhat ritualistic rubric of P.P.B.S. is another question.

One can distinguish at least four leading ideas in the P.P.B.S. package:

(1) government budgets should be presented on the basis of outputs not just inputs; for example instead of showing the costs of staff, materials, etc. (the traditional rubric), they should show the cost per school or hospital or missile system;*
(2) government expenditure should be tentatively projected forward up to 4 or 5 years, so as to show the cost implications of existing or prospective programmes. (This is the task of the Public Expenditure Survey Committee, P.E.S.C., in Britain);
(3) evaluation techniques should be introduced to test the benefits of public programmes; and
(4) selective studies should be made of problem areas of expenditure. (This element is represented in Britain by P.A.R. – Policy Analysis Review.)

In very general terms the whole package is supposed to amount to a dynamic process. Policy goals are matched against available resources and

* This corresponds to the earlier notion of 'output' or 'programming' budgeting. Since the traditional input type of budget is usually still kept for financial control one has to produce two budgets and build a 'cross-walk' between them, particularly if legislatures insist (as the U.S. Congress has done) upon retaining the traditional budget. The more novel feature of P.P.B.S. is the attempt to structure government outputs according to basic goals so as to facilitate subsequent evaluation. In practice this is very difficult – see below.

vice versa; alternative methods of pursuing the goals or using the resources are investigated (an element not specifically mentioned above); programmes are evaluated for goal and resource effectiveness; and the cycle is repeated. Another way of viewing the process is to say that 'planning' leads to 'programming' which is then incorporated in the annual budgetary cycle. But the general formulations are of limited help because they can be activated through a great number of organisational routes and methods, leading to varying emphasis on the possible aims. As the two examples from Britain in the last paragraph show, elements can be abstracted from the P.P.B.S. package and separately institutionalised. Thus in Britain the principal innovations have been systematic long-term budgeting (P.E.S.C.) and – more dubiously since the success of the experiment is much in doubt – selective programme studies (P.A.R.), whereas output budgeting and evaluation techniques are at a very experimental and tentative stage. By contrast, American administrators have become cynical about the possibility of persuading Congress to swallow long-term budgeting (and some also consider that since future decisions must be political, the reliability of future estimates is pretty thin);[3] but despite initial setbacks they have perhaps greater faith in output budgeting and evaluation techniques.

Coming to the central subject of resource efficiency it is obvious that element number (3), the evaluation techniques, is the critical one. We are back at the familiar problem that it is possible, at least in a financial sense, to know the costs of various public outputs, but how are we to evaluate and compare the benefits? To know the physical outputs of public expenditure – the numbers of children passing through school or patients through hospital, and so on – is not to know the social outcome (the effects on welfare or well-being) of a given block of expenditure. Failing the revelation of some uncontestable 'social-welfare function', one can do no more than judge the 'benefits' of a public programme in a variety of ways, by different tests.

(1) *By Reference to Policy Goals or Objectives.* This is often regarded as the test of *political* efficiency. However, it is a very slippery and uncertain one because political leaders are often vague or ambivalent about goals.[4] Also the targets may deliberately be set low to assist accomplishment or high to encourage effort; and goals or targets may be largely forgotten by politicians by the time evaluation becomes possible.

(2) *By Reference to Professional or Administrative Standards.* This is the usual test of *professional* efficiency and is often important and relevant. Such tests include safety standards for public works, examination standards for education, crime detection standards for the police. The snag with such tests is that they are often partly circular in the sense of using the achievement tests of those providing the service. For example, the figures of crimes solved by the police will exclude those that have not been detected and may be suspect for other reasons; the number of examination passes will depend upon the standards or decisions of teachers themselves and in any case may be a poor guide to the benefits of education. Standards are more objective

when set or scrutinised by independent investigators. (This is the function of administrative inspection, a possible snag being that the inspectors may be too influenced by the methods they are supposed to be reviewing, especially if they are in the same agency.) Sir Geoffrey Vickers generalises the value of this test to the point of claiming that 'goals' are very much less important than 'standards', because the aim of administration should be to establish tolerable minimum standards governing both social relations and those between human beings and their environment.[5] His point is well taken, but unfortunately many professional standards are (perhaps necessarily) much narrower and more inbred than his theory requires. The Vickers concept is also relevant to the next test.

(3) *By Reference to Social Indicators of 'well-fare' or 'ill-fare'.* The relevance of such indicators to the achievements of public programmes is obvious, and social indicators have attracted increasing interest from this standpoint.[6] For example, data about changes in housing conditions (slums, overcrowding, occupancy rates, household formation, and so on) are patently relevant for the success or failure of public housing programmes. The difficulty with this *social* test of efficiency is that social changes occur from a great variety of causes, some of which come only partially or not at all under the control of government, while, in addition, the overlapping effects of different programmes are hard to sort out. This test draws attention particularly, and very necessarily, to the indirect effects of public facilities, controls, and subsidies upon social behaviour; but one here enters a minefield of policy analysis in which causal chains can be traced only tentatively, and with the aid of much intelligent research, while even so value judgements about what has caused what are almost impossible to avoid. There is a sort of parallel here with electoral behaviour – just as an electoral majority does not scrutinise the work of government closely but gives a crude verdict of approval or disgust, so a scrutiny of social indicators offers guidance about the apparent success of public programmes; are conditions in this policy zone getting better or worse? Social indicators also show up danger points or points of regression in social and environmental standards, and thus become very relevant for the future agenda and policies of government, whether or not they can be accurately interpreted in a causal sense. But they are very indirect and uncertain, although politically important, tests of programme effectiveness.

(4) *By Reference to the Economic Benefits of a Programme.* This *economic* test of efficiency is the elusive goal of cost–benefit analysis, which in theory is supposed to be the most rational and comprehensive one because it matches like with like – benefits with costs, both in money terms – and thus seems central to the aims of resource planning. But the economic benefits of a public programme cannot be equated with its costs, which would be circular, and adequate independent tests of economic benefit are sometimes virtually impossible, at other times difficult or tendentious, to discover and apply. In the case of indivisible public goods, such as defence, law and

order, space exploration, and so on, no market for the good can be postulated other than the political body which votes the cost. Thus economic analysis has to rest content with cost-effectiveness, following the old idea in Defence for example of getting a 'bigger bang for a buck' (or the same bang for fewer bucks). But cost-effectiveness is critically dependent upon non-economic criteria of possible benefits. In evaluating alternative weapon systems the critical questions are whether they ever may be or can be used, what their effects will be (prospective or actual) upon possible enemies, allies, and neutrals, how they will affect the methods and morale of the armed forces, and other imponderables. Compared with these issues, the task of pricing the technical potentiality of a weapon system is child's play. The example of the war in Vietnam hardly suggests that McNamara's P.P.B.S. at the Defence Department payed off in policy analysis; where it did pay off was in checking some of the extravagant rival projects of the armed services, which is the old goal of public economy under a fancy name.

Very many public programmes, however, do offer divisible services that are assigned or available to individuals whose willingness to pay for the service (as a test of benefit) can often be estimated in a variety of ways. Unfortunately these tests are very partial and tendentious because of the existence of substantial externalities and welfare redistribution effects which are often prime reasons for government providing the service at all. Thus an educational programme for underprivileged children (such as the Headstart programme in the United States) can hardly be evaluated in terms of the increased earning capacity thereby produced – itself very difficult to guess at – because the benefits of the programme also should include enhanced social opportunities, leisure interests, and civic participation for the children in question. It is the height of artificiality to put money values on these intended results, being hard enough to guess at the results themselves. Moreover there is also the problem that a citizen's political estimate of some public benefit often seems to differ from his inferable market estimate for reasons discussed in Chapter 6.

The inferred market values of public benefits are most useful for analysis when they appear to be substantially either higher or lower than the costs of provision. The latter is the more usual situation. Thus Schulze points out that the costs of providing irrigated water to farmers in the West are very high in relation to the prices which the government charges and also to the inferred market value of the water. He then points out that possible redistributive goals such as aid to agriculture or to Western states could be accomplished in much more efficient ways. Of course if there is an unalterable wish to give a very large bonus to a small group of farmers, from some political compulsion, the analyst can say no more than that (as Schulze does say) it might be cheaper to retain the farmers on handsome pensions than give them an indirect subsidy sufficient to rehouse ten times as many homeless families.[7] But the force of this example is its prodigality, perhaps matched by other cases in the United States, which makes possible an unambiguous appeal to the old-fashioned virtue of economy.

These considerations about evaluation are also related to how a programme 'structure' and its constituent 'elements' are set up. Theoretically, especially if an *economic* input–output model cannot be plausibly constructed, the programme structure is often recommended to be based upon sets and subsets of policy goals; theoretically again, one might construct a logical hierarchy of such goals or a 'goals matrix'. But in practice: (*a*) policy goals are hard to clarify, and are multiple and often conflicting; (*b*) they cut across departmental and other organisational boundaries; and (*c*) they are resistant to presentation in tidy hierarchical bundles. Thus, in practice, the structure usually comprises lists of organisational tasks, partly rearranged so as to express major policy aims or supplemented with descriptions of such aims.

P.P.B.S. then can be used for a variety of purposes such as (*a*) clarifying the pattern of public expenditure, (*b*) forward projections and analysis, (*c*) evaluation of benefits, and (*d*) analysis of alternative options within some framework of assumed goals and evaluation techniques. The first two elements are 'macro' in nature, and must cover the whole system, while the latter two elements can be (and if done in depth must be) treated selectively. These latter elements represent tasks of policy analysis which ought to be the concern of public agencies anyhow, whether or not there is P.P.B.S. A critical question, beyond the scope of examination here, is whether P.P.B.S. facilitates or (as a few critics suggest) actually impedes specific policy analysis of a fruitful kind. It seems probable that a comprehensive 'systems' approach has tendencies in both directions.

However a budgetary system is set up, there are familiar problems about the comparative evaluation of different programmes which are toughest at the higher levels. How is one to compare the marginal utility of £100 million spent upon Education or on Defence? To attempt a reasoned as opposed to a crude value judgement one must analyse such matters as: (*a*) the respective force of *environmental* factors in relation to each service, for example changes in the school population or in the vulnerability of the country to air attack; (*b*) economies of scale and of increasing or decreasing returns, for example it might seem to be the case that only another £200 million more would make a significant difference to the effectiveness of Defence, whereas relatively little extra spent upon some Education services might raise their average effectiveness; and (*c*) judgements about the respective efficiency with which each service utilises its existing resources (an economy and organisational judgement). But while such judgements ought to be attempted, the relevant data is extraordinarily hard to separate out from the partisan claims being advanced for each service, and even a budget examiner will find it difficult to stand clear of his basic value judgements and prejudices – certainly no politician is likely to do so.

As one moves down the line it becomes increasingly meaningful to compare the benefits of different services, because these are easier to relate to the same or similar policy goals, and for results to be scrutinised from similar perspectives. The real gain concerns the number of meaningful questions that can be asked, rather than the improved scope for specifically economic evaluations, although that also will occur to some extent. For example, numerous questions can be asked about the respective worth of two different programmes of adult education. Economic evaluation necessarily comes in when the analysis of respective benefits is related to the schedule of costs, and the function of the economist is or should be not that of solving the equation but of providing some helpful information to the policy-maker. But because the cost information is indispensable, at any rate in a financial sense, it does not thereby follow that further economic analysis should occupy a dominant place in the final decision. The most fruitful economic contributions come as part of a team effort in which economic information about marginal costs and (to the extent possible) benefits is related to other contributions concerning institutional conditions and social behaviour. Such economic contributions need to be modest and undogmatic, and are being developed in particular fields.[8]

Critics or cynics sometimes say that P.P.B.S. and the like represent wasted effort because public expenditure decisions are inevitably political. If by 'political' is meant the sum of competing partisan pressures (parties, interest groups, public officials, and so on) concerned with the claims of particular services, the assertion is broadly true, although some reservations must be added. We now possess some informed accounts of the 'budgetary game' as a political process, and the same accounts show how partisans can absorb and use the new techniques to their own advantage.[9] Thus part of the effect of P.P.B.S. is to make the budgetary game more sophisticated without changing its broad character or results.

Therefore, as economists themselves sometimes recognise, the most important evaluative questions to raise about the budgetary process are political ones. How diffused or concentrated is the process? How many or few participants (interests) are represented and through what routes? Is it open or secret? What are the respective roles and influence of politicians and civil servants and of different *types* of politicians and civil servant? In so far as one can answer these questions, one can compare the answers with different normative models of the policy process and *their* possible justifications.

However, this political character of the budgetary process is fatal to the use of economic and other techniques only if one assumes (as some welfare economists do) that objective standards of social welfare could be discovered and applied quite independently of the political process. On any less absolute view, the techniques could still be claimed capable of improving the budgetary process in at least two principal ways within a general political framework.

(a) *By providing information that will increase the rationality of the bargaining process.* This notion requires elucidation. If one merely means that partisans will stick to the same goals, but argue for them more sophisticatedly with the aid of additional data, then the claim for improved results is not obvious. The net budgetary results might be the same as before, but reached after greater effort and expenditure; or if the more sophisticated protagonists are gainers why is this to be commended? The relationship between more information and social gain becomes much more convincing if the information enables partisans to apply their goals or their values more accurately. This development will not eliminate value conflicts, but will make the process more realistic in the sense that participants are more likely to achieve what they want; and more rational in the sense that the bargains struck should on balance produce a larger totality of desired benefits. It is certainly the case that even convinced supporters and opponents of some programme are often very ignorant about the programme's likely effects, or about alternative measures which might be preferable. Thus a general case for more skilled analysis is not hard to make out on these grounds.

But is P.P.B.S. actually useful for this purpose? It seems that most of the information that it provides is unusable or anyhow not used by politicians and other budgetary participants except for the technical experts.[10] It is not hard to guess why. The most natural approach to policy analysis is to start with some problem, goal, or presumed need and fan out to trace its implications (including resource constraints); or else to consider how given resources could be best deployed within a limited range of easily related alternatives; in other words, the bias runs from the micro to the macro, and from policies and their consequences to resource availability, rather than in the reverse order. At any rate legislatures have conspicuously failed to make much of the comprehensive expenditure analysis with which they have been regaled; the assumptions and interconnexions are difficult to grasp and seem too remote from urgent policy concerns. In Britain little has been made by Parliament of the P.E.S.C. exercises; the annual debates are occasions for pleas on behalf of particular services or disquisitions upon the general state of the economy. Following the logic of resource planning as recommended by economic consultants, Parliament set up a comprehensive Select Committee on Public Expenditure; but although the sub-committees of this body have published some useful information they have largely fallen back upon traditional kinds of policy review. They have not really addressed themselves to the interconnexions of public expenditure or to the assumptions behind expenditure forecasts. The idea of comprehensive planning fails because legislators, and to a large extent Ministers also, cannot follow the convolutions of the analysis.

It may be tempting to write off these failures as due to the inadequate intelligence or rationality of politicians, but this is certainly not the whole story. Policy analysis is intrinsically very difficult to do intelligently, and it is loaded with an agenda of specific problems about which much has already (as a rule) been said or written. New economic techniques embodied in budgetary requirements may sometimes be a useful stimulus to fresh thinking in an over-rationalised policy field; they may be a counter to inertia. But equally they may achieve nothing beyond the rationalisation of received opinion, or new but shallow prescriptions which cannot (through lack of time and knowledge) get to grips with problems which are all too familiar to the members of some policy sub-system. It is here that the intended *comprehensiveness* of resource planning can be an actual obstacle to careful analysis. Concerned as they are with the interconnexions of the system, and with the need to compress a great variety of considerations within the elaborate technical specifications of a total analysis, the analysts may mistake a sort of logical ritualism for the goal of greater efficiency. That at the very least is a besetting danger of the exponents of P.P.B.S.

(b) *By acting as 'efficiency partisan'*. This role is as old as the hills, and it is wrong for Schulze to claim that 'P.P.B.S. *introduces* the "efficiency partisan" into the debate'.[11] However public expenditure is allocated it must be kept within *some* global limit itself fixed by political decisions, although ones that are perhaps more influenced by technical economic arguments than are allocative decisions. The global level of public expenditure is strongly influenced by political and technical considerations about managing the economy, and the generally weak relations between the allocative expenditure decisions on the one hand and general economic and tax policies on the other is a blemish of all budgetary systems including P.P.B.S.

Keynesian economics made budget deficits respectable and possibly inadvertently spread the idea that 'public economy' was a false god. Simultaneously, as political demands for more public expenditure have grown rapidly, many professional groups inside as well as outside government have increased their bids for better services, and budgetary competition has become less tempered by public-interest norms of restraint and economy. Despite Keynes then, it is more necessary than ever to scale down and compress the totality of bids for public expenditure yet seemingly harder to do so.

Partisans for expenditure restraint have always been indispensable within government, but they now take the guise of 'efficiency partisans' concerned with the 'wise use of resources' rather than with the crude, old-fashioned idea of saving public money in any way that proved possible. The Dawes era in U.S. government when the Bureau of the Budget 'kept humble', eschewed policy issues, and prided itself upon economising in towels and soap or tracking down the rubber bands appropriated by a Federal employee,[12] seems today as quaint as Gladstone's ambition when Chancellor of the Exchequer to save candle-ends. No doubt the sophisticated P.P.B.S. and cost–benefit techniques of modern financial controllers represent an advance in many respects, although their most effective uses still occur when a case for economy can be plausibly demonstrated to the lay mind. Since the benefits of public programmes are intrinsically so difficult to analyse and estimate, the controllers must continue to walk the tightrope between economic considerations (however sophisticated) and political opinions. In the end too, when public economy becomes imperative, it *has* still to be imposed by the crudest rules of thumb such as across-the-board expenditure cuts, a sort of forced levy on each department according to its political standing, or axing the politically weakest (usually the smallest) programmes.

Thus the social utility of P.P.B.S. and similar techniques must remain a matter of doubt and speculation. It provides some, but not very much, information for increasing the rationality of policy judgements. It offers a more sophisticated setting for the role of efficiency partisan, but without radically affecting the institutional imperative of public economy or the basic devices that seem available in practice for this purpose. In particular it would seem that too much has been made (by economists and administrators and even politicians) of the supposed 'rationality' of economic techniques, at the expense of their attention to organisational and sociological factors whose influence upon decision outcomes may well be more considerable. For example, which *routes* to public economy have the better effects? Stepping up the sophistication of budgetary techniques or strengthening the organisational energy with which the *more* demonstrable examples of possible resource savings are followed up? Or inculcating (if such is now possible) a broader band of officialdom with the need to get 'value for money', even in a somewhat crude sense of that term? To ask such questions may at least serve to underline the extent of the faith which modern governments have reposed in the particular nostrum of economic techniques.

C. Economic Ideas and Government Operations

The influence of economic ideas and techniques upon the conduct of government has grown enormously since the Second World War. The number of professional economists employed by government has multiplied tenfold and more in some countries, and recently P.P.B.S. has created a large demand for economic and other analysts, especially in the United States.[13] More significant still for the influence of economic thought upon government operations, particularly in Western Europe, has been the emergence of economic training as an essential or at the least a highly valued qualification of government administrators. In France and in Germany, for example, economics is now as important as law for an administrative career, and more important for a successful one.

The importance of economics can be seen as a natural, and in some respects indispensable, consequence of the political agenda of modern governments, which accords great importance to the management of the economy, public intervention with industry, balance-of-payments problems, the doctrine of economic growth, and the finance and allocation of public expenditure. Other influences can also be detected. Traditionally European administrators were expected to possess good intelligence combined with legal and political understanding of the conditions of their work, but not particular intellectual specialisms which were often seen as inimical to a rounded or balanced administrative viewpoint. In a technically minded age, however, administrators have encountered the stinging criticism of being amateurs or jacks of all trades who lack appropriate 'scientific' knowledge.

How to meet this criticism? Administrators could not all become scientific experts, but they could all learn *some* economics. Moreover, it is scientific knowledge of *society* which has been particularly stressed by critics, and of the social sciences economics is apparently the most scientific as well as (apparently again) the most relevant to modern government. Only real experts can do scientific or technological appraisal, and 'social appraisal' is a vague concept, but economic appraisal seems relatively more specific and potentially useful at almost every organisational level and in relation to almost every policy issue. What more sensible then than to transform the administrator into a rational resource allocator, blending a minimal economic knowledge and capacity to use economic advice with his more traditional abilities? Even in Britain, the home of the generalist tradition, by the 1960s all administrators were being packed off to a Centre for Administrative Studies for a quick injection of cost–benefit analysis and quantitative techniques.[14]

Despite these developments professional economists often complain that their advice is rejected or frustrated by administrators and politicians. Certainly there are still administrators old-fashioned enough to regard any form of expert advice (even economic advice) with scepticism, and many politicians remain suspicious and ignorant of economic thought. However, the main reason for the rejection of some economic advice is not scepticism inside government about the value of economics, but conflicts over the advice that is proffered. Schisms of economic thought or belief affect all participants in the policy process, and tend to line up groups of politicians, administrators, and economic experts in competing teams. Thus a growth or interventionist-minded politician will work most easily with administrators and experts who share the same general bias, while those who retain some faith in free markets and in economic equilibrium may form a different working coalition. Such coalitions of experts, semi-experts, and laymen with economic opinions are natural enough, because economics as an operational discipline is not sufficiently neutral or objective to eschew the influence of value judgements.

My concern in this section is with the general influence of economic ideas or modes of thought upon the way that governments conduct their affairs. That there must be such influences is self-evident, but its direction is far from clear. Since economists themselves easily disagree at the levels of both theory and practice, the net effects of their influence upon any subject must be hard to judge. Still it does appear to me that a species of economic thinking about certain problems of government has been in the ascendancy during recent decades, although the ideas in question represent much more the vulgarised beliefs of economic administrators than the theories of professional economists. At any rate, a few reflections or speculations will be ventured.

When most economists extolled the virtues of markets operating under perfectly competitive conditions, the profession occupied a scholarly position upon the sidelines. Like theologians they could repel heresies and elucidate orthodoxy, but they were not for the most part required to get in on the action. Businessmen did not need economists to tell them how to make profits, and right to this day business opinion is much more sceptical of the value of economic advice than is political opinion. Adequately competitive markets are supposed to be self-regulating, and do not require economists to plan the use of resources.

The voracious spending of modern governments who swallow up to half and even more of the Gross Domestic Product, has drastically altered the conditions under which resources are allocated. Paradoxically, the economist is now called upon to achieve through his art what the market system was once supposed to do by the light of nature. Economists, as we have seen, have responded readily enough to these opportunities for influence and employment. But an interesting question concerns their intellectual image of the leviathan which they purport to serve or hope to master.

There are those who see political pluralism as being somewhat analogous to market competition. They include economists, notably some members of the 'Public Choice' school in the United States, who want closely to relate the provision and control of public services to the individual preferences of specific groups of clients or beneficiaries. But such opinions are not a usual, nor a very realistic, way of conceiving governmental operations. Whatever the degree of political or administrative pluralism, there are also strong political bonds (such as parties and pressure groups) and organisational bonds (such as administrative controls) which closely connect the different parts of the governmental system even within modern federations.

Prominent among the centralising influences in modern states are economic management and public finance. Almost invariably the great bulk of the revenue is levied and collected by a central agency and then allocated through a variety of routes to numerous agencies, central and local. Competition for resources within government must be directed ultimately towards some central point of control and allocation and cannot take the form of exchanges between autonomous units or enterprises. Success in this competition depends primarily upon political and administrative influence, and not upon market performance and innovation.

A critical question, therefore, is whether the state is viewed as a set of semi-autonomous enterprises which ideally would need to raise their own resources by demonstrating the value of their services to clients, or as a unitary system providing a comprehensive package of services out of a largely common pool of taxation. The second view is the more realistic even if it is not the ideal. But the second view may also lead economists to forget the values of pluralism altogether and to treat government like a single vast firm whose output is to be optimised.

If economic rules for 'optimising' the use of public resources exist or can be invented by economists, then it might seem logical to centralise all public resource decisions. It might also be logical to reorganise governmental machinery so as to assist this result. In practice, economists will concede that these aims are impracticable because of political and organisational constraints. But the very language that is used – 'constraints' and the consequent necessity to 'sub-optimise' at a lower organisational level – carries the message that comprehensive resource planning is the rational ideal, together with the assumption that the values embodied in traditional political or administrative arrangements must be less desirable, if desirable at all, than this quest for 'optimisation'.[15]

These are not just abstract beliefs or opinions. It is a frequent complaint of P.P.B.S. exponents that rational resource planning is impeded by departmental organisation, and by the semi-autonomous status of local or state governments who cannot be fully controlled (although financial controls over these bodies have been steadily increased). The implication is that the government system should be overhauled to facilitate the aims of the resource planners. The doctrine seems curiously utopian when one reflects upon the extreme difficulty of finding 'rational' economic criteria for the benefits of those public services which can be centrally controlled or guided.

To take a specific example from Britain, the major reorganisation of central government in 1970 was much influenced by these economic ideas. Sir Richard Clarke, one of the main civil-service architects of this reconstruction, has suggested that its most important aim was to improve the dialogue between departments over resource allocation and to facilitate P.E.S.C. and P.A.R.[16] The Treasury, Sir Richard explained, could not conduct fruitful negotiations over public expenditure with a substantial number of separate departments, nor could the Cabinet adequately discuss their various plans and priorities. But by creating a few giant departments through amalgamations (as was done), the process could be streamlined. In fact it then became necessary for each giant department to undertake a further substantial internal exercise in resource planning under weakened Treasury supervision, while the hoped-for systematic Cabinet reviews of departmental plans has not materialised. But even if we concede the logic of Sir Richard's argument as far as it goes, it is not apparent that the somewhat abstract possibility of more rational resource planning is truly the most important consideration about government organisation. It could indeed only appear so because of the faith being placed in budgetary techniques, in comparison with other important arguments both for and against this overhaul.

Another fashionable idea about government organisation concerns the economies of scale. In the economic theory of markets, the existence of increasing returns in some industries is conceded to be an advantage of oligopoly or monopoly in certain circumstances; but whether this advantage outweighs the consequent removal from consumers of the benefits of competition is left an unsolved issue or one that should usually be answered negatively. In relation to government, however, the value of competition is often treated as irrelevant. There seems then to be no economic objection to maximising economies of scale in government, and there arises a tendency on the part of efficiency-minded administrators and investigators to search for such economies.

Another British example will illustrate the point. The Royal Commission on Local Government in England and Wales which reported in 1969 recommended the wholesale abolition of smaller local authorities, save as primarily advisory bodies, and the concentration of all services in very large units. The Commission conceded that it had failed to unearth any definite evidence about economics of scale in local government, but it stuck to the opinion that large units expressed in terms of minimum population requirements were necessary for efficient services. Still more striking was the support which this argument received from almost all government departments in their evidence to the Commission, since only a few years previously the same departments had seen little case for enlarging the scale of local authorities in their evidence to a previous Commission investigating the government of London. Although many factors were at work here, one cannot but detect the influence of economic fashion about the relationship between size and efficiency.[17]

Of course, professional economists are not directly responsible for these organisational changes and some would disavow the arguments used. Moreover, the administrators and politicians who champion reorganisations generally have ulterior motives, which may be judged good or bad on their own terms. Thus the theory of P.P.B.S. and rational resource planning enabled McNamara to establish a stronger central control over the representatives of the individual services in the Defense Department in the U.S. structure of government than would otherwise have been possible. P.P.B.S. is sometimes pictured as primarily a device for strengthening organisational hierarchy. Similarly, the British departments who argued the need for more economic efficiency in local government were doubtless mindful (once the idea had become respectable) of the advantage to themselves of dealing with much fewer local authorities. Of course, the fewer local authorities should also be stronger ones, hence perhaps more resistant to central control – indeed this was an avowed aim of the reform. In practice this result was uncertain since a 'remoter' political base for local government might also prove to be a weaker one, and in any case life would be administratively simpler for the central departments.

But these considerations merely underline the respect which has come to be accorded to ideas of economic efficiency and rationality in government, vague as such ideas necessarily are and difficult as is their application. In fact theories of resource planning in government only makes sense within a framework of a much more complex argument, towards which theories of economic competition or concentration can make relatively little contribution. Competition does not and could not have the same meaning or virtues within government as in a market situation – for one thing the incentives and penalties are quite dissimilar, and competition cannot bankrupt an incompetent public agency in the way that it does an inefficient private firm. For this and other reasons the social value of administrative competition between public agencies is very qualified and conditional, and can entail – especially within the United States – palpable examples of waste and extravagance. Equally, however, the supreme virtue often accorded to 'administrative co-ordination' by European administrators can be equally simple-minded, and lends itself to the monolithic view of government activities which is so hospitable to the dreams of some economists and resource planners.[18]

The true issue concerns the extent and character of the political and organisational pluralism which will anyhow occur within a democratic government. Pluralism has the virtues of spreading political participation and of facilitating experiments and innovations in the provision of services. These are more important considerations than the theoretical claims of centralised resource planning, and they point towards a greater *decentralisation* of tax and fiscal arrangements than is now customary. Equally, pluralism becomes excessive where the multiplication of different power centres gives protective colouring to numerous special interests, creates wasteful duplication and empire-building by separate agencies, and scatters money and staff too thinly on the ground for the realisation of fruitful innovations. Economies of scale are relevant to this issue, but only within a framework of political and organisational considerations. Clearly no 'optimum' degree of pluralism can be specified, and each governmental system being the product of long evolution is open to change only within somewhat narrow limits. But the desirable *directions* of change can be discussed within the kind of framework that has just been sketched.

Economic doctrines cannot contribute a great deal to this debate, but their presumed importance lets them in on the ground floor with unfortunate results. The 'Public Choice' economists who recommend an economic model of extreme pluralism seem to be too unrealistic to achieve much more than an armchair defence of some tendencies of the U.S. system of government. The more influential economic doctrines are to be found inside government, urging a strengthening of the monocratic and centralising tendencies of the modern state. Save perhaps in the special American context of excessive or chaotic administrative competition, the advice seems often to be misguided in political or organisational terms.[19] That it should be aired suggests the simple-minded appeal of the welfare economist's ideal – a social-welfare function imposed upon society by the philosopher-economist.

Consider another example of economic fashion, or economic theology. In many countries public enterprises present an uneasy equipoise between managerial discretion and political control. Whatever the theoretical status of public corporations they are subject to numerous political pressures (which in Britain largely take the form of *ad hoc* Ministerial interventions of an informal kind) whose precise character is not known either to Parliament or to the public. The usual managerial belief is that such pressures confuse the location of formal responsibility and erode effective performance. The usual suggested cure is a strategic framework of government policy which will specify, without frequent changes, the goals and responsibilities of the public corporation.[20]

At this point economic doctrine appears with the injunction that public enterprises should follow 'commercial' criteria, while 'social' considerations should be decided by the relevant Minister or government department. This means that a public enterprise itself ought not to operate unremunerative services or make purchases above the lowest tender, unless some Minister is prepared to back and to subsidise the transaction on grounds of the 'public interest'. He can then order a cost–benefit study of the proposed operation or simply support it on political grounds, but the fact that a public subsidy is required will temper such uncommercial decisions, pin responsibility for their adoption, and clarify the goals of the public corporation. These doctrines were strongly espoused in Britain by the Select Committee on Nationalised Industries, under economic advice, and they have become orthodox public policy, at any rate in theory.[21]

Whilst this doctrine has points in its favour, it also represents in some respects a misapplication of economic theory to the circumstances of government. Many public utilities, such as the post and telecommunications, the railways, electricity, and gas, were nationalised in the first place partly at least because of 'social' or 'public service' considerations. Often such enterprises are or anyhow were legally enjoined to provide 'adequate levels of service', for example to inhabitants of rural areas, although this entailed financial loss. In any event cross-subsidisation is endemic in the public-utility field even where the services are provided by private companies. The licensing boards which award the franchises for air routes, bus routes, and so on, usually try to help poorer or more remote areas by linking the award of a remunerative route to that of an unprofitable one. Suburban bus routes are subsidised from main routes, postal services to the Orkneys from those in central London, and so on.

There are sometimes also good reasons for general subsidisation as opposed to cross-subsidisation. The railways are a classic example because of the social and environmental case for getting traffic off the roads, the possibly unfair terms of road transport competition, and the falling marginal costs of railway operation. Of course, one can concede that the public-service type of argument needs to be closely scrutinised because it can easily become an excuse for organisational inertia and extravagance; but it is also the case that a public-service ethic *can be* a boost to organisational morale and effectiveness in circumstances where there may be no other real incentive. Thus, in the case of the railways, the question arises: which policy will produce the better managerial performance? One that requires piecemeal and precarious Ministerial subsidies for 70 per cent of the railway track thereby encouraging the management to concentrate upon the 30 per cent of track which might conceivably be made viable? Or one that allocates a fixed subsidy to the management and enjoins it to provide the best possible services (including bus feeder lines, etc.), with a thorough review of performance every five years or so? The answer is admittedly not obvious even if the author's bias is.

These considerations gain much of their force from the restricted meaning which necessarily attaches to the notion of commercial behaviour in the case of most public enterprises. Peter Drucker says that the first rule of private enterprise is market innovation, but in a public enterprise this injunction (while still perhaps very valuable) must be understood restrictively. Public enterprises are not socially expected and often not legally allowed to switch or diversify their activities, for example from mining coal to making toys. They are not subject either, however their financial framework is set up, to market tests of profitability . There are a few examples, such as the Port of New York Authority, where a public enterprise has built up a financial empire and energetically diversified its operations; but the circumstances were exceptional – a public corporation created by bi-state compact which weakened public control, and a large city without the funds or credit to build enough public works itself. Social critics of the P.N.Y.A. would not in any case want the example emulated.[22]

What financial rules or methods of control should be applied to public enterprise? Here one is faced with competing applications of economic theory to the circumstances of government. On one view the appropriate course is to devise 'optimum' rules of resource allocation that can be applied uniformly to all enterprises. The parliamentary Select Committee suggested two such rules – marginal-cost pricing and a standard discount rate. From these basic rules specific targets could be derived for each enterprise, and the operation of central control would become semi-automatic. There are of course undeniable difficulties about this economic theology. Thus, whatever the merits of marginal-cost pricing, it cannot logically be applied only to the public sector without risking a worse result than some inferior pricing rule; and it cannot practically be applied either because of the large subsidies necessary in some cases.[23] Again, even if some principle of discounting should be agreed, it is clear that no defensible principle can be easily applied – extensive and arguable interpretations of the principle would be necessary which would point away from the idea of uniformity. It is not surprising that the Treasury refused to accept these precepts, although it was too craven to challenge the economic theologians directly.

Alternatively, one can accept the idea that no general financial rules are applicable to the public sector, and piecemeal cost–benefit studies could now be done to determine the flow of investment funds to each industry. Given the necessity of somehow determining levels of subsidisation, this is a field in which limited C.B.A. exercises have usefulness so long as the considerable limitations are recognised. But piecemeal methods of this type also lack any clear rationale, and can be justified only on grounds that there is nothing better. In this situation one can move a little closer to normal managerial incentives if one concedes that the credit of a public enterprise (as tested by past performance) should have at least some relevance for determining its entitlement to further capital.

This example has involved some delving into a complex organisational issue. A general conclusion, however, is that considerations of managerial effectiveness have too easily been subordinated to economic theories or doctrines which prove to be somewhat abstract. In this context nothing is more interesting, as showing the spirit of the times, than the willingness of a parliamentary committee to act as a mouthpiece for economic theologians.

To repeat, this section has been merely a speculative foray into dark territory. A book is waiting to be written about the influence of economic ideas upon the behaviour of governments. It can be conceded that the points made here are one-sided and thinly backed with evidence, and that the influence of economic ideas as opposed to administrative or political intentions may have been exaggerated. But it does at least appear that some simple notions of economic efficiency have been used by officials to advocate changes which ought to be assessed on a much broader basis. If this is so it is a natural enough result of the influx into government of economists and their techniques.

One should also recognise the basic difficulty of offering economic prescriptions for government problems. In Western countries most traditional economics has taken the market system as its model. This is obviously true of 'micro' theories of the firm but even 'macro' theories of the economy are not of much help for analysing the *internal* operations of the vast system of government. The thriving literature of welfare economics does deal with social and public policies, but the schisms within this branch of economics reveal how little it can be isolated from conflicting political or ethical positions.

Welfare economists tend to agree that 'consumer demand' or the sum of individual preferences should be in some sense the test of public policies. If the economist trusts in his own techniques for ascertaining and aggregating these preferences, he may be disposed to believe or to accept that resource decisions should be centralised because in that way available resources can be more efficiently utilised to meet a given schedule of demands – if that schedule is tolerably accurate. But if the economist is more modest and accepts that his tests are at best only a partial and unreliable guide to the preferences of individuals within a government context, it becomes more logical for him to stress the superior merits of political accountability and (within limits) decentralisation as ways of giving people what they want. That at least is one way of defining the problem.

Those economists who believe in the capacity of their techniques to interpret social welfare find natural allies in other efficiency experts and in the exponents of scientific administration. The result can easily become a doctrine of organisational efficiency divorced from considerations of political choice except at the highest, formal levels of political authority. The economists who support and stress political choice, on the other hand, hark back to an older tradition of economic thought – the rational, autonomous, self-interested individual who should be free to voice his preferences directly, both in market and political arenas, without the intervention of technical intermediaries. Thus one has the paradoxes that welfare economists can become authoritarian through faith in their techniques, and liberal economists can have more faith in direct democracy than political scientists or ordinary citizens. The positions sketched here are poles apart, which perhaps suggests that welfare economists exaggerate the schisms of ordinary mortals. But in any case there is no doubt as to which of these positions is the stronger influence upon and within governments.

Once again I must plead guilty to simplifying the position of economists. It might equally be said perhaps that numerous economists in the central places of government accept the system as they find it, and simply utilise the opportunity for an ambitious application of their techniques. In any case economics is too flexible and economists themselves are of too diverse opinions for any simple summary of positions to be accurate. It is enough to have raised some questions about the directions of economic influence.

D. Economics and Social Values

Invariably, when C.B.A. is under discussion, someone will say: conceding all the snags, what better or more rational way of making a public decision is there? Economic surveys of the subject, after conceding a host of unresolved theoretical and practical problems, still tend to finish on this optimistic note.[24] A brief review of the possible meanings of a 'rational decision' will help to pave the way for some final reflections about the use of economic techniques in modern societies.

The word rationality appears to have three different if related meanings. First, it stands for the notion of reflection as a prelude to action. Instead of acting upon hunch, the decision-maker should analyse the situation carefully, consider alternative options, list their pros and cons, and so on. A number of logical models can be employed for this purpose but it was pointed out in Chapter 7 that the usefulness of any such model, at the level of formal logical thought, is pretty limited. It has to be related to the circumstances of a policy process. The subject need not detain us here because economics cannot claim, and certainly does not have, any proprietary right to such models, either in a general form or as adjusted to the circumstances of public policy-making.[25]

Secondly, rationality is an *instrumental* value concerned with the maximisation of some goal or the application of some value judgement. Many kinds of information may be useful for such operations, and the usefulness of specifically *economic* information will vary with circumstances. If, to revert to the Roskill case, I am a naturalist whose value judgement is restricted to the wish that the airport site chosen shall do the least damage to flora and fauna, I need factual information to apply my judgement; but economic information will not figure high on my list (if at all) since other data is more directly useful and probably sufficient. Certainly economic information very often *is* relevant to the exercise of value judgements and raises the familiar conundrum: while such information seems logically more comprehensive than other information because of a common numerator, its significance is correspondingly more dubious and perplexing. It is wrong to accord any intrinsic superiority to economic over other types of information.

Finally, rationality stands sometimes for a principle of harmony between conflicting aims or values. This use of the word has a long and controversial philosophic history. There is Hume's view that 'reason always is and ought to be the slave of the passions' which confines reason to a series of unrelated instrumental roles. Metaphysicians, however, have often sought some principle of harmony which can order conflicting human desires in a right-and-just manner, for both the individual and society, as in Plato's famous vision of the proper relationship between the soul, the spirited element, and the appetites, within the constitution both of the just individual and also of the just state viewed as an analogue to the former. For Plato, reason, which was the soul, should be the controlling element. Moral philosophers such as

Kant have sought 'regulative principles' for ordering the diverse value judgements made by the individual.

At a more mundane level this sense of rationality is expressed as the popular idea of 'reasonableness'. A reasonable man is one who co-ordinates and balances his value judgements in some way, and avoids dogmatic excess. A reasonable society is one which tolerates a diversity of value opinions among its members (subject at least to protecting the value of toleration itself). An extended use of this notion brings in the other two senses of rationality, to allow for the desirability of introducing relevant information in support of individual judgements or claims, and for systematic debate about the grounds of a decision. Sir Karl Popper's view of the 'logic of democracy' sees this process as a systematic sifting of claims and counter-claims, supported by relevant information, which is somewhat analogous to the experimental methods of science. If this is so a composite notion of rationality must provide the connecting link between scientific and democratic activities.

The usefulness of rationality in this broad sense has already been suggested. Relevant information enables individuals to apply their values more accurately, hence to achieve more of what they want or believe in. If one adds an attitude of 'reasonableness' which is prepared to listen and where persuaded to make concessions to the claims of others, even at personal expense, social harmony is enhanced.

What has this discussion to do with economics? It is hardly to be expected that welfare economists shall have discovered the harmonising principles of 'right reason' which have puzzled and divided philosophers for centuries. Its function can more plausibly be seen as that of providing relevant information which is useful for rational debate as here described. But if economics is to bring disparate values into a common equation, there must be some unifying principle to enable them to do so. This necessity is recognised in the postulate of a 'social-welfare function', and economists usually although not always concede that the S.W.F. must be left indeterminate. But is this conclusion or concession simply a little theoretical top-dressing upon a practically useful body of information, or does it place very critical limits indeed upon the scope and uses of that information? This was the issue treated critically in Chapter 1. Let us reconsider the verdict.

To the layman, as sometimes to the economist himself, it is the ubiquitous scarcity of resources which underpins the value of economic analysis. In the public-policy realm, even if benefits cannot be satisfactorily quantified, it still seems possible and very useful to 'know the costs'. For limited financial purposes this proposition is true. Thus if the budget must be limited to £x millions for political, psychological and other reasons, it is essential to know the financial costs of particular items. It may also be useful, as Chapter 4 conceded, to modify these calculations by reference to certain considerations about 'real resources' because of their relevance to the total size of expenditure that should be allowed, and to some of its subdivisions. But this exercise amounts essentially to notionally repricing some of the factors of production employed by government so as to allow for certain 'externalities' in the economy as a whole, and to co-ordinating the transfer payments made by government with policies of demand management.

But at a deeper level neither costs nor benefits can be known in isolation. Since factors of production have no intrinsic worth (or so most economists now assume), their prices depend upon the interaction between the 'subjective' costs attached to these factors by their owners and the 'subjective' benefits ultimately attached by consumers to their alternative uses. Snap this market link and the only 'objective' meaning attached to the costs of government operation will derive from the competing demands of consumers for the same factors of production, and clearly this influence will be enormously affected by the vast scale of government operations.

Of course socialist economists would reject this conclusion and argue that factors can still be priced rationally even where government determines both demand and supply. Actually what this claim means is that in principle prices can be set according to consistent government rules, but the 'standard of value' which results is the product of political values.

The paradoxical relationship between welfare economics and the market system has been mentioned before. A competitive pricing system does, in principle, provide a standard of exchange value for linking the costs of production to the preferences of consumers. It may be, indeed *is* the case, that this standard must be understood conditionally and restrictively, for example as limited to certain transactions carried out under appropriate conditions. The working of the system should also be understood descriptively rather than normatively in the sense that it is subject to higher-level judgements about the ethical worth of any system. But still within this context the exchange value of money has a certain consistency which even a great deal of market 'imperfection' does not altogether vitiate.

But if welfare economics comes into existence because of extensive examples of market 'failure' (such as technological spillovers) and the wholesale replacement of individual by collective expenditure, this new discipline still carries with it the mental luggage of market economics, particularly its preoccupation with the 'sovereignty' of consumers' preferences. These signboards now have to be posted in a strange landscape wherein the old paths are largely obliterated. Hence there is not a little confusion as to precisely what tests of value do provide some genuine element of consistency to the figures in a C.B.A.

This confusion is certainly apparent in popular fallacies about the *purposes* of C.B.A. and similar techniques. The layman undoubtedly understands the notion of economic efficiency in a quite different way from many welfare economists. He may start also from the assumption that entrepreneurs are efficient in a market sense when they maximise profits, and then suppose that in government some loosely analogous test of efficiency can be found. This test may be located in some vague idea about the 'strength of the economy' which stands actually for a variety or amalgam of possible goals such as (1) increasing the economic basis of military strength, (2) increasing the capacity of the economy to withstand depression and foreign economic competition, and (3) economic growth. If economic growth is regarded as the single or overriding goal, this will usually be understood as maximising the value of the total bundle of goods and services that are produced (whoever provides them).

It is risky to invoke the layman's reasoning, but certainly goals such as these are frequently espoused by politicians and by many economists themselves, and it might be supposed that economic techniques were serviceable for their promotion. In fact of course the *bêtises* of such efficiency tests as economic growth are now often exposed, especially by some welfare economists. Leaving aside all the problems of achieving consistent measurements over time and upon a comparative international basis, figures of Gross National Product cover only those goods and services which enter into economic exchanges. Thus many unpriced elements even of material welfare are necessarily excluded, such as the services of housewives, vegetables from the back garden (save for the cost of seeds), and so on. Equally the figures *exclude* the adverse effects of the technological instruments of growth (which should be deducted) and *include* many items with a dubious or possibly negative relationship to material welfare such as high expenditure upon journeys to work, some advertising, the salaries of many bureaucrats, and so on.

However, these criticisms of 'growthmanship' are incidental to the main argument. The point is that popular ideas about economic efficiency have no association with the welfare economist's ultimate criterion. Market efficiency is not altogether a suitable paradigm for those who stress the inability of market prices to register welfare effects. Equally, collective goals such as economic growth or economic stability have no necessary relationship at all to the tests of policy which welfare economics would ideally apply. These tests refer ultimately to the content of individual preferences, and it has already been suggested that in its fully realised form (although not admittedly in its actual practice) C.B.A. would become a species of 'democratic science'.

Ideally, analysts would like to measure as many welfare effects as possible, and thus extend their coverage well beyond the range of economic transactions as these are normally understood. Equally at least some of them would like to drop any cloying assumptions about egoistic motives or *homo economicus*, and incorporate preferences of almost any type (altruistic ones for example). But if individual preference is supposed to be King, unqualified in any respect save for some definition of the term's logical categories, the directions which these individual preferences may take become completely indeterminate. If the collective preference (however this is summated) turns out to be increasingly inimical to work and favourable to idleness, then it is (on this view) economically 'efficient' to follow this preference. If people reject modern technology and revert to communal forms of society with little economic exchange, that also would be an 'efficient' result although not perhaps one that would prove very hospitable to the cost–benefit analyst.

Admittedly this utopian version of C.B.A. is practically impotent for reasons which are not without relevance to its *actual* tendencies. Some economists, notably in recent years James Buchanan, have stressed the crucial difference between estimates of hypothesised costs and benefits as these appear to a decision-maker *before* the decision is made, and the stream of realised costs and benefits that are measured *afterwards*. This explains some of the curious problems of 'business-decision theory' and may account for the limited respect for economics held by most business-men; the economist is not in the entrepreneur's chair, wrestling with his uncertainties, but is viewing business decisions *post facto*. Buchanan makes the point that it is wrong to take the economic outcomes of a choice (supposing these can be predicted) as a test of the *desirability* of the choice which must be related to all the considerations that appear relevant to the decision-maker.[26]

Business decisions, however, gain some degree of consistency on the not unreasonable assumption that they are related to calculations of individual economic advantage, whereas there are critical uncertainties about the decision-maker's values in the arena of collective decisions. As Buchanan points out, an egoistic dictator would have little use for C.B.A. because he would not himself bear any of the costs, and the same point applies in a modified way to decision-makers in democracies. Philanthropic philosopher-economists might lay down benevolent rules about the distribution of costs and benefits but how would these relate to individual preferences? If we assume (mythically) the fullest possible democratic decision-making, each citizen must logically be enabled to express his preference about the effect of a collective decision upon other citizens, which may range all the way from indifference to impartial altruism, including many possibilities of selective benevolence or malevolence.

While ethical rules for tackling these dilemmas can be propounded and debated, there is absolutely no way of answering them in terms of a schedule of individual preferences. Not only does the data not exist, it could not exist. In the first place the opportunities and incentives for 'cheating' by disguising one's preferences are obvious in the case of collective decisions. In the second place, as Chapter 6 showed, individual preferences seem to have a great deal of ambivalence depending upon which chord is struck in the individual personality. In their market behaviour individuals often seem to put a low value upon their own health or safety, whereas in their political capacity they may require or expect paternalistic rules for restraining this behaviour and demand expensive curative treatment. Again the generally egoistic assumptions behind market choices are modified or replaced in collective decisions either by a less scrupulous egoism (the cheating syndrome) or by partial altruism or, alternatively, by both attitudes.

This 'ambivalence' of behaviour refers both to a differentiation of roles and (linked with it) to a conflict of values which it is merely ludicrous to suppose capable of compression within the strong-box of the economist's preference functions. Of course this does not rule out the possibility of a fuller integration of relevant roles and norms, and a large arena of social debate has for long been concerned with this very issue. Economists have freely entered this debate on opposing sides, their technical arguments being employed in support of possible normative positions. For example, Kenneth Arrow diagnoses some of the imprudent market behaviour of individuals in relation to personal health and safety hazards as related to imperfections or failure in the market for private insurance.[27] If market mechanisms could be improved, state provision would presumably be less expected or demanded (although public action would be needed to improve the market), and the ideal of the autonomous, responsible individual determining his own destiny by private economic initiative would thereby be furthered. The converse position would contend that collective health provision is a civic duty that is owed not only by the rich to the poor but also (and more relevantly here) by the healthy to the unhealthy. And economists can and do support this position, not only by reference to the unpredictability and heavy expense of sickness, but by suggesting appropriate technologies for implementing the goal.

This instrumental or technological function of economics in relation to values was stressed in a famous book by Gunnar Myrdal, and Myrdal's theory indicates the maximum role which economists can legitimately play.[28] For example, the lengthy economic debate over the correct discount rate to be applied to public projects is meaningless unless this rate is conceived as a technical instrument for implementing possible value positions. Should governments discount the future at a lower rate than the market because of having a 'trustee' responsibility for the future? What does a 'trustee' role mean, since presumably it does not apply logically to all but only to some public projects such as those concerned with 'conservation'? How to define conservation? As the debate unwinds economics can assist with the information needed to define and to apply social positions, but has no title to determining those positions at any level of the debate.

A set of economic techniques then which propose or purport to relay individual preferences about collective decisions in a comprehensive way is a psychological absurdity and an ethical monstrosity. Hence the idea of a grand democratic science of C.B.A. is simply a fallacy, and the more hard-headed economists certainly do not believe in it. But their analysis must consequently (in Western countries) try to realise a concept of welfare maximisation which has been derived from a market system under markedly non-market conditions. A weak 'efficiency' principle is then derived which places a heavy weight upon the weak reed of ascertainable 'costs' and compares these (where possible at all) with figures of 'benefits' derived from dubiously inferred market indicators or else from cruder direct statements or snap-shots of consumer preference which cannot, under the necessary circumstances, be expected to have much consistency or much relevance.

This simplified 'efficiency' principle is then supplemented, on paper only, by a sliding scale of 'distributional' principles which are supposed to allow for some of the infinity of positions which a social-welfare function might theoretically take. These 'distributional' principles express the economist's conscience over the implications of his advice for the distribution of wealth, and no doubt it is not his fault that they can do no more. They do not in any case attempt to cope with the rich mine of prudential, altruistic and other valuations which appear powerfully to affect individual judgements about collective decisions. As already suggested it would be the ideal end-product of C.B.A. to incorporate such judgements, and it is not the economist's fault that no way can be found. Thus, ultimately, the actual criterion of efficiency employed by analysts does bear some resemblance to the layman's image; and although technically it can be rendered precise, intellectually and normatively it remains rather fuzzy.

No doubt this verdict will be regarded both as too harsh and too abstract, because insufficiently mindful of the exigent conditions of public decision-making; and while I have certainly missed out much of the subtle reasoning by economists themselves on the subject of economic value, it may also be thought that the spirit of economic scepticism pervades the argument to a point where Dr Johnson's treatment is called for – of kicking a wall hard to show that an external world exists. Perhaps this is so. But it may at the least be suggested that critical issues in the modern world are unlikely to be solved with the aid of cost–benefit analysis. The results (if honestly done) are usually too indeterminate, and there can be little consistency between the various exercises. The critical values for a decision must either be omitted or conditioned to fit the techniques; and no dramatic breakthrough in the techniques is intrinsically possible. We are not here, as some economists occasionally aver, in the pioneer days of flight because a normative 'science' is a contradiction in terms.

If the use of these techniques has any general effect upon the *directions* of modern society, one suspects that it is one of reinforcing the trends or fashions prevalent at a point in time. This is to be expected because C.B.A. takes the economic preferences currently held as the normative basis for choosing the future, and has no affinity with either historical continuity in policy-making or composite and visionary social ideals. It may be that these decision trends oscillate within critical limits set by the difficulties of managing and maintaining the given system of political economy. Certainly economic techniques are not the tools for proposing radical changes in society, although they would doubtless confirm the direction of such changes once in movement.

One can only speculate also about the reasons for the respect and deference accorded to economics in modern society. One explanation might be that the increasing pressure of demands for more consumption in societies in which work is steadily losing its prudential and its normative character can only produce an acute crisis of resource allocation; within a semi-collectivised economy the economist is then turned to as the relevant expert. Another explanation is that an age uncertain of its values and its social direction will attach correspondingly more attention to the distribution of that which it has. For similar reasons techniques will be enlisted to substitute for the lack of agreement upon values and to dissect the values themselves. It is an age of analysts. Just as the psychoanalyst seeks to dissect the psyche but finds its re-assembly none too easy, so perhaps does the cost–benefit analyst proceed within his realm of operations.

Howsoever these things may be, it is to be expected that future historians will be surprised at the credence and importance accorded to economics in the 1970s.

Notes and References

Chapter 1

1. Introduction (p. vi) to W. A. Johr and H. W. Singer, *The Role of the Economist as Official Adviser* (London, 1955).
2. E. J. Mishan, *Cost–Benefit Analysis* (London, 1971).
3. J. Margolis, 'Secondary Benefits, External Economies, and the Justification of Public Investment', reprinted in *Readings in Welfare Economics*, ed. K. J. Arrow and T. Scitovsky (London, 1969).

Chapter 2

1. I. M. D. Little, *A Critique of Welfare Economics* (Oxford, 1950).
2. J. Bentham, *An Introduction to the Principles of Morals and Legislation* (London, 1789).
3. Mishan, *Cost–Benefit Analysis*, p. 309.
4. D. W. Pearce, *Cost–Benefit Analysis* (London, 1971), p. 52.
5. J. K. Galbraith, *American Capitalism: the Concept of Countervailing Power* (London, 1952).
6. Little, *A Critique of Welfare Economics*, chapter 2.
7. *Ibid.* chapter 4.
8. L. Robbins, 'International Comparison of Utility: A Comment', *Economic Journal* (Dec 1938), 635–91.
9. Sir Geoffrey Vickers, *Value Systems and Social Process* (London, 1968).
10. The two definitions are from Mishan, *Cost–Benefit Analysis*, p. 311; and Pearce, *Cost–Benefit Analysis*, p. 14n.
11. A. K. Dasgupta and D. W. Pearce, *Cost–Benefit Analysis, Theory and Practice* (London, 1972) p. 25.
12. K. J. Arrow, *Social Choice and Individual Values* (New York, 1963).
13. A. K. Sen, *Collective Choice and Social Welfare* (Edinburgh, 1970).
14. A. K. Sen, *Behaviour and the Concept of Preference* (London School of Economics, 1973).
15. N. Kaldor, 'Welfare Comparisons of Economics and Interpersonal Comparisons of Utility', *Economic Journal* (1939) and J. R. Hicks, 'The Foundations of Welfare Economics', *Economic Journal* (1939).

Chapter 3

1. J. M. Buchanan and W. C. Stubblebine, 'Externality', reprinted in *Readings in Welfare Economics*, pp. 201–2. The quoted definition relates actually to a *potentially relevant* externality.
2. See for example Otto A. Davis and Morton I. Kamien, 'Externalities, Information and Alternative Action' in *Public Expenditure and Policy Analysis*, eds R. H. Haveman and J. Margolis (Chicago, 1970) pp. 74–95.

3. For example, Mishan, *Cost–Benefit Analysis*, pp. 107–8.
4. Ibid. pp. 125–37.
5. Trevor Newton, *Cost–Benefit Analysis in Administration* (London, 1972) pp. 41–5 and 89–91, and Ministry of Transport, *Roads for the Future* (London, 1969).
6. Ministry of Transport, *Road Pricing, the Economic and Technical Possibilties*, Smeed Report (London, 1964).
7. See the analysis in J. M. Thompson *et al.*, *Motorways in London* (London, 1969).
8. C. D. Foster and M. E. Beesley, 'Estimating the Social Benefit of Constructing an Underground Railway in London', reprinted in *Readings in Welfare Economics*, pp. 462–520.
9. See for examples City of Coventry, *Coventry Transportation Study: Report on Phase I* (Coventry, 1968); N. Lichfield and associates, *Stevenage Public Transport, a Cost–Benefit Analysis* (Stevenage Development Corporation, 1969).
10. E. J. Mishan, *The Costs of Economic Growth* (London, 1967) pp. 233–40.

Chapter 4

1. Sir Geoffrey Vickers, *The Art of Judgement* (London, 1965) pp. 31–4.
2. M. H. Cooper and A. J. Colyer (eds), *Health Economics* (London, 1973).
3. Charles L. Schultze, *The Politics and Economics of Public Spending* (Washington D.C.: The Brookings Institution, 1968) p. 91.
4. M. Blaug (ed.), *Economics of Education*, 1 (Harmondsworth, 1968), chapters, 5, 7, 11, 13.
5. *Report of the Commission on the Third London Airport* (London: H.M.S.O., 1971) pp. 274–5. Anyone who reads this appendix and still believes the figures therein is surely very credulous.
6. Mishan, *Cost–Benefit Analysis*, pp. 153–74.
7. Ibid. pp. 175–9. See also G. H. Peters, *Cost–Benefit Analysis and Public Expenditure* (London: Institute of Economic Affairs, 1973).
8. G. P. Wibberley, *Agriculture and Urban Growth* (London, 1959). See also Peters, *Cost–Benefit Analysis and Public Expenditure*, pp. 38–42.
9. *Docklands: Redevelopment Proposals for East London*, Volumes 1 and 2 (1973). Report to Greater London Council.

Chapter 5

1. For a discussion of some of these issues see B. M. Barry, *Sociologists, Economists and Democracy* (London, 1970), which includes references to much of the voluminous literature.
2. A. Downs, *An Economic Theory of Democracy* (New York, 1957). For evidence supporting the rationality of voting (in the sense described in the text) see V. O. Key Jr, *The Responsible Electorate: Rationality in Presidential Voting* (Harvard University Press, 1966).
3. M. Olson Jr, *The Logic of Collective Action: Public Goods and the Theory of Groups* (Harvard University Press, 1965).
4. E. C. Banfield, *Political Influence* (New York, 1961). Schultze, *The Politics and Economics of Public Spending*.
5. On this and other theories of democracy a useful book is R. A. Dahl, *A Preface to Democratic Theory* (University of Chicago Press, 1956).
6. P. Self, *Administrative Theories and Politics* (London, 1972) pp. 277–89.
7. J. C. Davies, *The Evangelical Bureaucrat* (London, 1974).
8. J. Plamenatz, 'Interests', *Political Studies*, vol. 11, no. 1 (Feb 1954) 1–8.

9. P. Self and H. J. Storing, *The State and the Farmer* (London, 1962) chapter 10.

10. B. M. Barry, *Political Argument* (London, 1965) chapter 10.

11. So called after the journal *Public Choice*. Individual works cited subsequently.

12. Downs, *An Economic Theory of Democracy.*

13. D. B. Truman, *The Governmental Process* (New York, 1953).

14. D. Braybrooke and C. Lindblom, *A Strategy of Decision: Policy Evaluation as a Social Process* (New York, 1963).

15. C. Lindblom, *The Intelligence of Democracy* (New York, 1965).

16. A. Wildavsky, 'The Political Economy of Efficiency', *Public Administration Review*, vol. XXVI, no. 4 (Dec 1966) p. 228.

17. See the discussion in V. Ostrom, *The Intellectual Crisis in American Public Administration* (University of Alabama Press, 1973), chapter 3, pp. 114–22.

18. Mishan, *Cost–Benefit Analysis*, pp. 68, 309–10, 323–4. R. Layard, *Cost–Benefit Analysis* (London, 1972) p. 37.

Chapter 6

1. See Chapter 2, pp. 25–31.

2. Dasgupta and Pearce, *Cost–Benefit Analysis: Theory and Practice*, pp. 36–7.

3. Layard (ed.), *Cost–Benefit Analysis*, pp. 28, 37.

4. A. Downs, *Inside Bureaucracy* (Boston, 1967).

5. J. M. Buchanan and G. Tullock, *The Calculus of Consent* (University of Michigan, 1962) pp. 4, 18, 27–30.

6. B. M. Barry, *Sociologists, Economists, and Democracy* (London, 1970), chapter 2.

7. Too familiar to repeat here. See for example: A. K. Sen, *Behaviour and the Concept of Preference* (London School of Economics, 1973) pp. 10–13.

8. A. K. Sen, *On Economic Inequality* (Oxford, 1973) pp. 96–9.

9. See Chapter 5, p. 112.

10. *Report of the Commission on the Third London Airport* (London: H.M.S.O., 1971), p. 258, para. 51.

11. Ibid., p. 261, para. 63.

12. J. Rawls. *A Theory of Justice* (Oxford University Press, 1972) pp. 22–7, 183–92.

13. Summarised in Dasgupta and Pearce, *Cost–Benefit Analysis*, pp. 66–9.

14. C. D. Foster, 'Social Welfare Functions in C.B.A.', in *Operational Research in the Social Services*, ed. M. Laurence (London, 1966).

15. Mishan, *Cost–Benefit Analysis*, pp. 310–15.

16. Rawls, *A Theory of Justice.*

17. Sen, *On Economic Inequality*, chapter 4.

18. N. Lichfield, 'Evaluation of Methodology of Urban and Regional Plans: A Review', *Regional Studies*, vol. 4, no. 2 (August 1970).

19. I. D. M. Little, *A Critique of Welfare Economics* (Oxford University Press, 1950) chapter 10.

20. Ebenezer Howard, *Garden Cities of Tomorrow* (London, new ed. 1946).

21. D. L. Foley, *Controlling London's Growth* (University of California Press, 1963).

22. J. N. Jackson, *The Urban Future* (London, 1972) chapter 8.

23. Peter Self, *Metropolitan Planning* (London School of Economics, 1971) chapter 6.

Chapter 7

1. Herbert A. Simon, *Administrative Behaviour*, 2nd edn (New York, 1957) chapter 2.
2. R. Hare, 'Contrasting Methods of Environmental Planning' in *Nature and Conduct*, (forthcoming).
3. M. Meyerson and E. C. Banfield, *Politics, Planning, and the Public Interest* (New York, 1955) p. 317.
4. Sir Geoffrey Vickers, *The Art of Judgement* (London, 1965) p. 40.
5. C. Lindblom, *The Intelligence of Democracy* (New York, 1965).
6. Peter Self, 'Is Comprehensive Planning Possible and Rational?', *Policy and Politics*, vol. 2, no. 3 (March 1974) 193–203.
7. Lichfield, *Regional Studies*, vol. 4, no. 2 (August 1970) 151–65.
8. *Report of the Commission on the Third London Airport* (Chairman Mr Justice Roskill), (London. H.M.S.O., 1971). The Commission published nine volumes of Paper and Proceedings, including two volumes of written evidence, four volumes covering local hearings, two volumes of research studies, and one volume of public evidence at the research stage (the final stage of public hearings was not published). Cost of preparing the report was £1,131,000. Useful critiques of the Report include *Regional Studies* special issue, vol. 5, no. 3 (Sep 1971; John G. U. Adams 'London's Third Airport', *The Geographical Journal*, vol. 137, part 4 (Dec 1971); Christopher Foster *et al*: *Lessons of Maplin*. The Institute of Economic Affairs Occasional Paper 40 (London, 1974). The only basic criticism of the Commission's methodology during its proceedings was Peter Self: 'Nonsense on Stilts: Cost–Benefit Analysis and the Roskill Commission', *Political Quarterly*, vol. 41, no. 3 (July 1970).
9. House of Commons Official Report, 20 May 1968, cols 32–9.
10. Roskill Report, ch. 4 para. 2.
11. For the Commission's treatment of noise see F. A. Sharman 'The Third London Airport as a Project Assessment Problem', *Regional Studies*, vol. 5, no. 3 (Sep 1971) pp. 135–43, and Adams, *The Geographical Journal*, vol. 137, part 4 (Dec 1971).
12. For the final cost–benefit table see Roskill Report, p. 119.
13. N. Lichfield 'Cost–Benefit Analysis in Planning: A Critique of the Roskill Commission', *Regional Studies*, vol. 5, no. 3 (Sep 1971) pp. 157–83.
14. See the discussion in *Regional Studies* special issue, vol. 5, no. 3 (Sep 1971) pp. 145–55, 185–200.
15. *Roskill Report*, p. 123.
16. Ibid. ch. 6, paras 76–8.
17. Ibid. ch. 12, paras 59–66.
18. Commission's Papers and Proceedings, vol. VIII, part I (Airport City) and *Report*, ch. 6, paras 28–45.
19. *Report*, ch. 6, paras 2–28.
20. Ibid. ch. 13, paras 29–36.
21. Ibid. ch. 11, paras 1–29.
22. Ibid. pp. 149–62.
23. A. Etzioni, *The Active Society*, (London, 1968).
24. Peter Self, ' "Nonsense on Stilts": Cost–Benefit Analysis and the Roskill Commission', *Political Quarterly*, vol. 41, no. 3 (July 1970) and Alan Williams, 'C.B.A.: bastard science and/or insidious poison in the body politik?', in *Cost–Benefit and Cost-Effectiveness Analysis*, ed. J. N. Wolfe (London, 1973) pp. 30–63.

Chapter 8

1. Aaron Wildavsky, 'Rescuing Policy Analysis from P.P.B.S.' in *Public Expenditure and Policy Analysis*, eds R. H. Haveman and J. Margolis (Chicago, 1970), p. 467. Parts 4 and 5 of this book provide an introduction to the uses of P.P.B.S. by the U.S. government.
2. Charles L. Schulze in ibid. pp. 145–73.
3. Fred S. Hoffman in ibid. p. 436.
4. Peter Self, *Administrative Theories and Politics* (London, 1972) pp. 64–72.
5. Vickers, *The Art of Judgement*.
6. Raymond A. Bauer (ed.), *Social Indicators* (Cambridge, Mass., 1966).
7. Schulze, *The Politics and Economics of Public Spending*, pp. 90–2.
8. For examples both of *a priori* economic theories and more useful contributions related to institutional conditions, see for example M. H. Cooper and A. J. Culyer, *Health Economics* (London, 1973).
9. Aaron Wildavsky, *The Politics of the Budgetary Process* (Boston, 1964) and H. Heclo and A. Wildavsky, *The Private Government of Public Money* (London, 1974).
10. Admittedly politicians continually press for 'more information' irrespective of whether they use information which they already have. If it can be had cost-free the tendency is natural. See also Helco and Wildavsky, *The Private Government of Public Money*, pp. 198–264.
11. Schulze, *The Politics and Economics of Public Spending* p. 95. To be fair Schulze's concern here is not with the budgetary controllers but with the programme evaluation staff in the agencies who, although identified with the same basic values, are 'more likely to be interested in questions of efficiency than the rest of the bureau'. But the need for public economy has always resulted in some internalised checks upon expenditure being located within each agency. The interesting question is whether a programme evaluation staff is able to establish much leverage on the bureau's policies whilst retaining its interest in economy and efficiency.
12. Quoted in ibid. pp. 11–12.
13. In the United States Federal Government expenditure for personnel concerned with P.P.B.S. (including contract services) was $60 million in 1970. Haveman and Margolis, *Public Expenditure and Policy Analysis*, p. 378.
14. Desmond Keeling, 'The Development of Central Training in the Civil Service 1963–70', *Public Administration* (spring, 1971).
15. The classic critique of this utopian view of budgeting is C. E. Lindblom, 'The Science of Muddling Through' *Public Administration Review*, xix, 2 (Spring, 1959) 79–88.
16. Sir Richard Clarke, *New Trends in Government* (London, 1971).
17. *Report of Royal Commission on Local Government in England 1966–1969* (London: H.M.S.O., 1969) chapter 4, *Report of Royal Commission on Local Government in Greater London* (London: H.M.S.O., 1960).
18. Self, *Administrative Theories and Politics*, pp. 87–120.
19. Vincent Ostrom, *The Intellectual Crisis in American Public Administration* (The University of Alabama Press, 1973).
20. A. H. Hanson, *Parliament and Public Ownership* (London, 1961).
21. Select Committee on Nationalised industries, 1967–8, First Report: *Ministerial Control of the Nationalised Industries*, volumes 1–3.
22. See for example 'Gotham in the Air Age' in *Public Administration and Policy Development*, ed. Harold Stein (New York, 1952) pp. 143–99.
23. For discussion see R. Turvey (ed.), *Public Enterprise* (London, 1968).

24. See, for example, A. R. Prest and R. Turvey, 'Cost–Benefit Analysis: a Survey', *Economic Journal*, LXXXV, (Dec 1965) 683–736.

25. For a much broader survey see Y. Dror, *Public Policy-making Re-examined* (San Francisco, 1968).

26. J. M. Buchanan, *Cost and Choice* (Chicago, 1969).

27. K. J. Arrow, 'Uncertainty and the Welfare Economics of Medical Care', *American Economic Review*, 53 (1963) pp. 941–73

28. Gunnar Myrdal, *The Political Element in the Development of Economic Theory* (London, 1953).

Index